Benjamin Graham

The Memoirs of the
Dean of Wall Street

Benjamin Graham

The Memoirs of the Dean of Wall Street

Edited and with an Introduction
by Seymour Chatman

McGraw-Hill
New York   San Francisco   Washington, D.C.   Auckland   Bogotá
Caracas   Lisbon   London   Madrid   Mexico City   Milan
Montreal   New Delhi   San Juan   Singapore
Sydney   Tokyo   Toronto

Library of Congress Cataloging-in-Publication Data

Graham, Benjamin.
    Benjamin Graham, the memoirs of the dean of Wall Street / edited
and with an introduction by Seymour Chatman.
        p.   cm.
    Includes bibliographical references and index.
    ISBN 0-07-024269-0
    1. Graham, Benjamin. 2. Capitalists and financiers—United
States—Biography. 3. Investment analysis. 4. Securities—United
States. I. Chatman, Seymour Benjamin, II. Title.
HG172.G68A3 1996
332.6'092—dc20
[B]   96-19261
                                             CIP

McGraw-Hill

A Division of The McGraw·Hill Companies

1 2 3 4 5 6 7 8 9 0 DOC/DOC 9 0 1 0 9 8 7 6

ISBN 0-07-024269-0

*The sponsoring editor for this book was David Conti, the
editing supervisor was Jane Palmieri, the designer was North
Market Street Graphics, and the production supervisor was
Pamela Pelton. It was set in Century Expanded by Teresa
Leaden of McGraw-Hill's Professional Book Group
composition unit.*

Printed and bound by R. R. Donnelley & Sons Company.

All photographs courtesy of the Graham family collection.

McGraw-Hill books are available at special quantity discounts
to use as premiums and sales promotions, or for use in corporate
training programs. For more information, please write to the
Director of Special Sales, McGraw-Hill, 11 West 19th Street,
New York, NY 10011. Or contact your local bookstore.

This book is printed on acid-free paper.

Contents

Introduction by Seymour Chatman   *vii*

1. Childhood in New York   *1*

2. Family Tragedies and My Mother's Perseverance   *19*

3. At Public School   *37*

4. High School Days: Brooklyn and the Bronx   *55*

5. The Farmhand and The Mechanic   *73*

6. The College Student   *93*

7. My Career Begins   *123*

8. Early Years in Wall Street   *141*

9. The Beginnings of Real Success   *163*

10. The Great Bull Market of the 1920s: I Become a Near Millionaire   *185*

11. The Northern Pipeline Contest   *199*

12. Family and Other Affairs   *217*

13. The Midpoint of Life's Way: The Deluge
    Begins   247

14. The Road Back, 1933–1940   267

15. My "Career" as a Playwright   279

16. The Commodity Reserve Currency Plan   293

Epilogue: Benjamin Graham's Self-Portrait
         at Sixty-Three and his Eightieth
         Birthday Speech   309

Chronology   317

Notes   327

Bibliography of Writings by and about
Benjamin Graham   337

Index   343

Introduction

In his sixties and seventies, Benjamin Graham, retired and living variously in Beverly Hills and La Jolla, California, Aix-en-Provence, and Madeira, wrote an account of his life which he called "Things I Remember." He put down as much as he could remember of his family and business life, and of the sights and sounds of his hometown, New York City. But he puzzled over the capriciousness of memory: why could he remember trivial things even as he forgot important ones? He wrote:

> How we remember some things and forget others intrigues me, yet few writers of memoirs acknowledge memory gaps. To write honestly "I don't recall" seems to vitiate the very goal of a memoir; yet psychologists, if no other readers, might arrive at valuable insights into the 'real character' of the writer by comparing what he remembers with what he forgets. I wrote a little self-epitaph which turns on this very point:
>
> This man remembered what the rest forgot
> Forgetting much that everyone recalled;
> He studied long, worked hard, and smiled a lot,
> By Beauty nourished and by Love enthralled.

In some respects, this memoir shows great recall, and associates have attested to Graham's astonishing memory for professional details—corporate assets, prices, yields, and the like. Already on his first job he set out to memorize whole tables of bond figures. Later, his lectures, books, and articles were studded with the particulars of corporate history.

Still, he confessed to an inability to remember oft-dialed

telephone numbers or the names of familiars. He was legendary for his forgetfulness: he once drove two of his children
to the Rockefeller Center ice rink, parked the car, took them
skating, and then all three went home by subway. A son's
mother-in-law reports that, once when she went to visit him in
Aix, he stuck out his hand and introduced himself as if he had
never seen her before. Of his "peculiar" memory he wrote:

> It retains and can reproduce countless historical and
> literary items that were stored there as long as sixty-
> five years ago. But it is completely useless in such mat-
> ters as telephone numbers (looked up a hundred
> times), the location of friends' apartments (visited al-
> most as often), the very names of people I have met
> frequently—although I may surprise comparative
> strangers by addressing them properly after a long in-
> terval. I have often had occasion to rescue myself from
> embarrassment by the formula of Italo Svevo (author
> of the great *Confessions of Zeno*). Not remembering
> someone he should have known well, he remarked
> wistfully: "You really must excuse me. There are three
> things I always forget—names, faces—and—I can't re-
> member the third."

More than most, Graham's memory was highly focused and
selective: he remembered what was important to him. He *did*
remember a student's name if he had had an interesting discussion with him. Ideas, perhaps, were more important to him
than people, statistics more than telephone numbers, and,
from the beginning, but increasingly as he grew older, culture
and the life of the mind more than money.

Though they cover only the first forty-plus years of his life,
these pages are being published as "Memoirs" rather than
"Things I Remember" to underline Graham's consciously literary intentions.[1] Obviously, a memoir is not the same as a journal, which strives to keep a record of experiences as they

occur. Recollected in tranquility years after the events it narrates, the memoir takes a longer view. Perhaps because he was too busy studying the market to keep a personal journal, Graham wrote memoirs in his sixties and seventies as compensation.

A memoir also subtly differs from an autobiography. Presuming to tell the whole, continuous story, the autobiographer pretends, if as a necessary fiction, to complete and accurate recall. The memoir, on the other hand, suggests a more casual and ruminative approach. It frees the author of the shackles of sequence, allows him to introduce flashbacks and flashforwards without restraint, to skip between the historical "then" and the compositional "now." It gives freer rein to meditation, to philosophical weighing of the meanings of raw experience. As Gore Vidal put it recently:

> A memoir is how one remembers one's own life, while an autobiography is history, requiring research, dates, facts double-checked. I've taken the memoir route on the ground that even an idling memory is apt to get right what matters most.[2]

Dates, facts, figures, and percentages mattered a great deal professionally to Benjamin Graham; but when he wrote his memoir, "getting it right" clearly mattered more. Graham sought not just a record of his life but an honest assessment. He confided to his memoirs his frankest thoughts—thoughts long meditated and in some cases hard won. They reveal a man for whom truth to himself was the most important objective, even when that meant contradicting received opinion. Just as he had questioned Wall Street lore during his investment career, in the privacy of his memoirs he questioned orthodox attitudes about personal belief and conduct. For example, he tells us how the nine-year-old Benjamin really felt (as opposed to how he should have felt) about the death of his young father: the sky somehow was supposed to fall in, but it didn't. His account of his mother is no less frank: his description of her modest shortcomings makes the tally of her strengths all the more persuasive. The text is full of expressions like "Honesty compels me..." and "A man of mental integrity could only think..."

And then there is religion. Jewish readers may be put off by Graham's early interest in Jesus (as an ethical, not a religious, figure), or his belief that Jews might have been better off being born Gentile, or that their true purpose in life should be to intermarry with other faiths to enrich the common gene pool. Obviously, it would be absurd to interpret these opinions as antisemitic. He was, after all, a prominent figure in Jewish causes, a vital president of the Jewish Guild for the Blind, for example. But Graham was too cosmopolitan to be tied to anything like parochial faith. Besides, what he criticized was not Judaism per se, but the shallower, more puritanic attitudes of some of its practitioners, attitudes which, in his view, narrowed and inhibited mental growth and cultural breadth. It is true that he came to accept many values inimical to Orthodox Judaism. But in that, he differed little from a goodly number of the offspring of Jewish immigrants, as Irving Howe has so thoroughly documented in *World of Our Fathers*.[3] Unlike Eastern European Jews or the previous generation of German Jews, Graham was born in England. His parents spoke the Queen's English, not Yiddish, and that doubtless accelerated his assimilation into American culture.

Graham came to his convictions after long, searching, and realistic meditations about history, garnered from extensive reading and daily immersion in the intricate values-testing of Wall Street. Emotionally, he envied those able to believe; but reason (backed by serious reading) kept him skeptical. Yet it was a positive skepticism, a skepticism grounded in the Enlightenment, steeped in Classical and Judeo-Christian values. His skepticism fed and was fed by an increasingly justifiable confidence in his own powers of reasoning, a confidence essential to a professional investor.

The term *memoir* resonates with the literary values so precious to Graham. He was an avid reader of the great authors, many in their original languages: Homer, Euripides, Virgil, Cicero, Horace, Lucretius, Tacitus, Catullus, Dante, Cervantes, Shakespeare, Bacon, Milton, Descartes, Pope, Fielding, Gibbon, Lessing, Macauley, Schiller, Kant, Dickens, De Quincey, Emily Brontë, Tennyson, Nietzsche, Hugo, Whitman, Tolstoy, Housman, Baudelaire, Ibsen, Conrad, Proust, Kafka, Rilke, Svevo, and especially relevant to this book, memoirists like Benjamin Franklin, Rousseau, La Rochefoucauld, Chateaubriand, and the Goncourt brothers. Clearly, he aimed at a memoir no less literary than his poems and plays, and his memoir is the most successful of his literary efforts. Always deeply interested in literature, the theater, the opera, and the concert hall, retirement gave Graham the leisure to immerse himself in these pleasures. (He was not, however, sensitive to the visual arts; he would spend more time reading the commentary than looking at the paintings and sculptures. Nor was he much interested in natural landscapes.) Not that he gave up the financial world entirely, but he watched it from an increasingly disinterested and lofty perspective. He felt no desire to make more money than he had and was relatively casual about his personal finances. Still, he was clearly pleased when his old students and associates sought out his advice about the market, especially when it was down. And in his very late years he mustered the energy to join James Rea in the Rea-Graham mutual fund.

This memoir is a personal account, not a practical guide to investment. For that, the reader must consult Graham's *Security Analysis* or *The Intelligent Investor*, investment books which many believe to be the best, and certainly the wisest, ever written. (Copies of the first edition of *Security Analysis*, 1934, currently command four-figure prices.) Still, the insights into Graham's early life that emerge here suggest how he got to be the superb investor that he was. His personality and talents can be explained in terms both of heredity and environment. His prodigious intellectual inheritance (he was a grand-nephew of the Chief Rabbi of Warsaw) inclined him to research, at a time when research was not a serious project in brokerage houses. The environment in which he grew up—his mother's permissive "let boys be boys" attitude and the tough streets of Manhattan, Brooklyn, and the Bronx—instilled a sharp sense of reality. He learned how to handle himself, not with his fists but with his brains. At the same time, he managed to avoid the aggressiveness that sometimes goes with a New York upbringing. Those who knew him describe his demeanor as gentlemanly, even courtly.

Along with its mean streets, the city offered the bounty of its school system, in all its turn-of-the-century splendor. In high school—Townsend Harris Hall, the "subfreshman" division of City College and Boys High in Brooklyn—Graham met and gloried in the challenge of what was arguably America's best public education. Today, one can only marvel at this excellent free instruction—imagine having one of America's great philosophers, Morris Raphael Cohen, as your high school geometry teacher. Call it elitism if you like, but Graham's retrospective plea that gifted students be adequately challenged must strike a chord in every thoughtful parent's heart.

The story of the bureaucratic mistake that temporarily blocked Graham's admission to Columbia (see Chapter 5) is poignant, but his own rejection of the same CCNY that he had previously admired as a "subfreshman" may seem a bit snobbish. Another way to consider his decision, however, is that he was looking for quality, for the best college education that money could buy—not his, of course, since he didn't have any, but what a scholarship would provide. He thought about Harvard—and would doubtless have been admitted if his mother had not insisted on his staying in New York. When he finally entered Columbia, he took no courses in business or anything even resembling it. He was fascinated by the humanities, by language and literature, by history, by philosophy. His career provides ammunition for the counterargument to the thesis that the MBA is the only real educational path into business.

Graham's memoir also documents what many teachers suspect: that the best, and perhaps the only, durable education is self-education. The most important thing that he learned was how to learn—on his own—and how gratifying it was to do so. He was astonished to discover that his fellow students forgot most of what they had prepared for school, forgot it deliberately, as if assignments were mere day work, obstacles to hurdle on the way to the "important" thing in life—making money. Graham built assignments into the furniture of his mind; this was the first kind of wealth he acquired, and, indeed, ultimately the kind that meant the most to him.

Even early on, the acquisition of money for its own sake was less important to him than it has been to most professional investors. Still in his twenties, he reacted negatively to Bernard Baruch's decision to give up his clientele and invest solely for himself:

> What a discreditable thing, I thought, for a highly gifted and enormously wealthy young man to decide to do with his life—to dedicate himself formally to making a lot more money, all for himself. And then, into the bargain, to write this down in his memoirs, without the slightest pang of regret or self-criticism.

But honesty compelled him to take a more charitable view of Baruch's decision, especially since it coincided with his own acceptance of an invitation to start his own fund:

> But was my decision any more creditable than Baruch's? I too was leaving the brokerage business, where at least I was giving helpful counsel to the public, to limit myself exclusively to a money-making venture. But I was far from a rich man by Wall Street standards. And I had been making good profits for friends and relatives who needed the money.

Graham's later preference for culture over money was elo-
quently expressed in his eightieth birthday speech (see pages
312–315), in which he recommended to his grandchildren the
incomparable richness of intellectual endeavor—for its own
sake, independent of material acquisitions. Of course, investing
does entail making money; but one feels about Graham that after
a certain point in time, his motive had less to do with personal
enrichment than with proving that his theories were indeed correct.

Why did he go to Wall Street in the first place? Graham's
father died young, but his mother and two brothers (though
scarcely older than he) nurtured without spoiling him. He inherited both the family's poverty and his mother's taste for luxury.
This combination put him into something of a quandary:

> Mother tried hard not to talk too often and with too
> much regret of our former and vanished splendor. But
> there remained so much to remind her of it that she
> found it difficult to put it out of mind. No doubt the
> chief of her chagrins came from the best-meaning
> source—our old friends. They remained faithful and
> did not desert us. But the contrast between their finan-
> cial state and ours was only too visible to Mother's
> eyes. More tangibly, their visits to us and ours to them
> imposed a constant pressure on Mother to disguise our
> poverty as much as possible, to cultivate all the stra-
> tagems of seedy respectability, to live always and pre-
> cariously a little higher rather than a little lower than
> our means allowed.
>
> We boys were steeped in that frustrating atmo-
> sphere, and on one of us at least it made a strong, un-
> wholesome impression. My natural inclination, I be-
> lieve, was always away from the material and towards
> the intellectual and even the spiritual side of life. But
> the difficult conditions of my childhood existence af-
> fected me no less than my brothers; I became too con-

scious and respectful of money. I took it for granted that the primary mark of success in life lay in large earning and large spending.

At the same time, and as if in compensation for this dilemma, his mother passed on a determination and grit that was to stand Benjamin in good stead. He learned to stick to his guns, whether it was eating the Grape-Nuts he had ordered in his earliest solo venture into a restaurant, or insisting on mailing his mother an apple from the farm over the postmaster's warning that it would rot, or standing up to the management of the Northern Pipeline Company. It was through his mother's insistence that he found the courage to reapply at Columbia after his incomprehensible failure to receive a scholarship. And doubtless it was a fortitude like hers that enabled him to weather both personal and business catastrophes like his two divorces and the Crash.

Perhaps his mother's financial plight and his family's experience as poor relatives helped to persuade Graham to choose a profession that would guarantee a decent income over the relatively penurious life of the college teacher. But his "natural inclination" to the life of the mind was to prevail. He came ultimately to care little for luxury after he mastered "the simplest and most important of all the rules of material welfare: The most brilliant financial strategy consists of living well within one's means."[4]

And he ended up being a college professor anyway, first to supplement his income during the Depression, but later out of the sheer love of teaching. Once he had made enough, money seemed decreasingly important. If he had gone in the other direction, what would he have been professor of? Practically anything, apparently, since his interests were so wide and his competencies so great. Even in 1914, it was quite remarkable that a graduating senior (especially a Jew) should receive offers to teach in no less than three departments, as diverse as English, philosophy, and mathematics, in an Ivy League university.

Instead he became a financial analyst—indeed, the first—
and has been canonized as such by Wall Street.[5] We can already discern the lineaments of Graham's investment theory
in his early development and influences. His family's situation
stimulated a penchant for caution. Still, he was to forget it
temporarily during his (and the nation's) feverish twenties.
What young man in his situation could resist the temptation of
easy money? Hence the Savold Tire fiasco described in Chapter 9. But unlike other young men, he learned his lesson early
and well. The need for caution was intensely reinforced by his
experience of the Crash and Great Depression. Like an engineer—one of the several careers he once contemplated—he
came to insist on an extremely wide margin of safety for his
investments. He deplored speculation as a form of gambling
(recalling the warning of his first boss, Alfred Newburger: "If
you speculate you'll lose your money"). He began to look for
securities that were *so* undervalued that, in the long haul, they
had only the remotest chance of losing market value. Neither
he nor anyone else (except perhaps the clairvoyant Baruch)
could have guessed the depths of the market plunge of 1929
and the length of the ensuing Depression. But despite the mis-
eries of the era, Graham persisted, and his techniques ultimately proved sound. His confidence in his own powers of reasoning enabled him to formulate and test his theories of value
investing and to ignore Wall Street's perennial claim to antici-
pate the market's direction and timing. Not only did he ignore
prognostication, but he profited from other investors' lem-
ming-like adherence to it. He preferred more reliable sources
—the actual facts and figures of corporate performance, which
he learned and taught his disciples to decode. John Train offers
a good metaphor to describe the way he ignored the clamor of
the marketplace:

> Graham, like a doctor working over a patient who has
> fallen to the ground in a riot, rarely lifts his head to
> contemplate the madness around him, but in his books

you can always hear that madness howling in the back-
ground.[6]

Perhaps it is not an accident that Benjamin Jr. decided to
study medicine and is today an emergency room physician.

How did the Graham-Newman company work? Here is a
good description:

Graham-Newman's operations were restricted to a few
well-defined categories, each of which promised a satisfactory rate of profit—say, 20% per annum, or better—against relatively minor risks. The latter were
further minimized by wide diversification. The categories were entitled: arbitrages; cash payouts (liquidations); related hedges; unrelated hedges; current-asset
stocks ("bargain issues"), and controlled companies—
the special province of J. A. Newman. A careful check
was kept on the result of each operation and class of
operations.

One consequence of this continuous evaluation of
results may seem surprising. The "unrelated hedges"
—in which a "cheap issue" is bought and an entirely
disconnected "dear issue" is sold against it—were
found to be more trouble than their overall profit was
worth, and they were accordingly dropped. The Graham-Newman "value approach" did not work well
enough in the short-selling of highly popular and hence
apparently over-valued issues, *unless* there was adequate protection through holding of a senior, convertible issue of the same company.

The "bargain issues" were practically all restricted
to the purchase of common stocks at less than two-
thirds of their net-current-asset value. Remarkably
few final losses were shown in this category, comprising [sic: "considering"?] the purchase of many hundred
such issues over a period of more than thirty years.

However, it is both paradoxical and typical of financial experience generally that the most profitable Graham-Newman operation of all did not meet this exacting requirement. This was the purchase of a 50% ownership of Government Employees Insurance Company at a price only slightly below its asset value.[7]

Graham was an inventive man, even in the literal sense. He devised an improved version of the slide rule and composed a list of words whose memorization would guarantee rapid learning of the Morse Code, each word immediately identifying the pattern of dots and dashes of the letter in question. His attempts at an electric door release and a pie-plate that cut pie into exactly equal pieces may have been less successful, but they were of a piece with the mind that invented new ways of determining stock values, ways then unknown in Wall Street. His mind was teeming with such inventions. He wrote them down in a tiny notebook which he called his "pillow book."

Aside from sheer brain power, Graham's greatest strength was his intellectual independence and his integrity. He was affable, but affability seems to have had little to do with his success. He was no salesman. He pretty much failed at peddling ice cream–making machines, shirtboard advertising, phonograph records, and bonds. But neither did his affability interfere with the hard logic of his decision making. In his own words:

> B. [Benjamin] achieved a degree of independence in any area in which his judgment told him that his conduct ought not to be dictated by mere convention or prejudice.[8]

Graham sought profits not only safely and by careful research but by the most honest means. IIis morality stands at the opposite pole of Wall Street operators of the sort played by Michael Douglas in the film *Wall Street*. Graham was so known

for his probity and even dealing that state and federal governments sought him for objective opinions about the values of
corporations in litigation and about establishing regulatory
agencies like the SEC. He was scrupulous to a fault: he felt
obliged in the memoirs to list even the most trivial "peculations"—stealing a penny from his mother's purse, making a
dollar or two as an usher giving better seats to theatergoers
than their tickets warranted, tacitly accepting the proceeds of
a bit of state government graft during his business career,
helping a playwright continue to receive disability insurance
payments though he was able to work. These minuscule lapses
only humanized him, persuaded him to adopt a charitable tolerance for the more serious misfeasances of relatives, friends,
and ex-employees.

Not only Graham's passive but also his active ethics were
impressive. He acted for unknown fellow stockholders in
demanding the distribution of excessive corporate capital (for
example, in the Northern Pipeline Company affair, Chapter 11).
And, though he drew no salary or commissions during the
Depression, he continued to do his best for his clients. He felt
genuine concern about not staying in touch with his resigned
superior at the U.S. Express Company, or about ousting the
less than competent president of the Unexcelled Fireworks
Company. Graham had neither the mind nor the inclinations of
the modern takeover artist cynically prepared to wreck a company for personal profit, regardless of the fate of employees,
management, and creditors. And we can imagine what he might
say about a financial world where feckless young traders could
bankrupt huge banks by pressing a few keys on their computer.

This memoir suggests that Graham's political stance is not
different from contemporary moderates: fiscally conservative,
but socially liberal. Consider, for example, two proposals presented at the Economic Forum at the New School of Social
Research, one

for large-scale slum clearance and its replacement by

low-cost housing, with subsidies for the former slum
tenants to the extent needed to meet the new rents.

Another,

> a plan whereby people who had lost their jobs were
> entitled to personal credit based on their skills and
> experience, credit to be advanced to them by the fed-
> eral government in the form of unsecured loans, bear-
> ing small or no interest and repayable on appropriate
> terms when they found jobs. While the latter two pro-
> posals appeared radical in the extreme to believers in
> the laissez-faire philosophy of the pre-Roosevelt days,
> they are not far different from schemes actually
> adopted in later years.[9]

In a letter to his daughter Marjorie, Graham sketched out
two proposals, one called "FANN"—Free Adequate Nourish-
ment principle—and the other "FFEB"—Food for Everybody.

> *Principle*: Everybody is entitled to have available
> nourishment without paying for it—no less and *no
> more...*
> *Scheme:* Establish in every school for which there is
> a demand for the service, a canteen which will supply
> two meals a day of adequate nourishment for any and
> all who may come in and ask for it. No frills of any kind.
> No questions asked, no investigations, no sermons...
> *Major control*: By an administrator who will have
> two functions of *equal* importance:
> (1) To assure that everyone—as nearly as possible—
> who wants adequate nourishment will have it within
> reach.
> (2) To assure that *nothing beyond this* is offered or
> accomplished by the plan. (Any other kind of service—

including special diets, extras of any sort—must be provided outside of the plan.)

My comment: The success of the plan will depend on two factors, viz: (a) Will the number of "free riders" (who "ought" to pay for their meals) be tolerable or excessive?

(b) Can the various bureaucratic excrescences be held to a really low part of total effort?

The idea of a *strict limit* implies meals on the order of those of the Salvation Army etc. but adequate.[10]

Graham was assuredly a capitalist, but a capitalist with a social conscience.

Little, of course, need be said about Graham's box score as an investor. The record speaks for itself. Recently, *The Wall Street Journal* placed him in the pantheon of the greatest investors of all time, with his student Warren Buffett, Peter Lynch, and George Soros. His average return was 17 percent—not as high as the others in the list, but then it was a record achieved over a period that included the Crash and the Great Depression, from 1929 to 1956.[11]

What is less known is Graham's prowess as an economist. Chapter 16 in the memoir explains his thoughts on one of the most serious problems of the Depression—the fluctuation of commodity prices and its volatile impact on markets and the economy as a whole. This interest gave rise to two books whose importance and current relevance is, unfortunately, obscured by the fact that they have been out of print for more than fifty years. They are *Storage and Stability* (1937) and *World Commodities and World Currency* (1944). These books discuss problems that are in greater need of solution than ever.

The first book was prompted by the widespread deflation accompanying the Depression. It proposes a way of stabilizing the American economy through replacing the standard tender for the dollar—then gold and silver—with "a basketful of commodities," that is, nonperishable goods like wheat, cotton, and

iron that could be purchased by the government with dollars
and stored for constant availability to consumers in exchange
for dollars. Graham describes his commodity reserve plan in
clear terms in Chapter 16.

World Commodities and World Currency presents essentially the same theory but transferred to the international
scene. The situation in 1944, of course, was quite different
from that in 1937. The war was over, and with it the Depression, since the American economy had been enormously stimulated by military production. Graham now saw the problem
not as deflation from overproduction, but inflation from scar-
city. But the market-basket commodity reserve principle, he
felt, was equally applicable to the new situation:

> The peoples of the earth have been promised a fuller
> peacetime utilization of its resources, the pattern for
> which has already been exhibited in the stupendous
> achievements of war production. Not only must sub-
> stantially full production be attained after the war; it
> must be *maintained* as well, without the once familiar
> aftermath of a pricked bubble and a deep depression.[12]

Graham was deeply concerned—even offended—by the standard practice of destroying commodities for the sake of sus-
taining prices. Taking coffee as an example, he notes:

> We have seen that ultimate absurdity of modern eco-
> nomics—the destruction of the earth's bounty—pro-
> ceeding not only in years of deepest depression but
> season after season, in good times and bad. From 1931
> through 1943, more than 75 million bags were burned;
> that is over 100 billion pounds, enough to supply the
> whole world for four years.[13]

He argued that there was no reason that the world economy
could not permanently expand, constantly increase abundance,

and provide goods to those who had never known anything but poverty. His motive was humanitarian, but also practical. Stockpiled commodities, or "buffer stocks," which could be eaten or transformed into useful finished products would also be more efficient in controlling economic swings than buried bars of lustrous metal destined never to be used. The granary was a better and a more meaningful depository for mankind than the mint, for both lean years and fat. It could at once stabilize prices (and hence the economy as a whole), a task that cartels pretended to but could not actually achieve, and provide resources that would prove a Godsend during times of unforeseen catastrophe. The book offers a close argument for the viability of this thesis, an argument that certainly deserves to be re-examined.

In his personal life, Graham has the reputation of having been a womanizer, with all the shallowness that that characterization implies. Symptomatic was the published eulogy for his posthumous induction into the U.S. Business Hall of Fame in April 1988. The author speaks of him as "a susceptible man in some ways—he was married three times, and leaped from blonde to blonde like an Alpine goat springing from peak to peak." His friend and student, Warren Buffett, more generously describes this aspect of his character—"It was all open and everything, but Ben liked women. And women liked him. He wasn't physically attractive—he looked like Edward G. Robinson—but he had style."[14] Buffett added that Graham wanted "to do something creative, something foolish, and something generous every day." *Fortune* could not resist putting a flippant twist on Buffett's compliment: "Inventing security analysis and value investing is evidence enough of Graham's creativity and generosity. And the foolish? Graham usually took care of that before getting out of bed."[15]

Whether or not love-making is a foolish act, it is a mistake to think of Benjamin Graham as a playboy. He did admire women and enjoy flirtation, though his demeanor in public was widely perceived as correct, even gracious. Much of his flirtation was

elegant, and often intellectual. He was indeed married three
times—to Hazel Mazur, Carol Wade, and Estelle Messing—
and also had his share of extramarital affairs. But unlike most
womanizers (except perhaps the learned Don Juan himself),
he seriously weighed his behavior, using his considerable understanding of the workings of the conscious and rational
mind. His blind point seemed to be that he tried to apply to his
love life the same sort of reasoning that made him a professional success. The women in his life should, he felt, repay his
courtesy and sweet reasonableness in kind, by following *his*
notions of fairness and decent behavior. It is easy enough to
agree that Graham was a reasonable man, but he reminds one
of Mr. Higgins in *My Fair Lady* (a musical which he surely
must have seen[16]), who plaintively asks "Why can't a woman
be more like a man?" He actually tried to get one of his wives
to sign a contract to "behave." By his own admission, it took
him a long time to learn how to relate to women emotionally.
An interesting passage in Chapter 10 of *The Intelligent
Investor* compares the haphazard ways in which "most
investors" pick a stock to the way they pick wives:

> It is difficult to describe exactly how most investors go
> about the business of choosing common stocks. By
> exactly what mental processes does A decide that he
> wants Bethlehem Steel at 35, while B prefers Wool-
> worth at 46, and C selects Allied Chemical at 190? The
> operation seems to be something like choosing a wife.
> A number of concrete factors are weighed more or less
> carefully, to which is then added a strong and perhaps
> controlling component of unreasoning favoritism.[17]

"Unreasoning favoritism" says as much about his own view of
love and marriage as it does about investor habits. But how
much can one hold against a man who explicitly acknowledges
his difficulties, as he does so often in the pages that follow, and
tacitly in some of his literary efforts, like the play, *China Wed-*

ding (described in Chapter 15)? At least Benjamin Graham did not live the unexamined life.

Nor is there much point in defending someone born in 1894 against charges of sexism. He was doubtless unconscious of the extent to which he used power to get his way with women. He does show a degree of insensitivity that few would find tolerable today. But the issue is complicated, and his own acknowledgment of emotional limitations seems honest enough to deserve a hearing. Beyond flirtation and casual affairs, he links his amatory difficulties to a *general* problem with personal intimacy—with men as well as women, with family as well as strangers. He complains of an inability to acquire close friends—"chums or cronies," as he calls them.[18] A colorful metaphor ascribes this to shyness and sensitivity: "Very early in life he set to work like a beaver to build a breastwork around his heart. He embraced stoicism as a gospel sent to him from Heaven." With women—who seemed, to the boy, creatures from another planet—he felt the problem was compounded, at least until he found his ultimate mate, Malou. Before he met her, his relations with women were hardly as joyous as *Fortune* implies. In his self-portrait, Graham writes:

> A large area of comparative failure was his dealings with women. Throughout his life he had no difficulty in finding women who attracted him and for whom he had sufficient appeal. Nor was his sex life inadequate or unvaried after he had overcome the copybook puritanism of his first manhood. In his view his troubles with women came about merely because they chose to take umbrage at his good qualities—particularly his even temper and his intellect. In return he developed some feeling of persecution and exploitation at their hands. Partly out of real experience, partly perhaps out of imagination, he felt that nearly all women were unreasonable, dominating, unappreciative of his kind-

ness and patience, too insistent on penetrating into the
forbidden sanctum of his private self.[19]

Yes, his language is defensive, especially its insistence on his
own "good qualities...good temper and intellect." But he
acknowledges—as few men do—that the failure was partly his
own and recognizes that his feelings of persecution and exploitation may have been fanciful.

No one can deny the brilliant applicability of his reasoning
powers to his profession. Liberated from parochialism and
prejudice by temperament and a brilliant secondary school
and college education, he was able to see through the mumbo-
jumbo of inside Wall Street, to question traditional practices,
in brief, to invent value investing. But it took him longer to
become truly independent emotionally, to free himself of the
claims of tradition. In an era when everybody praises "family
values" (whatever values they privately practice), it may be
difficult for us to see the positive side of Graham's personal
morality. For one thing, his sense of family was strong. His
daughter, Elaine Graham Sofer, observes that his paternal values were traditional enough: "When I was about ten, I freely
roamed our extensive family library in search of grown-up
books. I soon became immersed in some art books which fea-
tured classical Greek statues in various degrees of undress.
When Dad discovered this, he did not scold but he did firmly
remove and lock them away."

It's become all too easy (and not a little hypocritical) these
days to ridicule men in the public eye who are attracted to
(and attract) women other than their wives. But in Graham's
case, another way to look at his womanizing is as a search,
even late in life, for the right companion. When he found her,
his womanizing ended. He writes:

[V]ery late in life...B. met a woman who possessed the
qualities of soul and mind, of character and tempera-

ment, which he had sought vainly in many others. To her, he felt, he could lower the barriers that had separated him from the rest of humanity. Under this new influence he inquired for the first time into the nature of these barriers.[20]

It sounds like Graham yearned for—and finally found, in his sixties—someone with whom he could relax his defenses, understand the foundations of his "beaver breastwork" and so dismantle it, or at least escape its excessive constrictions. By all accounts, his commitment to this woman, "this personage from *outre mer*," was deep and total. He learned the price he had paid for traits which once seemed exemplary: his "pleasant conduct," his "basic reluctance to criticize others...[or] to sit in judgment upon them," his invariable affability, courtesy, agreeableness, and patience, his avoidance of "conflicts of all kinds, even those of abstract opinion if any emotion might be involved." In retrospect, he found these not to be the virtues that they had once seemed. Instead, he saw

> smugness, selfishness, snobbery, a certain contrived artificiality in his generous gestures, a touch of calculated egoism in his unruffled serenity. His third wife said of him that he was humane, but not human—the phrase struck home. He lacked genuine sympathy, a true sharing of the joys and sorrows of others. His enthusiasms were either entirely impersonal—for ideas, for artistic creations—or else for those things that contributed to his own development, his inner glory. He [had] "turned from praise" with unfeigned modesty, but that modesty was itself a manifestation of a pride so perfect as to be indistinguishable from vanity. His was Horace's *mens sibi conscia recti*—"a mind conscious of its own rectitude"—wrapped in the insulation of confident superiority. Like Landor, he strove with

none, for none was worth his striving—at least in his own estimation. He recognized only one close companion, only one kindred spirit—himself.

That's pretty subtle insight (and note how the classics helped him achieve it). The capacity for such insight, and the frankness to express it, makes it easy to forgive the self-scrutinizer many of his failings.

Much changed after he met Malou; he came to understand

the need for less superiority and more humanity... At age 60 and beyond he was to begin his emotional development all over again; he must accept Love not as an experience of life, but as *the* experience of life.

Graham was proud of his achievements, and in the privacy of his memoirs, he is not adverse to name-dropping[21] nor to celebrating the privileges that wealth brought him. He had no false modesty; indeed, the memoir shows a faint tendency to boast, though the trait is more than compensated by his readiness to put himself down, often in humorous terms. He was an inveterate and clever punster (however one might feel about that genre). Beyond puns, his subtle sense of humor lightened both his conversation and his exposition of economics and investment theory in writings and lectures. (A nice example is his proposal that the French pay off their World War I debt in wine, Chapter 16.) According to relatives, friends, and students, sly and enigmatic humor marked his ordinary demeanor.

Graham was not only well versed in letters but wrote with some distinction. The style of his professional books and articles is clear and forceful, though tending a bit to the impersonality of business prose. His vocabulary was crafted in the tradition of *The Magazine of Wall Street*, an influential investment journal of the teens and twenties. The photographs and drawings of the dignitaries who wrote those articles—Irving Fisher, Professor Hollander, Richard D. Wyckoff, and the rest—with their wing collars and severe miens, is of a piece with the antique ponderousness of their prose. The style contained little of the hype or figurative language that characterizes modern business writing: profits were not "sensational" or "boring," they were simply "satisfactory" or "attractive." The market didn't "go south," it simply fell. The subtitle of *The Intelligent Investor* is "A Book of Practical Counsel." In his goals and practicality, Graham reminds one a bit of Benjamin Franklin, whom he admired greatly. Though his search for objectivity led him to overuse the passive voice and other impersonal constructions, his style is generally lively and evocative. For example, this memoir catches the sights and sounds of early Manhattan brilliantly:

> Little locomotives like that in Central Park used to draw the elevated trains in those far-off days. They would go by overhead with a fine roar and sizzle, and in the winter evenings we could watch the flame and sparks. When later the El was electrified, we could still see a flock of these minute steam engines gathered together in a little raised yard along the tracks. Eventually they disappeared, having been sold, I believe, to some South American country.

Graham did less well with poetry and playwrighting, as he acknowledges. Despite his appreciation of the great literature of the ages, poetry was not his strong suit. But he wrote at least one good poem, a poem which combines rather well his affection for cats and the Renaissance man's concern for the big picture. He called it "Tempus Felis" ("Cat Time"):

> O Time, that with your kitten-tongue
> Lap up the scant cream of our lives,
> And even whilst you purr a song
> Sink in our flesh your tiger-knives;
> O Time, that with your felon paws

Pounce crafty-cruel on scampering men,
Whom for a subtle God's applause
You trap, release, and seize again;

O Time, that gazes incurious
Past all our prayer and snivel-curse,
As we in you you live in us,
Your prize, your prey—your universe.

Graham's short-lived career as playwright suggests that his ability to craft character and plot was not great. The production on Broadway of his play *Baby Pompadour* seems due more to good connections in the theater world than to the play's intrinsic merit.

But Graham's devotion to literature was deep and genuine, and it did find another outlet, namely, translations. His English versions of Latin verse (colleagues assure me) are quite respectable. He also translated a novel by the Uruguayan author, Mario Benedetti, *La Truega*, "The Truce." Though there is no report of formal study of Spanish, his linguistic gifts led to a professional, publishable translation. Benedetti's novel concerns an accountant turning fifty and contemplating retirement. A widower, he has raised two boys and a girl. They live at home but are not close to him. One of his sons leaves home; the other angrily refuses to discuss his life with his father. Only with the girl can the accountant hold a reasonable discussion. Into this gray life enters a young woman recently hired as his subordinate. To his surprise, he is attracted to her, and to his greater surprise, she reciprocates. He sets up an apartment for her, though she continues to live part of the time at her parents'. (Her mother knows of the romance and does not disapprove.) The couple are very happy but very discreet. Still, he tells his daughter (who becomes fast friends with his mistress). Finally, the day of the protagonist's retirement arrives. But in the tragic denouement the young woman suddenly dies of heart failure, leaving the poor man twice a widower.

There would seem to be parallels between the protagonist's situation and Graham's own, particularly the love affair with the young mistress. In middle age, Graham also had a relationship with a young and beautiful woman, Carol Wade. It resulted in a brief marriage which ended considerably less idyllically than the Uruguayan accountant's. The alliance put a certain strain on relations between father and children. But that strain was relieved by Graham's later marriage to Estelle Messing (the mother of Benjamin Jr.), and his final relationship with Malou.

One detail of Benedetti's novel that strikes a resemblant chord is the description of the accountant's habits at work. It reminds one of Graham's description of his employment at Loeffler's telephone shop (Chapter 5). Much of the accountant's work is of a mechanical sort; he keeps himself from getting bored by "thinking of other things, and even (why shouldn't I say that to myself?)...dream[ing]." At Loeffler's, Graham's solution to the problem of boredom was to mentally recite classical poetry; but occasionally he got carried away and ended up shouting the lines aloud, much to his boss's annoyance. Perhaps his feelings at such moments were like Benedetti's protagonist's:

> It's as if I were divided into two beings, different, contradictory, independent. One who knows his work by heart, who is completely master of its ins and outs, who is always sure of what he's doing; the other dreamy and feverish, full of frustrated passion, a sad chap who, nonetheless, had, has and will have a call to joy; an absent-minded fellow who has no concern with where his pen is running or what things are being written by that blue ink which will turn black in eight months.[22]

Whatever the thematic connections between Graham and this fictional Uruguayan accountant, there is no denying the quality of Graham's translation. There is none of the elaborate

Victorian diction of his own verse and of his translations of classical and French and German poems. His prose reads succinctly and smoothly, conveying with accomplished ease the essence of Benedetti's simple tale.

The divisions of "life" and "work," "personal" and "professional," "feeling" and "thinking" were to preoccupy Graham throughout his life. Although no Freud,[23] in his later years he increasingly sought for emotional wisdom to match his understanding of the economic and financial ways of the world. A part of this quest led to a deeper understanding of the opposite sex and of his family.

He remained at bottom a man who was "rational, brilliant, and emotionally guarded."[24] But all three of his surviving children attest to Graham's capacities as a father, though in degrees and qualities that varied through the stages of his and their lives. At the very least, he was always conscientious, responsible, and more than adequately supportive. He was not only generous financially, but shared with his growing children the pleasures of literature, music, sport, and travel. At his best he could be a "marvelous father," especially towards an appreciative daughter in the stage that he most appreciated, mid-adolescence.[25]

What is finally so redeeming about Graham's character is his lifelong capacity to learn not only from books but from his personal experience—especially his mistakes.

Seymour Chatman
University of California, Berkeley

CHAPTER ONE

Childhood in New York

Many people seem to recall innumerable details of their earliest childhood, but I am not one of them. Very few impressions remain of events prior to my father's death, when I was only eight and a half years old. And some of the incidents I do recall are suspect, in the sense that I am not sure whether I remember the experience itself, or only someone's later account of it.

For example, I used to say that the earliest event I could clearly remember was being awakened, together with my brothers, by the eager voice of my mother crying "Leon, Victor, Benny, get up and run to the window! It's the twentieth century!" I was then five and a half, Victor a year older, Leon two years older. Very likely I remember her excitement, but, on reflection, I must concede that the story was told fairly often by my mother in after years and I may confuse her anecdote with the fact.

Remembered or not, I *was* born on May 9, 1894, at 87 Aberdeen Road in London, England, and my original name was Benjamin Grossbaum. (That date makes me one month younger than Khrushchev and one month older than the Duke of Windsor—two men who lost their jobs.) I was the youngest of three children, all boys. In fact, mother once told me—as a joke, I now suppose—that, being "the Benjamin of the family," I was naturally given that name. (Out of delicacy or a lack of the inquisitive sense, I never asked mother how it came about that there were none after me.)

My mother was quite explicit on one point: I had grievously disappointed her by being a boy. After one still-born son and two other male offspring, her heart was set on a daughter. She had no hesitation in telling me that her first impulse was to "throw me out of the window." But to spare my feelings, she always added that she was happy she hadn't done so.

I have looked up my namesake in the Bible, to find out what I could about his character and accomplishments. In Genesis, Benjamin is called the apple of his father's eye and the favorite of his brother, Joseph. But he does only two things in the narrative: (1) He weeps upon Joseph's neck (45:14), and (2) produces more children than any of his brothers—no less than ten, all boys (46:21). This was the more noteworthy achievement since he was a mere lad at the time he moved down to Egypt with all those sons. Daughters were mighty scarce in Jacob's family. He himself had only one, Dinah, along with twelve sons. These sons, in turn, had some fifty-odd children, of which only one—Sarah, daughter of Asher—was a girl. "Surely, it was the Lord's doing; it is wondrous in our eyes." The Bible says nothing directly about Benjamin's character, but Jacob's prophesy about him "in the last days" is far from flattering: "Benjamin shall ravin as a wolf; in the morning he shall devour the prey, and in the evening he shall divide the spoil" (49:27). Later, his descendants made plenty of trouble, and once were almost exterminated by their brother-tribes.

Sixty-one years after my birth, on a short trip to London, I felt the urge to revisit my birthplace. I gave the cabby the address I remembered, 14 Aberdeen Road. After considerable difficulty he found the street, an obscure one in the northeastern part of town. I descended—as one really does from those old London taxis—and with a slight beating of the heart walked up to number 14. It turned out to be one of a row of dingy, two-story brick houses, evidently occupied by workmen. Its appearance was a blow to my ego; family tradition had it that we were in comfortable circumstances, could afford several servants—at a pound per month apiece—and that we lived in a comfortable house with a pretty garden. Later I found that I had confused the number 14 with a house we occupied some summers later in Brighton, on Cambridge Road. So my disappointment had proceeded from error. The next year my cousin Wilfred brought me an authentic photograph of my first home as it appeared in 1956. The structure was by no means imposing, but it did have three stories and a large bay window. At the turn of the century it might have been a suitable example of bourgeois respectability. I visited it in 1960 and found it a pleasant little corner house, well-preserved for its age and with a minuscule garden running around two sides. It seemed more spacious when I had last played in it as a boy of seven.

Victor was born fourteen months after Leon, and I appeared thirteen months after Victor. This closeness of our ages proved most disconcerting to me as the youngest. But from the practical point of view it had numerous advantages, since it facilitated our being brought up as a unit. For example, we all learned a little French at the same time from our mademoiselle. I still have a letter I wrote in French at the age of four to "Cher Papa et Maman," then away on some trip. It is nicely done, on carefully ruled lines—too nicely, in fact, making me suspect that practically all of it, except that little boy's handwriting, must have been the work of Mademoiselle.

Whether we had more than one of these governesses over the years, I do not remember. She (or they) left no impression on me, other than a curious gastronomic one. We often had homemade charlotte russe for dessert—delicious sponge cake (not ladyfingers, as at present) filled with ineffable whipped cream. I still have a mental picture of some mademoiselle cutting up Uneeda biscuit cartons and forming the pieces into cardboard shells to hold the confections.

At the time of my birth our family had already begun a series of removes which were to continue many years. My brothers were born in Birmingham, England, where Father and his father imported china and bric-à-brac from Austria and Germany. Shortly after Victor's birth the business and the tributary families moved on to London. A year later a momentous decision was made: an American branch was to be set up, and my father—second of a large line of brothers—was to operate it. Thus, sometime in 1895, when I was not more than one year old, the five of us sailed to New York. We traveled second class, and when we reached America, we were looked over casually by a government doctor, and then we walked down the gangplank into our new country. There were no papers required or other formalities of immigration. Those were reserved for the fourth-class, or steerage, passengers, who were processed at Ellis Island in New York Harbor.

I do not know whether Father expected to live permanently in the United States. Probably not, since we boarded in a private home, instead of setting up one for ourselves. I do know that he was proud of his British nationality, which he retained to his death. In those days Englishmen were specially loath to change their allegiance, and it was only after World War I that the rest of us became American citizens.

In my early years I was a fiercely patriotic Englishman to whom the superiority of the British in practically every respect was so obvious as to make any challenge absurd. Needless to say, I found challenges to this view all about me in our new abode. At the turn of the century the United States had a strong inferiority complex vis-à-vis the mother country, and this was expressed to me in continuous criticisms and taunts. British manners and pretensions, the British accent, British clothes were all considered ridiculous in American surroundings.

The Myers family, whom we lived with—in the Sixties just off Park Avenue—consisted of a widowed mother and four each of sons and daughters. Practically all the children were living at home, apparently disinclined to get married and move out. How the one house could hold all of us comfortably, I have no idea. But I do remember that the Myers were most amiable towards us and especially affectionate towards me as the baby. But that did not prevent them from teasing me unmercifully about my Britishness. One altercation turned on the yacht race for the America's Cup. Naturally, I made no bones of my conviction that Sir Thomas Lipton's *Shamrock* was bound to win. It didn't, and I still smart from the ribbing I received.

Later, when I went to school, I found my pro-British bias confronted by anti-British feeling among my classmates. They were always refighting the Revolutionary War with me, comparing George Washington to George III—much to the latter's disadvantage—and even insisting that they had also won the ambiguous War of 1812. For a number of years, I spoke with a pronounced English accent, which our family had naturally imported with it to America and had communicated to me when I was learning to talk. At school I couldn't say "coffee" or "dog" without being derisively imitated. But, happily, by the time I was ten, very little of that accent remained.

There is a large photograph of us three boys, taken when I was two years old, at Richfield Springs, New York. Several portrait-size enlargements of this came into existence, and they hung through the ensuing years on various walls. They show the three of us, in descending order from left to right, the brim of one large straw hat meshed with that of its neighbor. We all have long, curly hair and are attired in white sailor suits with black silk scarves, white socks, and black patent-leather, one-button shoes. But woe and indignity to me! Instead of the masculine short pants worn by my brothers, I am captured for posterity in short skirts. In those far-off days that was the habit for very small boys who had not reached the state of functional dependability. The skirts made it easier for the nursemaid to change things. As to the effect on the victim, parents did not concern themselves much with the emotional reactions of their offspring.

The portrait came into being in a rather unusual way. Our family was in Richfield Springs—then a fashionable summer resort—because Father had leased a shop there for the season. Much of his business was done through auction sales at such places as Saratoga, Bar Harbor, Mackinaw Island, and even the more proletarian Atlantic City. Thus on July 4, 1896, we were spectators at the annual Richfield Springs Independence Day Parade. Dressed in our finest, we were placed in the window of our store to watch the celebration. According to Mother, we stood so intent and motionless that a lady came in to inquire whether the sculpture of the three children was for sale.

This sounds a bit apocryphal. But it is undoubtedly true that a professional photographer was so struck by us that he offered free prints if we would let him exhibit the portrait in his shop window. As a result we acquired quite an assortment of these photographs, in various sizes. Our visitors would fall into polite, and maybe genuine, ecstacies at the view of us three cherubs, but it was a long, long time before I could regard that white skirt with an indulgent smile instead of acute humiliation.

Of my father I remember very little indeed. This is the more regrettable because he was, by all accounts, a marvelous person. In later years I never heard anything said about him except in enthusiastic praise. He had "a heart as big as this world"—that was the common verdict—and he showed it by innumerable acts of consideration and financial assistance to his parents and ten brothers and sisters, as well as to others. Furthermore, he was handsome, vivacious, charming, and nearly always in high good humor. He was also an excellent business man, keen-witted, energetic, and unfailingly resourceful. In his last years the British branch of the business was proving unsuccessful, and the profits he made in America supported not only ourselves but also our parents, uncles, aunts, and cousins in England—a veritable army. This Father managed to do, somehow, but at the cost of enormous labor and nearly constant traveling about the country.

When I was five, my parents took me on a short trip to Hot Springs, Virginia, where Father hoped to recuperate from one of his illnesses. Of the trip three impressions remain. The first was that we were immured in the hotel for some days by spring floods, which brought melted snow from the nearby mountains coursing and eddying through the streets. Then there was a friendship which I struck up with a member of the Swift family (of meat-products fame), whose wealth my parents referred to most respectfully—though I think now it must have been at its early and comparatively modest beginnings.

Then there was the Grape-Nuts incident. One morning Mother told me I was a big enough boy to go down to the restaurant by myself and order my own breakfast. No doubt my parents were eager to have the use of the bedroom without the incommoding presence of a third party—at least I hope so. But I considered it a signal favor, and when I took my solitary seat at our dining-room table, I was too proud for words. I don't remember whether, as a precocious lad, I was already able to spell out words on the bill of fare, or whether I asked the waiter to read them to me. In any case I was struck by a new concept—"Grape-Nuts"—of whose existence I was up to then unaware. Naturally that was what I ordered. "Have you eaten them before?" asked the waiter skeptically. "No, but I want them," I replied. "I don't think you'll like them," said he. "Better take something else." My vanity was at stake. Didn't I know my own mind? I insisted, and the Grape-Nuts were brought. In those days and long afterwards, my teeth were abnormally sensitive, and that excellent breakfast food rubbed them like gravel. The waiter stood by, looking on with a superior air. I ate every last kernel, and added a defiant, mendacious: "I liked 'em." But I didn't order Grape-Nuts again, and not for many years to come.

When I was seven, Leon and I were taken by our parents to spend a summer in England. (Victor was by then proving to be something of a problem child, and it was thought best to send him to Dr. Davidson's well-known summer camp at Coolbaugh, Pennsylvania, for increased discipline.) While this was an exciting and memorable experience for us, I don't recall Father as part of it. Apparently he only took us to England and later fetched us back, spending the intervening weeks at auction sales somewhere in the United States. Only one incident in which he took part has stuck in my memory, and it was not altogether a happy one. On the return voyage I was a favorite of the passengers, who loved to persuade me—and little enough persuasion I needed—to stand up before them, chin high in the air, and recite "Oh Captain, My Captain" with tremulous feeling. Two nights before reaching port, there was to be the traditional captain's dinner and entertainment by passengers and crew. I was told that, by popular request, I had been invited to perform Whitman's elegy again. I was in seventh heaven with pride and anticipation. Then came the cold shower. Father had decided that I was much too young to stay up so late, and besides so much adult attention would be bad for a little boy's upbringing. My appearance was canceled, and I went to bed early and disconsolate. The next day I learned that Father himself had recited a long poem in my stead at the celebration. The painful impression I carried so long—that Father had intentionally appropriated my glory to himself—undoubtedly did him an injustice.

In contrast with the frequent praise of others, I find it strange that most of my own memories of my father are on the silly or menacing side. One of his favorite expressions was "he's a left-handed imitation of a paralyzed gridiron" which I found, or was supposed to find, highly amusing, even though I hadn't the faintest idea what a gridiron was. Unfortunately, too, I remember expressions such as "I'll knock you into the middle of next week," "I'll thrash you within an inch of your life," and "I'll break every bone in your body." The last two were certainly not pleasantries, and were directed against my frequently misbehaving brother Victor. Why do I remember these horrendous threats, and not the charming and genuinely amusing things Father must certainly have said?

While I treasured our trip to England and boasted about it ad nauseam to my playmates, I recall only a series of detached scenes: a seemingly interminable train ride from Southampton to London; my three young aunts with tennis rackets—all the gift of my generous father, as I later found out; the pleasant garden of Grandfather's house, where, I assume, all of us were somehow accommodated. The year was 1901, Queen Victoria had died some months before, and I was struck by the sight of the woodwork of the shop fronts painted black in mourning. I recall being told that Edward VII was ill that summer, and hence his coronation had to be postponed. Also, the Boer War was then in full progress. Leon and I were duly provided with little khaki uniforms—a new color then—and wooden rifles, and we paraded up and down our street in military formation. I remember, too, riding on top of one of those famous double-decker open omnibuses, and eagerly trying to attract the attention of the numerous soldiers on the street. As soon as I saw one looking up at me, I would salute him furiously. When someone returned the salute, I was overjoyed.

We spent only a short time in London, however, and then moved down to Brighton, to pass most of the summer at the home of Mother's parents—the Gesundheits, a name which was the cause of much amusement to others and embarrassment to us. The house was a large brownstone affair at 14 Cambridge Road. I remember Grandfather Gesundheit as a stout, jovial man with a white beard, Grandmother as a stout, emotional, and domineering lady just returned from Paris with a glass bottle full of hard candy for us, and our young aunts, Margaret and Caroline, as being very sweet to us.

I have a special picture of services in the synagogue which we must have attended regularly, since our family was Orthodox Jewish on both sides. What I see is a procession of five sons of the rabbi, entering their pew in file, all attired in Eton suits, with turned-down collars and top hats. During that summer a gas heater exploded in the rabbi's house. He was badly burned and long confined to his room. I remember our paying him a courtesy call, and finding him forbiddingly swathed in bandages.

At once a delight and a torment was the frequent bathing at Brighton Beach. A little way out into the water the sand was smooth and pleasant to the feet. But then (where a boy of seven perforce had to hold on to a guide-rope) commenced a wicked assemblage of pebbles which the waves sent flying against our legs. We were always eager to go bathing—why I can't imagine, unless we thought real boys were supposed to be eager—but since the water was cold, the beach pebbly, and we had not the faintest notion of how to swim, the whole experience was a Spartan trial.

There was real fun, however, in the Brighton bathing machines. These were enclosed wagons, used as dressing rooms by the bathers. At low tide you could find them, in serried rank, down by the water's edge. At high tide they would be way up the beach, but still at the water's edge. The pulling up and down was done by several horses, hitched between the wagon shafts of each machine. The purpose was to permit the bathers to undress and dress near the water, and thus escape the long and uncomfortable walk on the stony strand. One lovely scene I can still see. It was after a great storm. The waves had come flooding in so suddenly that there had been no time to pull the wagons up to safety and most of them had been carried out to sea by the receding tide. There they were, floating on the ocean, within sight of us curious spectators on shore. Sailors were out there in rowboats, lassoing them one by one with ropes, and then laboriously tugging them back to shore. How Leon and I wished for another great storm and another such sight!

Years later, as a dedicated Latin scholar given to extracurricular reading, I came upon the famous lines of Lucretius:

Suave, mari magno turbantibus aequora ventis,
E terra magnum alterius spectare laborem.

(Sweet, when the sea is great and the winds are
    rough'ning the billows,
Safe on land to behold, far out, the toil of another.[1])

Instead of bringing to mind the picture of a storm-tossed, laboring vessel, these lines have always summoned an image of two boys on the beach watching men in rowboats struggling with a flotilla of bathing machines.

Throughout my childhood I was very well-behaved, rarely getting into any kind of scrape unless led astray by my brothers. Victor was the *enfant terrible* of the family. During his teens he developed into a real problem child—the sort referred to as "delinquent"—but he came out of a period of institutional discipline much changed for the better. Leon, the eldest, had the best-balanced personality of us three. He was a normal, mischievous, down-to-earth youngster, who was often in hot water—but never at scalding temperatures. An enthusiastic fisherman at nine, Leon rarely caught anything more than a shiner or two, but he kept on trying. One day he landed an eel. What to do with this repugnant and—for us Hebrews— entirely useless specimen? What indeed, if not to cut it up into small segments, and to place one of these neatly under each napkin which appeared on the service-plates at our Sabbath dinner table. When the napkins were raised by the rather large assemblage, which included some honored guests, the result was minor pandemonium. Everyone knew instinctively that he—or mainly she—was gazing at some weird substance strictly forbidden by the Mosaic code. It was touch-and-go whether the expensive service-plates would have to be thrown away, or whether they could be redeemed by numerous lustrations. Leon was duly punished for his dereliction.

Some time before our vacation in England we had moved

from the Myers' boardinghouse to our own four-story private residence at 122nd Street near Seventh Avenue. I took delight in operating the speaking tubes. You blew very hard into the mouthpiece, thus activating a shrill whistle in front of your lips. You then pushed a little lever which drew the whistle out of the way, and listened for Cook to reply. Her loud Irish voice would come through clearly: "Yes, Mum, what is it, Mum?" And I would answer gleefully: "It is only me, Benny." Then she would say disgustedly "Get along with ye, and don't bother me again."

A delightful dumbwaiter operated between the kitchen in the basement and the dining room on the first floor. What fun it was for a little boy to imagine himself a soup tureen, cram himself into the lower half of the dumbwaiter, laboriously hoist himself up and laboriously hoist himself down. Is it memory or fantasy that tells me of the day when we three boys got into the dumbwaiter together, and the cord broke?

I remember following Father and Mother through every room of our house, including one or two on the top floor—servants' quarters, no doubt—which impressed me as strange territory. Father was carrying a large feather and an ordinary dustpan. These were symbolic instruments, employed in a traditional ritual which we called "looking for *chometz*" (leavened bread) on the eve of Passover. The entire house was cleaned scrupulously, to remove every trace of our daily food, and two complete sets of dishes and pots and pans, reserved only for these holy days, were pressed into service. As if for a siege, large supplies of special provisions were laid in—tens of pounds of matzoth in large oblong packages, big blue paper cones of extra-hard sugar that had to be hammered into awkward pieces, and a special supply of milk, jams, and spices. And the search? That was to prove to our own satisfaction, and perhaps that of a very exacting God, that nothing contravening the Passover canon remained in the house. Of course, we never found a leavened morsel on these expeditions, but the search was exciting.

When I was five or six, we moved to a brownstone private

house at 2019 Fifth Avenue, near 125th Street. The second floor had a plate-glass window, and the large parlor behind it was used as a showroom for our chinaware. We boys were denied access to that region on threat of painful punishment for it would have been sheer folly to allow three young bulls into the family china shop. But we were taken on carefully chaperoned tours of inspection. My mental picture is genre Omar Khayyám, who found in a potter's house:

> Shapes of all sorts and sizes, great and small,
> That stood along the floor and by the wall.

It was the big Sèvres vases—above a certain size we always called them "vahses"—that impressed me most. Some of them seemed of mountainous height, but then I was not only young but small for my age as well. I don't recall exactly how the biggest one looked, but I can never forget my awe at being told that it was worth a thousand dollars. That was a lot of money in those days.

We played in Mount Morris Park, which was only a stone's throw away. We also went shopping often with Mother on 125th Street, then a fairly fashionable center for upper-class trade. We bought meat and groceries at Weisbecker's large market. For most other items we went to Koch and Company, a good-sized department store. But for major purchases, or a larger selection, we journeyed down to Bloomingdale's, then as now on 59th Street. You took the trolley car to get there, for the subway was not yet built, the El was inconvenient for us, and autos were still curiosities. The streetcar system was well developed, with a number of competing and collaborating lines, involving elaborate inter-car transfers. These were provided by uniformed gentlemen who sat under large umbrellas, at various important street intersections. And every umbrella carried a large slogan printed twice or thrice on its body: "All cars transfer to Bloomingdale's." That was one of the household expressions of my childhood.

For many years we were outfitted with shoes at Wright's store on 125th Street. They advertised their wares as "Wrightform Shoes," and my youthful mind was greatly impressed by the neatness of the pun. It wasn't long before my own career as inveterate punster began. ('Tis a vocation wherein fame and infamy are one and indistinguishable.) For my birthday, perhaps the sixth, I was given a much cherished express wagon. There was a late spring or early summer day when Mother allowed me to go shopping with her, taking my wagon along. We piled the parcels in the conveyance, and then Mother bought some bunches of sweet peas from a street vendor; these she spread around the wagon. We must have made a striking sight—a pretty young matron and a boy in sailor suit and black curls, tugging a gaily bedecked wagon behind him—for I recall how vain I felt as I noticed passersby stopping and admiring us.

At five, my schooling began—ignominiously. I was sent to a public kindergarten nearby, located on the second floor of some building. I remember only sitting in ecstacy before a box containing sand and a large shell, with which I played to my heart's content. But I was soon to be expelled from Arcadia. I had not yet mastered the difficult art of unbuttoning and buttoning my pants, although all the other pupils had passed that critical point in their education. Thus my visits to the toilet required the assistance of the busy teacher. After a few days of that nonsense I was sent home, never to return. Thus I was compelled to wait until September 1900, when I was almost six and a half, before I could begin again, in the first grade. I was very impatient to start, my brothers having taken on insufferable airs because they were in school and I was still a baby. One day I heard Leon complaining of some punishment he had received for talking on line. What did "on line" mean? I wondered. How wonderful to stand on line, even if it brought a punishment!

When at last I did enter the first grade, I proved an eager and successful student. We learned both separate letters and whole (small) words—the inevitable *bat, cat,* etc. The latter were printed on cards which the teacher exhibited to the class for their recognition. I did so well at this work that I was quickly passed from 1A into 1B. (In those days the year's grades were divided into separate halves, each of which began both in September and February.) My first school was No. 157 at St. Nicholas Avenue and 123d Street. Since we came home daily for lunch, we would make the trip to or from home four times a day. My walks were enlivened by the appearance of a St. Nicholas Avenue streetcar drawn by two horses. People from other towns often made fun of New York for being the last to retain animal transportation (along with many electric trolley lines, of course). Our St. Nicholas Avenue horsecars were actually the final survivors of that ancient institution; at the very end the service was limited to one trip a day (usually without passengers) as a gesture required "to keep the franchise."

It early became evident that I was cut out to be a good boy and an excellent scholar, but not much else of consequence. I was healthy but small for my age, and well below average in athletic sports. In those days, good students were not expected to be athletes. Nevertheless, I *was* required to participate fully in games and exercise of all sorts. I did as much as anyone else, only I did so less successfully. Thus my ego was constantly being bruised. Because my muscular coordination was poor, I suffered from a general awkwardness. I would drop things and break them, or run into things and damage them and sometimes myself. Besides that, I was incurably absentminded, constantly given over to meditation or mere daydreaming. Hence the angry cry from others that sounded so often in my ears: "Why don't you watch what you're doing!" or "Why don't you look where you're going!"

These were rhetorical questions. If I ever had tried to explain that a little boy might have his head full of many intriguing ideas entirely peculiar to himself, and that these ideas prevented him from noticing the physical world around him—no doubt I'd have been treated as young Joseph the Dreamer was by *his* brothers, and perhaps I'd have deserved it.

On our mademoiselle's day off, we three boys were on our own. Once we decided to pay a visit to the little locomotive that pulled the train for kiddies at 65th Street and Fifth Avenue, just inside Central Park. (Later the tracks were taken up, and it became the site of the pony rides.) Naturally, we covered the three miles plus on foot. It was a delicious and languid hour or two watching the puffing engine and the little cars make innumerable round-trips. We couldn't be passengers, of course, since we had no money; but that didn't seem to make us too unhappy. Then came the long walk home. It was quite dark when, exhausted, we reached the brownstone house. We paused briefly to decide on strategy, for we suspected that we had committed a major misdemeanor and that severe punishment was in store for us. Leon, as the eldest—all of nine years old—and nominally the responsible head of the undertaking, bravely volunteered to go in first, while Victor and I cowered behind in the protecting shadows. It was indeed a frantic household which greeted its prodigal sons. The police had been notified some time before, and horrible prospects of kidnapping or accidents were frightening Mother and the help out of their wits.

My recollection is that Leon and Victor both received sound thrashings, while I—as the youngest and presumably a pliable tool of my brothers—got off virtually scot-free. Perhaps, after all, there was some compensation for being low man on the family totem pole.

Little locomotives like that in Central Park used to draw the elevated trains in those far-off days. They would go by overhead with a fine roar and sizzle, and in the winter evenings we could watch the flame and sparks. When later the El was electrified, we could still see a flock of these minute steam engines gathered together in a little raised yard along the tracks. Eventually they disappeared, having been sold, I believe, to some South American country.

The New York Central lines on Park Avenue were not electrified until later. The trains ran by steam in an open cut, crossed by passenger bridges at every block. As a boy of four or five, I would often be taken over one of these bridges, to look down in wonder and delight as the engine came racing towards me and then beneath me. Not only have all these locomotives, tiny and huge, disappeared from the New York scene, but so have all the Elevated Railroad lines themselves—those tremendous structures of thick steel columns and interlaced ironwork, which used to cast their fretted shadows on the streets below them. It is as if they had never existed. These changes, and many others more striking and portentous, have occurred within my own lifetime. When I was a college youth I read appreciatively the famous lines of Ronsard's sonnet:

> Le temps s'en va, le temps s'en va, ma dame,
> Las! le temps, non, mais nous, nous en allons
>
> (Time passes on, time passes on, my Lady;
> Not time, alas! 'tis we who pass away)

We go, while time and the world remain. True enough, yet often I feel as if the world I once knew, and the kind of leisure peculiar to that less complicated world, have died—except for my own surviving memory of them. A brief survival, indeed; yet in some sense it is I who have both buried Time and kept it alive, whatever Ronsard may sing.

CHAPTER TWO

Family Tragedies and My Mother's Perseverance

Our summer trip to England proved to be the high spot of our prosperity and happiness for many years to come. Not long after our return Grandpa Grossbaum died in London. The news came suddenly in a cablegram. I remember my father's reading it and straightway bursting into a loud lament. Even clearer is the picture of him sitting in a low chair, with slippered feet on a footstool, and wearing an old suit with the sleeves wilfully slashed and buttons torn off. This was part of the Orthodox custom called "sitting shiva"—an elaborate ritual of mourning for a departed parent.

Fifty years were to pass before I learned the dramatic particulars of Grandfather's death. I was walking in London with my Uncle Sol, when he stopped at a certain corner between Bond Street and Regent Street and said, "Here's where we had our store when your grandfather was alive." Then he told me that Grandpa had had a trusted assistant, whom he found was stealing large sums from the business. He threatened to turn the man over to the police, but the manager drew a revolver and cried: "My life is ruined in any case, and I shan't be much worse off if I killed you and was hanged. You are a pious, God-fearing Jew. I shall spare your life if you will swear solemnly to me on this Bible that you will not tell a soul about my thefts." Grandfather swore the oath, and the man was never prosecuted. But the double shock of the large monetary loss and the threat to his life ruined Old Grossbaum's health and made him an easy prey to pneumonia some months later.

I said "Old Grossbaum" because he was the head of a large family with eleven living children and innumerable grandchildren. He lives in my memory only in a large portrait-photograph—a man with a square, expansive, grey-black beard, a skull cap, a severe expression, and a fanatical gleam in his eyes. During my younger years I heard many stories of his extreme piety, with special emphasis on the fact that he had his own Beth Hamedrash, or House of Learning, next to his home, where scholars and the devout would come to pray and study. Much later the tales told me by my uncles, his sons, were in a different key. They emphasized the oppressive strictness of their upbringing in his home and his flat prohibition against all amusements or secular activities. Even whistling was strictly banned. Yet this bearded patriarch was only fifty-six years old when he died!

On a previous trip my father took along one of the newly invented phonographs, which he demonstrated to his younger brothers and sisters in the ground-floor parlor of Grandfather's house. It just happened—can this be true?—that what he played was a whistling record. Whereupon my grandfather rushed out of his upper-floor study and shouted, "Who's that daring to whistle downstairs?" Father shouted back, laughingly: "It's none of us, Father. Come down and listen to my new phonograph." As my Uncle Will told the story, the older man returned to his study without saying a word. After all he couldn't antagonize the financial mainstay of the entire family.

I remember a phonograph in our home on 128th Street. The

year must have been 1900. I was most impressed by the horn, which was considerably larger than myself. The records were on wax cylinders, similar to those used much later for the Dictaphone. Each record started by announcing the name of the selections and the artist, and by adding in a kind of triumphant sing-song: "Edison Recccord!"

My father liked possessions and was especially interested in the new and unusual. At his death he left three gold watches. One of them was a "repeater": when you pressed a button—presumably in the middle of the night—it would first ring the number of hours, then the quarter hours, then the remaining minutes. After Father's death, Mother told us that each of us would have one of those watches at our bar mitzvah—when at the age of thirteen we assumed all the duties and privileges of a full-fledged Jew. This promise, alas! could not be kept. It was not long before the watches, with many others of Father's proud possessions, had been sold or pawned, never to be reclaimed. Among those other possessions was an assortment of special canes, one shielding a really ugly-looking rapier, another an umbrella, and the third, a long, very thin bottle and three glasses to match. The bottle was supposed to be filled with whiskey or brandy. Actually, of the many personal things that Father left, I can remember benefiting from only one. It was an English blazer coat that Mother had somehow managed to save and keep over the years. I used it a few times as part of my tennis costume when I played on the public courts. Father had evidently been quite slender, for the coat seemed to fit my eighteen-year-old frame quite well. However, I still remember that my friends, far less foppishly attired, would pass some unfavorable remarks on my outfit, and I regretfully gave up wearing my one and only heirloom.

When my grandfather died, Father's health was already sadly impaired. His color was bad, and we were told he was suffering from a mysterious ailment called "yellow jaundice." Nonetheless, we made another of our innumerable changes of residence. This time we moved into an apartment house. It was The Ferncliff, on 120th Street and Seventh Avenue, which I considered at the time to be quite an imposing building. May 1 was then the universal moving day. It must have been a cool spring afternoon, because I remember coming into our parlor for the first time, to find my parents warming themselves before a wall of blue flame in the fireplace. I learned that it was a new heating arrangement, based on gas, and it fascinated me.

Directly south of us, on Seventh Avenue, there was a large florist establishment, with greenhouses stretching back behind the store. I was then getting old enough to be led into minor mischief by my brothers, especially Victor. Under his instruction, I prepared a knotted cord which was attached to a large screw, which in turn had been passed through a special kind of red rubber washer used in the beer bottles of the period. You moistened the rubber pad with saliva and applied it to a glass pane of the greenhouse, where it stuck fast by suction. Then you ran the knotted cord through your fingers. After each knot the screw head would fall back against the glass with a loud click, the ensemble sounding a bit like machine-gun fire. The exasperated proprietor would dash out of the store, shouting invectives and threats, but we always managed to escape up the block, our torture contraption clutched in our fists.

Another practical joke was also practiced by our set. Materials needed: a pebble and a milk bottle. You threw the pebble against a lower-storey window, making a sharp sound, and simultaneously you dropped the milk bottle over the railing into the depressed areaway. The ensuing noise sounded as if the glass from a broken window had fallen to the ground. This could generally be counted on to produce great excitement among the family selected for the experiment.

When we moved to The Ferncliff, my schooldays were firmly launched. I entered the primary department of Public School 10, situated at 117th Street and St. Nicholas Avenue. Even then it was an old school, as its low number probably indicates. But it had a fine reputation for scholarship and athletic prowess. I spent just one term or half-year in the primary department, starting in the 3A grade in September and being skipped next February into 4A, which was the beginning of the grammar school proper. The elementary department had its own principal, a Miss Roberts, who seemed to me some very ancient and very powerful divinity. (She had probably just turned forty.) There was an assembly of all the primary classes once a week. For this purpose a number of classrooms were opened up, by an ingenious arrangement of sliding walls, to create an auditorium. In front was a dais, on which Miss Roberts was throned, sometimes flanked by a visiting dignitary. My one clear recollection is of a quotation inscribed on a glass window behind the dais. It read:

> Honor and shame from no condition rise;
> Act well thy part, there all the honor lies.
> —Alexander Pope

How many times I read those lines, while the ritual of the assembly droned boringly along! How many times did I puzzle over the meaning of the word "condition," which at that time I associated with matters of health, cleanliness, and good repair.

On February 1, 1903, though less than nine years old, I proudly took my place among the grammar-department boys in Miss Churchill's class. She was blonde and beautiful, the recipient of marked attention not only from some of the men teachers in the school, but even from older and bigger boys in her class who seemed pleased to be kept after hours for extra work, or to help with various chores. All this took place in another universe, far removed from the ideas or dreams of an underaged, undersized youngster. But I did love Miss Churchill, because she seemed as sweet as she was beautiful.

Alas! It was under these pleasant surroundings that the great tragedy struck our family. Father's health grew suddenly worse; he was taken to the German Hospital (now

Lenox Hill); he underwent an operation for an unnamed internal condition. (Years later I learned it was cancer of the pan-
creas.) At the end of February we three boys were summoned
out of our classrooms and taken down to the hospital by our
governess. There we were told that we could see our father for
just a few minutes and that we were to be very quiet. Ever
since that day I have the mental picture of entering the sick-
room to find him swathed in bandages; but obviously that
detail was added by my imagination. I am sure, however, that
he placed his weak hand on each of our heads in turn and gave
us his final blessing. I kissed him, I know, feeling at the time
more apprehension and bewilderment than filial affection.
Then we tiptoed out.

We were brought back to lunch at my Uncle Emanuel's
home. On the way our mademoiselle made the suitable reas-
suring statements, which in my innocence I took at face value.
So when my cousin Ethel, aged fifteen, asked anxiously what
was going to happen, I replied bravely that Father was getting better. "So then he isn't going to die?" she exclaimed half-
relieved, half-incredulous. "Of course not," I said—but my
brothers were strangely silent. Then Victor—our "bad"
brother, who was at the same time the most openly emotional
of us three—found a prayer book, and with tears streaming
down his face began to stumble through some Hebrew
prayers.

We went on to our own apartment and waited. At last the
door opened, and someone led our mother in. She was weeping
piteously. At the sight of our scared faces, she cried out, "My
poor, poor boys. You are all orphans."

I suppose we started to cry too, for even I was not too young
to understand that from that moment on everything would be
different, unhappily different. In later daydreams, I relived
that pathetic moment many times. And always I imagined
myself running up to Mother, throwing my arms around her,
and exclaiming, "No, Mother, we are not orphans. We still
have you."

Father was buried in Washington Cemetery on Long Island, then considered quite distant. I remember that we drove out in four-wheeler cabs behind the hearse, that we all threw some dirt on the grave after the coffin was lowered, and that we stopped at a place just outside the cemetery for food and hot drinks, for it was a bitterly cold day. The next year we returned to the spot, to dedicate the gravestone. The address was made by Alexander Rosenthal, a close friend of the family, a lawyer, and an orator. He compared our father's life to the monument now standing above him. The front portion, bearing the inscription, was smooth and finished; the rear portion was rough, unfinished. So Father, dying at the untimely age of thirty-five, had finished only half his life. The second half, so full of promise, was now destined to remain uncut and undeveloped forever. Many people were there, and all of us cried. The loudest lamentations came from a group of professional mourners—old men who frequented the cemetery, forced themselves unbidden on every funeral or memorial party, and beat their breasts and called upon the Lord—for a few pennies.

The almost-effaced memories of my father's funeral were destined to be revived for me a quarter of a century later. I was then about his age at death, and myself a father. Now there was another boy of eight, my beloved firstborn Isaac Newton—named after the grandfather he had never seen. But this time it was the son who lay in the coffin and we weeping parents who threw the last handfuls of earth over his little grave.

How did the loss of my father affect my inner being? Surely I had suffered a more devastating loss than I could realize. Psychologists would assure me that I had been deprived of an essential ingredient of security and normal development—that the experience could not fail to have deeply traumatic effects upon my nature. Yet frankness compels me to acknowledge that in my own soul-searching, I cannot find these disturbing consequences. We do not miss what we have never really had; perhaps my father's continual absences on business, and the consequent lack of any feeling of companionship with him, had somehow diminished the impact of his death upon his three sons. On the other hand, perhaps it is the special quality of childhood to be less overwhelmed by major disasters than by relatively small problems of family relationship which later turn into neuroses. It seems to me that Leon, Victor, and I must have felt and behaved somewhat like the band of children in Richard Hughes' classic, *The Innocent Voyage.* When one of their leaders dies through accident, his name disappears overnight from the conversation and the consciousness of the others.

It is a tribute to our mother's wise parenting that we grew up as genuine *boys*, entirely free from any attachment to her apron strings and ready to assume masculine responsibilities as early as possible. Adversity is bitter, but its uses may be sweet. Our loss was great, but in the end we could count great compensations.

With our father's death a new chapter opened for our family's material life. It was a long and distressing one, beginning as a kind of dégringolade which carried us down into evermore straitened circumstances, and continuing for several more years in a struggle to keep from falling still lower. We had various assets of the business, mainly of a certain stock of bric-à-brac, some thousands of dollars in life insurance, and quite a lot of personal possessions, including furniture and jewelry. Practically all of this was to disappear in the next few years. At the beginning, various efforts were made to carry on the business. Father's older brother Emanuel and two of his younger brothers had been working under his direction. They did their best, no doubt, but they proved to be completely ineffectual. They soon dropped out, and then Mother's brother, Maurice, took over. He was an engineer, and by common acceptance an intellectual genius. He was later to make quite a success as one of the earliest of the "systematizers," or "efficiency engineers." But he had neither the engaging salesmanship nor the day-to-day resourcefulness that had been the foundation of Father's achievements. By the end of a year or so the business had lost so much money that the remaining stock was sold for what it would bring, and the business given up completely.

Later on, Mother was led by her own hope or desperation, or by the advice of others, to take in paying guests—in more brutal language, to open a boardinghouse. This adventure, too, proved unsuccessful, and after two years was abandoned. Mother also tried a little speculating in the stock market. I remember her calling her broker often for quotations on U.S. Steel. Her account was undoubtedly a very small one, and was carried with a member of the then existing Consolidated Stock Exchange, where the unit of trading was ten shares, instead of one hundred, as on the New York Stock Exchange, or "Big Board." The broker himself was an old friend, but Mother's picayune operations were handled by his extremely young son. Thus there was a time when as a small boy I would open our paper at the financial page each day to see what U.S. Steel had done. Ignorant as I was of finance, I knew enough to be glad when the price advanced and sorry when it was down. Needless to say, Mother's margin account was duly wiped out in the panic of 1907, in addition to which she suffered great inconvenience through the closing of her bank.

Not that Mother ever had any considerable sum in her bank account. But however small her assets, she insisted on the dignity of paying by check. That was easy enough, since the banks required no minimum balances and made no service charges. In our later Bronx days I recall being sent to our bank to cash a small check. As I stood at the window, waiting, I heard the teller call back in not too low a voice, "Is Dorothy Grossbaum good for five dollars?" Fortunately, the answer was yes. But the experience must have been vaguely humiliating, since I remember it so well.

Little did I or anyone else suspect that many years later the financial pages were to become an open book to me and that the dreamy, impractical, ink-stained Benny G. would become a figure on Wall Street. Nor could anyone have foreseen the later fate of my mother's brokerage company. Let us turn the clock ahead twenty years. The son is now in full charge; his father, an old man, is but a figurehead. Miraculously, the little firm has become a large business trading heavily on the fact that it had been established in 1887.

The dingy cubbyhole of an office has been replaced by a suite, beautifully furnished, equipped with countless telephone booths used by high-pressure salesmen pouring tales of easy money into the ears of thousands of foolish people, their names taken almost at random from the directories. The company has become one of the biggest "bucket shops" in the country. Its customers' purchases are not actually made. The hundreds of thousands of dollars invested to margin these accounts are appropriated—virtually stolen outright.

To carry out the swindle successfully, the bucket shops depended on the inevitable market breaks to wipe out their customers. At the beginning of the great bull market of the 1920s, a large number of these fraudulent establishments were running full blast—unimpeded by the incredible heedlessness (or worse) of the authorities, of the newspapers that accepted their flamboyant advertising, and of the New York Stock Exchange houses who accepted business from them. As the market continued its advance, the bucket shops found their position increasingly vulnerable. In the end they all closed their doors, thus finalizing the despoilment of their clients. The failure of my mother's brokerage company was one of the most spectacular of the lot. The son was one of the few plunderers who actually went to jail—for a short stretch. Shortly thereafter, his father died—of a broken heart, everybody said.

In a few distressful years every cent of what Father had left us was used up or lost. Mother's jewelry went to the pawnshop, never to return. We were saved from misery, though not from humiliation, by the fortunate chance that some of Mother's numerous brothers and sisters had become wealthy. They carried us through the three years of our Purgatory.

My guess is that Mother and her three boys lived for a while on around $75 per month: quite a comedown for a lady who not too many years before had been mistress of a large house, with cook, upstairs maid, and French governess. Let me portray my mother as accurately as I can, for she was a lily who needed no gilding.

My memory is of a stately lady, but actually, she was very small—under five feet—and when she walked the street surrounded by her three grown-up sons, she seemed like something tiny and precious, entrusted to the care of robust guardians. Her stateliness must have stemmed from my own pygmy stature at the time, and from the fact that she always held herself with dignity and grace. Mother was not a dazzling beauty, but she was pretty enough to excite admiration everywhere. She retained the delicacy of her features and her fine-china skin up to her sudden death at the age of seventy-six.

Mother had many virtues, and also a few faults. Her great strength lay in her courage and her philosophy. The untimely loss of her husband took everything from her but her children. She made no parade of wifely devotion and fidelity to the memory of her Isaac. Yet no man after him could claim her thoughts; and despite several offers of marriage, with tempting material advantages, she steadfastly refused to wed someone she did not love. Some five years after her widowhood she was energetically courted by a middle-aged gentleman who had lost his wife. It was at one of the lowest points in our fortune, when we were sharing a house in Borough Park, Long Island, with Uncle Maurice and his family, and we felt keenly our position as impecunious relatives. Mother was taken to dinner and the theater. She proudly returned with a box of expensive chocolates—which had for us the *éclat* of so many jewels. Not long afterward she summoned us into council, announced that she had received an offer of marriage, and asked us to think the matter over and tell her how we felt about it. We were then boys of sixteen, fifteen, and fourteen, respectively. Though we discussed the matter among ourselves with great gravity and decorum, I am ashamed to admit that we were all inwardly overjoyed at the prospect of financial salvation. Our decision was quickly reached and communicated: "Mother's happiness was our first consideration. If this marriage would relieve her many burdens and bring her contentment, we were not at all inclined to stand in the way. On the contrary we would welcome this important change in our lives, and do our best to be loving and dutiful sons to our new father."

Mother smiled at us when we had finished. Then she told us in a quiet voice that she, too, had been thinking the matter over and had decided *not* to accept the proposal. The man was suitable enough, perhaps, but she didn't love him and didn't think she could ever love him. Without love she would never marry, regardless of the advantages. There was nothing for us to say, so we kissed her and left—very disappointed.

Mother's refusal to remarry was a romantic defiance of Fortune. Yet her general outlook on life was neither romantic nor impractical, nor even especially idealistic. Her scale of values was comfortably bourgeois. Money was important to her, not only to provide the necessities of life, but—more interestingly—as the key to luxury and magnificence, and as the proof of worldly success. She was ambitious for her sons, and in her darkest hours she was buoyed up by the confidence that in due time we would restore the family fortunes.

In fact, she had more confidence than we ourselves, as an incident will illustrate. I was about to graduate from high school, and my brothers were already at work, earning not more than $10 per week. A newspaper poll had indicated that the average worker would be well satisfied if he could earn $30 per week for the rest of his life. Mother asked us what we thought of that attitude. One by one we replied that $30 per week seemed like a pretty substantial salary, not too easy to attain, and that we would be quite content with it. Mother looked at us with a disdainful smile, and said she would be deeply disappointed if she thought that our ambitions were really as mediocre as all that.

Mother was rather hedonistic, fond of delicate and beautiful things, averse to work or concentrated effort—unless absolutely necessary. She would say proudly that she was known in her family as "die Erbsenprinzessin," the Princess of the Pea, who proved her claim to royalty by detecting the presence of a pea beneath a large number of mattresses in her bed. But after the loss of her husband she seemed overnight to develop an unsuspected toughness, resiliency, and resourcefulness. She did whatever she had to do—even to scrubbing the kitchen floor, for her the ultimate trial of Job. She went without what she could not have, and with remarkably little complaint.

But she also developed quite an art of transferring household chores to her sons. We got our own breakfast while Mother slept late. Her habits were not that of the valiant woman priced above rubies in the Book of Proverbs. She arose when it was quite light—about ten o'clock—and retired at one in the morning. She marked these events with a cup of tea, *à l'anglaise.* For this there were always a few drops of cream on hand, even in life's darkest moments. We boys didn't cook dinner, but we dried the dishes, made the beds, pushed the carpet sweeper. I ran most of the errands—which meant that I did most of the shopping.

She somehow retained small luxuries of the past. She tried not to indulge her love for dainties too far, but some desires she could not resist. From time to time, she would make a batch of delicious cookies, with butter shortening. These were expensive, and she persuaded herself that they were too ethereal for the gross palates of mere boys. She kept them hidden in a tin box among the lingerie in a large wardrobe that had followed us around (on the backs of swearing moving men). My own sweet tooth led me to her cache. By great exercise of willpower I limited my depredations to one cookie at a time, not more than twice a week. But one day Mother came into the bedroom and found me with the box in my hand. I expected the heavens to fall on my head. Instead, her reproof was so gentle that I felt all the more ashamed of myself, and she quickly departed. It was only many years later, as I recalled that scene, that I understood that Mother's conscience must have troubled her even more than mine.

We were very careful with the butter at home—Mother would never allow us to spread butter *and* jam on our bread—but what we did use was the expensive sweet butter. Salt butter, good enough for everyone else, could never win Mother's acceptance. Another extravagance was powdered red sugar for berries and other dishes. She kept the sugar in a crystal container, and to meet her exacting taste she always flavored it with a genuine black vanilla bean. She also liked to add chives, grown in a little pot on the kitchen windowsill, to the cream cheese on her bread.

Mother had a lively mind, but hardly a deep one. She made it a point to be interested in worthwhile subjects, and this raised her conversation considerably above the *terre-à-terre* level of most of her lady friends. In her youth she had had a good education (for a Warsaw girl of the 1880s); she had read poetry and good novels, and was reasonably at home in several languages. But intellectual drive was not one of her virtues, and as the years passed she felt less inclined toward serious reading. But she did retain a deep respect for learning and study. Her counsel, if not her example, was a constant inspiration and encouragement to me to make the most of my mental capacities.

Mother was an inveterate cardplayer. She always played for money, but the stakes were never high enough to constitute true gambling. At a very early age we were all initiated into the mysteries of solo whist, pinochle, and the various stages of bridge. Mother enjoyed playing with us and teaching us the fine points as we went along; she used to say that cards were about the only thing that she could handle better than we could, and she drew innocent enjoyment from her superiority. She liked to quote a famous Frenchman—was it La Rochefoucauld?—who remarked to a non-cardplayer: "What a lonely old age lies in store for you, my friend." This would have been particularly true for Mother, who could not abide more than a few minutes of women's small talk.

Mother left us free to encounter the risks of youthful masculine activity. She never suggested that we refrain from any sport, however hazardous. We often came home with bruises and contusions. Although reasonably sympathetic, she shocked us more than once by remarking that cuts on the legs would heal by themselves, whereas a tear in our trousers meant either labor or expense.

She forced courage on us, too. In our boardinghouse days, Mother slept in a room on the basement floor, in a large double-bed which I shared with her. (Our hours of retiring and awakening were so completely different that I cannot remember any problems of privacy or prudishness arising from this arrangement.) One night—probably about 2 or 3 a.m.—she woke me out of my invariably deep slumber to tell me that she had heard a noise in the house and thought that it might be a burglar. Then, in a perfectly matter-of-fact way, she announced that we would have to go through the house and see, since she could never fall asleep with the question unsettled. Whereupon she lit a gas lighter, and the two of us started on a tour of the house. I haven't the faintest notion of what we would have done if we had discovered an intruder. I was scared to death, but I was ashamed to show any sign of fear before my mother. No one was found, and we both went back to sleep.

Mother was happy to have her boys living with her, but she had a deep dislike of living with anyone else. She found the years that she shared her brother Maurice's home highly distasteful. Uncle Maurice was as ill-tempered and tyrannical as he was intellectually brilliant. His first wife, Aunty Eva, was a sweet, benevolent, completely ineffectual person, exposed without defense to his reproaches and biting sarcasm. We were present at many painful scenes at the card table, where my uncle would berate my aunt for some foolish play. She would try to justify what she had done, he would attack her more savagely, and she would burst into tears. Then Mother would rally to Eva's defense, and the argument would continue between sister and brother—the language suddenly changing from English into Polish, so that we children would not understand. (Years later, all this was brought back to me by a scene in Sardou's *Madame Sans-Gêne* in which Napoleon and his sisters have a quarrel-royal, and switch suddenly from French to Corsican-Italian. There was much of the Napoleonic in Uncle Maurice—including a short stature and a visible paunch.) Mother showed considerable courage in daring to take her sister-in-law's part in a house where she and her sons were living at the sufferance of her domineering brother.

Later, after I married in 1917, economic conditions dictated that Mother live with my wife and me. This arrangement worked out very badly, for the usual reasons. A year later it became possible for her to have her own apartment, and thenceforth she lived alone until her death twenty-six years later. She refused all our suggestions that she share a flat with one of her numerous cronies; there was no dearth of widows among whom to choose. We were concerned, of course, about the possibilities of accident or illness striking her as she grew older. In her youth Mother's health was called "delicate," and in her intermediate years she suffered from both a "heart condition" and a "stomach condition." Her doctor put her on a strict diet, which she ignored almost completely, saying that there was no point in prolonging her life at the expense of most of the things that made life worthwhile. Despite this apparent self-neglect, she never had any really serious ailments. In all the years she lived by herself, there were not more than a few days that she needed help because of an indisposition.

At Mother's death, her independence, courage, and inveterate card-playing all contributed their part. One evening in October 1944 she spent playing pinochle at a friend's house on West End Avenue. Some time past midnight she started alone on her way home. She was accosted by a thief, who seized her handbag. In the hospital, she told us that she refused to give it to him. He struck her, wrenched the bag away, and fled. She sustained a fractured skull, and died the next day. The pocketbook contained about $3.

Ironically, Mother was always concerned that robbers might brutalize her sons. When she read in the newspaper of someone killed in a holdup, she would ask us to promise her not to offer resistance if we were held up, but immediately turn over all we had. Of course, she knew that that was the only sensible course for herself as well. But when confronted by a criminal who seized her property, she refused to be robbed—even of $3. She resisted instinctively, as during all her life she had resisted injustice and unfairness. Mother's death was tragic in its circumstances, but in her own eyes, I think, she would not have considered it a tragedy. Her one personal fear had never been of sudden death, but instead of lingering illness or helpless old age. These intolerable indignities she was spared, and I am sure that she would have chosen her violent end in preference to long years of suffering for herself and—by consequence—for her loved ones.

CHAPTER THREE

At Public School

The years that formed my character were the three that followed Father's death. Between 1903 and 1906 I lived at 244 West 116th Street and attended P.S. 10 nearby. When I entered, I was an innocent and sensitive child; when I graduated, just past twelve, I knew how to steel myself against Fortune's slings and arrows, to earn a little money in a variety of ways, to concentrate hard on whatever I had to do—and, above all, to rely mainly upon myself for understanding, encouragement, and pretty nearly everything else.

Was this transformation on the whole good for me? I feel that it was, but others have disagreed sharply. They say that the pressures and privations I experienced during that formative period distorted my character, created too much of a wall between me and the world around me, made it impossible for me to achieve relations of lasting and truly intimate friendship or love with other human beings. I shall discuss these negative possibilities when I deal with later phases of my life. At this point let me merely describe the process of adaptation of a small boy to what struck him as a largely unsympathetic world.

Considering the affection and attention lavished on children these days, one might imagine that I was relatively neglected. But the opposite was true. I received support when I needed it. Otherwise, I was left to grow strong on my own. For example, on an extremely cold winter's day I went ice skating on the Central Park lake just below 110th Street. Of course I had walked there and back. I recall coming home half-frozen and nearly in tears from the bitter discomfort. Mother helped me off with my wraps, sat me near the fire, chafed my hands to bring back the circulation, and gave me some hot tea to drink. All perfectly normal, you say: what does it prove? But this scene left an indelible impression with me, for it was the *only* occasion I can remember—except, perhaps, when I was sick in bed—that my mother (or anyone else) ever showed such solicitude for a minor physical malaise of mine. In our household we were supposed to cure our own wounds, unless they were serious, and to complain about practically nothing.

Obviously, my relations with my brothers were also bound to toughen me. They were in no sense bullies; indeed, they had a special fondness for me which was destined to endure sixty years and more. But they were older, bigger, stronger, and much more practical. As early teenagers they could scarcely be expected to show much unselfishness or delicacy of feeling towards me. Fortunately, I am unable to remember any specific example of injustice or mistreatment at their hands. (This forgetfulness of injuries, or of disturbing events generally, became one of my most characteristic traits, sometimes carried to lengths which amazed others and even surprised myself.) But I do recall my general feeling of being ill-used. With some bitterness, I once resolved to inform them of their wrongs. For their birthdays I planned to write a list of their sharp words and unfair actions and to present these to them marked "FORGIVEN" as birthday gifts. But I never did so.

We were a very crowded pair of families, living in a nine-room flat with a single bathroom. At first there were four each of Grossbaums and Gesundheits, the latter group consisting of Uncle Maurice, Aunty Eva, Cousin Helen (coeval with Victor), and Cousin Ralph, seven years younger. Then another cousin, Elsie, was born. She was delivered at home, as were nearly all babies in those days, and somehow room was made for her. It must have taken a miracle of management and consideration to make that single bathroom suffice for so many users. I do not recall any special difficulties or discomforts arising from our very scanty resources.

Somehow or other we managed to get the things we needed—food and clothing, of course, but also skates, baseball equipment, and, later, tennis rackets and balls. Not only were prices infinitely lower then than now, but as a matter of course we bought only bargains. Our baseball was usually a 5-cent Rocket, sometimes replaced by a 10-cent extravagance. My tennis racket, a birthday present, a Spalding Favorite, cost a dollar. We bought tennis balls secondhand, from the Manhattan Tennis Club, then situated at 123th Street and Manhattan Avenue, quite good ones at three for 25 cents, and they lasted a long time.

Where did the money come from for these things? I think we always had an allowance—perhaps as little as 10 cents per week—plus some extra money on our birthdays. But we all tried to earn small sums in whatever employment we could find or invent. Like most families, we subscribed to *The Saturday Evening Post,* in those days the most popular weekly magazine by far. The publishers advertised in each issue for boys to sell the *Post* on the street and to canvass for annual subscriptions. When I was no older than nine, I signed up (or rather Mother signed my application). They sent me thirty copies a week; I was charged 3 cents each, and I sold them for a nickel. Along with the first shipment came a nice cotton apron with a pocket for holding change. I remember stationing myself at one of the exits of the Elevated line at 116th Street and 8th Avenue, crying to one and all: "Get your *Saturday Evening Post,* just out, five a copy." I also remember a brief stint as a newsboy on the street; but Mother soon put a stop to that, saying "Father wouldn't have liked it." Apparently, our family's snobbery made some fine distinction between the respectable and character-forming career of selling the weekly *Saturday Evening Post* on the streets of New York, and the demeaning, character-corrupting business of selling daily newspapers.

After school we played in the street. In those days I had two or three really close friends my own age whom I saw practically every day. My nearest chum was Sydney Rogow, who lived on 111th Street, in comparative splendor. (His father and uncles owned a small department store out in Brooklyn.) Most days I would go over to his block, and a number of us would play stoopball or street hockey on roller skates. There were virtually no autos then, and the horse-drawn traffic offered little interference to anything the boys might want to do in the streets. One game we played often was "cat." The cat was a sharpened piece of wood, like a large clothespin. You would strike its nose with a larger stick, and as it jumped in the air you would hit it again as far as possible. Your opponent would try to catch it, failing which he would have to throw it in towards the stick which you placed on the ground. There was a scoring system, based on the final distance between the thrown cat and the stick.

How many years have passed since I last saw American boys playing cat! Yet this very year (1967), on a visit to the little isle of Santa Maria in the Azores, I found a group of kids playing the identical game. It was as if the clock had been turned back a half-century. I asked for the stick, which they gave me in wonderment, but I couldn't come anywhere near hitting the cat. I gave 20 escudos to the oldest boy, to buy candy for the bunch, and they—at least—were happy.

Once I inadvertently gave Mother a terrible fright. While playing some game, I found myself in the middle of the street with streetcars approaching from both directions and clanging their bells vociferously. Whether from bravado or helplessness, I elected to stand in the narrow passage between the tracks. The cars passed each other with their bells clanging. I disappeared from view—all right before our window, out of which by unhappy coincidence my horrified mother happened to be looking. I waved to her nonchalantly as the cars separated, but Mother seemed too overcome to speak. I didn't feel too comfortable myself, as those cars came awfully close to me.

Across the landing lived the other tenants on the second floor, the Vermilyes. They had a boy named Joseph of my age and a girl, Hazel, about three years older. We four children were reasonably friendly with them, but any real intimacy was out of the question, given our difference in religion. Not that such a question ever arose expressly between us, but in a kind of subterranean manner it controlled and limited our relations. The grownups spoke civilly enough to each other when they met in the hall, but they never passed over each other's thresholds in three years of living only a few feet apart— except on one occasion only a month or two before we moved away. The Vermilyes invited Mother, Uncle Maurice, and Aunty Eva to come over for tea. Returning, Uncle Maurice remarked that they were very nice people indeed, and that it was too bad that the families were getting to know each other just before we were leaving. Was it the case that the reason for the Vermilyes's hospitality was that the Jewish families next door were moving away?

The only fistfight in my life was with young Joseph Vermilye. How it started I don't recall. But there we were on the street in front of our house, surrounded by my brothers, Cousin Lou, and other kids all urging us on to do battle. The encounter couldn't have lasted more than a minute or two; we swung mightily, probably without landing a single blow! Along came a grownup and stopped the fight, much to the relief of both us eleven-year-olds and the disgust of the spectators.

How was I able to avoid other physical conflicts in the years that followed? To my credit it was not because I let myself be bullied or chased away from a fight, or begged to be let off. Since I was extremely peaceful by nature, I was never the one to pick a quarrel. But why did others refrain from challenging me? The truth is probably that I have been lucky all my life. A less probable explanation is that in my boyhood—the fighting period—I was almost always with youngsters older and bigger than I, and it was against the rules of junior chivalry to force a fight on a smaller kid. ("Why don't you pick on someone your size?" was the always effective question put by those in attendance.) A third explanation—which may sound farfetched—is that there was something about me that sheltered me from hostile acts by others. Nearly every one seemed to like me, if in a patronizing and protective way, and at the same time to feel that I really wasn't one of the bunch.

One of my friends was the son of a tailor across the street from us named Kaufman. He used to place a poster or two in his shop window announcing the current or forthcoming show at one of the neighborhood theaters. For this he received two free admissions. A few times young Kaufman invited me to go with him to a Saturday matinee, and those were great events in my life. But there was a certain wrinkling of brows and turning up of noses at home when it was known that I was associating with a tailor's son. Though our family could afford very little else, it could always afford the luxury of snobbery.

Then there was a mysterious rich boy—a friend of my brother Victor—who came to our flat from time to time. He had a stepfather—a strange sort of animal to us—and always a lot of coins in his pocket. I have a mental picture of him sitting on a bed or a chair, throwing a handful of pennies in the air, to fall all over the room, and yelling "Scramble" with a condescending expression on his face. And we three boys would go on our hands and knees before him to grope as fast as we could for those miserable coins—so important to us. One day he gave us a lecture on how babies were born. He opened up his shirt and showed us the large space below the navel which he said opens up for the mother and allows the child to emerge. (According to his private information, all babies were born like Julius Caesar.) This boy—I've forgotten his name—brought a great adventure into our lives. He told us that every Christmas the Tammany Hall organization gave a party for poor children at Tony Pastor's Theater (right next to the Tammany headquarters on 14th Street), at which toys would be distributed to one and all from a huge Christmas tree. He said he could get all three of us tickets of admission. But would Mother allow us to go to a celebration of the great Christmas festival, which all Jews of that time and before were accustomed to view with resentment and fear rather than envy? But Mother proved remarkably pliable, and we actually went! Of that celebration I recall vividly the great moment when we were allowed to pass in front of the theater stage and to ask for one of the toys hanging from or placed below the huge Christmas tree. I came home with a small Flexible Flyer sled—a windfall beyond my wildest dreams.

Alas! I was not destined to enjoy that heavenly gift for long. At the first big snowfall in January I took it to the long slope that runs around Morningside Park. It started high up on Morningside Heights to the west—at about 113th Street— then turned sharply left to run down 110th Street to Morningside Drive below, then sharply left once again for about a block at the bottom.

After a few runs, I was hit from behind by a big bobsled manned by a half-dozen grownups. I must have been unconscious for some moments; when I came to, nobody seemed to be paying any attention to me, nor was my sled anywhere in sight. I never found it again, though I walked up and down that slope countless times looking for it desperately. I came home, almost in tears.

Besides Christmas—less extensive then than now—there were three holidays which have left a strong impression on me. The first was the Fourth of July. It was the day of unremitting but heavenly noise, numerous fires, and even injuries and deaths. We were awakened at dawn by the staccato sound of revolvers being fired in the street. Any young man worth his salt had a small 22-calibre or a more impressive 32-calibre pistol, with a large supply of blank cartridges for the occasion. (Some idiots made it their boast to fire nothing but real bullets.) By afternoon the streets were littered with cartridge shells, and we would scour the neighborhood to pick up as many as our pockets could hold. (What did we do with them? All I recall is that by inserting a shell between two fingers, near the knuckles, and properly blowing into it, one could create an exceedingly loud whistle.) Kids too young for revolvers had cap pistols—some with enormous powder caps—and a great variety of firecrackers, including bunches of one hundred very small ones made in China and called "salutes." They came tied together in a package that could be bought for a single cent. Usually these bundles were fired off as a unit, making a brave little display. But those for whom pennies really counted—and that meant Leon, Victor, and Benny—would detach the inch-long cracker "salutes" and set them off singly in many different ways. One favorite was to make little boxes out of old paper, insert the lighted firecracker, and throw it out of a window or from the roof. The explosion was quite satisfactory.

There would also be posters announcing that at a certain time and place—usually on 125th Street—"the biggest firecracker in the world" would be ignited under the auspices of some business concern. We would join the crowd assembled in a large circle, kept at a safe distance from the explosive by several high-helmeted policemen, gaze in wonder at the enormous paper cylinder with its rope-like fuse, and wait in mingled ecstasy and apprehension for the deafening boom. There would be fires and horse-drawn fire engines aplenty, which children from six to sixty would chase, but most of the fires were too small to be worth our time to watch. Most families would have some supply of evening fireworks—rockets, roman candles, St. Catherine wheels—which would be set off from apartment windows or in the street as soon as the belated darkness arrived. Today all pyrotechnic exhibitions are set off by licensed specialists and rigidly controlled by the authorities. We oldsters can feel nostalgia but no real regret for the vanished holocausts of the great and glorious Fourth. The price in death and dismemberment was indeed too high to pay for a mere bacchanalia of noise and colored lights. But I write this with mixed feelings, for in 1928 I was to become a director and (rather nominal) vice-president of the largest fireworks manufacturing concern in the country, and for a number of years I was to observe with a natural dismay the rapid inroads made on our business by what was called succinctly the "safe and sane" Fourth.[1]

As for Halloween, none of us had any idea what this holiday was really about. We never heard it referred to as "All Souls' Eve" or "All Saints' Day." For us then, as for most kids now, it was associated with pictured hobgoblins, witches, and hollowed-out and lit-up pumpkins—none of which actually entered our Jewish home. But what Halloween really meant in our lives was a lot of boys roaming the streets in the early evening; wearing their coats turned inside out and carrying long stockings stuffed with a lot of flour at the bottom. With these they would strike each other and anyone else nearby, leaving a hard-to-erase white streak on the victim's suit.

Election Night came every November (because the mayor of New York City was elected for a two-year term in odd years). For youngsters the most important aspect of an election were the bonfires. These were the province of various gangs of teenage boys, who caused much less trouble to the police in those days than their successors. Before Election Day the members of a gang would assemble wooden objects of all kinds—chiefly empty packing cases from the grocer's—and store them as a cache in cellars or the corner of a vacant lot, to await conflagration night. If the secret hiding place became known to another gang, that could prove disastrous. "The 110th Street gang stole our 'Lection"—meaning "our wood"—might be the heart-breaking tale. Come Election Night, in the middle of every few blocks the wood piles would be duly assembled, set fire to, and left to blaze away for a nice long while, surrounded by hordes of entranced spectators.

Thanksgiving in the streets of New York in the early 1900s was the day for kids to dress up in their elders' clothes and roam the streets asking for pennies. "Anything for Thanksgiving?" was a ritual question posed to every passerby. We were never allowed to take part in these disguises or this mendicancy. That would not befit our respectable, albeit penniless bourgeois status. How times have changed! The dressing up and the begging now take place on Halloween instead of Thanksgiving.

My chief interest in life in those and later years was my schoolwork. I was a good student, devoted to learning for learning's sake, and also extremely ambitious to make an outstanding record. There was plenty of homework, but I did it very quickly and in all sorts of odd moments. Mother used to say, with the usual exaggeration, that she did not understand how I got such good marks since I always seemed to be doing something other than homework—generally some nonrequired reading.

When I was in the sixth year, an important event occurred in the New York City schools, known as the "Maxwell Examinations." The superintendent of schools, a forbidding character named Dr. Maxwell, had announced that he was dissatisfied with the level of teaching and scholastic competence in the city. He personally drew up a series of examinations, in English and mathematics, to be given to everyone in the elementary system. They were considered to be exceedingly difficult for their respective grades, and severely marked. In English I was disappointed to learn that I had gotten only sixty-eight; but that seemed more impressive when it appeared that the second-highest child had received only forty-two. But a heart-breaking event occurred in the mathematics test. There were five questions on the front blackboard. They did not seem so difficult; I finished them rather quickly, turned in my paper, and walked out while every one else was still at work. Later I was called into the office of the principal, the well-known Dr. Birkins, remembered by countless graduates of P.S. 10.

"Benny," said he, "Why on earth didn't you answer the last

two questions?" You can guess the story. Questions 6 and 7 were on the blackboard at the back of the room, where I hadn't seen them, nor heard the teacher's announcement. I had answered the first five questions perfectly, and so received a seventy—which was the best record in the school. Said Dr. Birkins to me, shaking his head sadly: "If you had only *answered* those other two questions, you would have made a name for yourself—and for the school."

My schooldays became really interesting when I entered the "Departmental System" in the 7A grade at P.S. 10, but the first day of that new dignity was anything but dignified. Shortly after the beginning of the term I was suddenly promoted from 6B to 7A. (Each year was divided into two separate grades.) Since this was the fourth time I had skipped, I was barely ten years old when, together with a few other boys, I was brought up to my new class by the assistant principal. The forty-odd pupils, all boys, took one look at me and burst into raucous laughter. Instead of the Norfolk suit, *de rigueur* among those twelve-year-olds, I was still wearing the sailor blouse and pants combination that marked the little boy. They regarded me as some kind of freak, and I began to regard myself with a sort of desperate loathing. That very afternoon I made such a fuss at home that Mother reluctantly took me up to Koch's on 125th Street and bought me my first Norfolk suit.

My cousin, Louis Grossbaum—universally known as Louie—exercised a great influence on my life, most of it for the good. He was the second son of my oldest paternal uncle, and the same age as my brother Leon. I have never met such an extraordinary collection of abilities as he possessed. On the one hand, he was an extremely brilliant scholar, outstanding in Greek, Latin, and mathematics, winner of the fabulous Pulitzer Scholarship and of many prizes at Columbia College and Engineering School. By my modest standards, he was an excellent athlete, in days when the studious were expected to be weaklings. Most surprising of all, he seemed to be a businessman to his fingertips. At first, he earned money delivering bread and rolls in the early mornings on Madison Avenue, where he lived. Later, he tutored the children of wealthy residents just west on Fifth Avenue or just east on Park. To my junior and impractical mind, he seemed to know everything about everything—including girls, a subject long destined to remain a closed book to me. The born leader of our cohort, he discovered an opportunity to make money by selling "Baseball Mailing Cards" at the Polo Grounds and the Highlanders' (later renamed the Yankees') stadiums. The cards were arranged like elaborate scenic postcards, with a long strip that unfolded and showed photographs of each member of the team. The playing schedule and a scoreboard for the game completed the package. Our profit was 2 cents on each pair of cards. As I remember it, each of us made about 20 cents per average weekday; but weekends and doubleheaders could net us as high as a dollar.

Somewhere among my papers there molders a brown-covered notebook, containing my diary, kept during one of those Baseball Mailing Card summers. I kept track of my daily takings, the result of the game, and my other doings. Sometimes I composed the whole thing in rhyme, and a messy doggerel it was. When I showed my new notebook to Louie, he condescended to start it off with his own composition, in the form of words of advice to his younger cousin. They began *Gnothi seauton* ("Know thyself"), written in Greek characters, and ended with a commentary in Louie's original Latin. I was lost in admiration of all this erudition, and solemnly vowed that I too would become a scholar of Latin and Greek.

It was my talent in mathematics that earned me my first big money. A friend of ours, Chester Brown, who was a grade ahead of me and several inches taller, was doing badly in algebra. His mother paid me 50 cents a week for three lessons in the subject. I can't figure out now how I was able to tutor in a subject I hadn't yet reached at school; so the story is probably wrong in some detail. But I did start tutoring then, and continued it more or less steadily until I ended tutoring the son of

General Leonard Wood and of other officers at Governors Island.

In those days, once it got dark there was practically nothing to do except hang around the street corners, or stay home and do schoolwork or read. I didn't care for the street life in the evening; the boys struck me as coarse and uninteresting. Thus I had plenty of time to read, and the amount I did seems prodigious. Each two weeks I would take four or five books out of the library, and in addition I consumed a number of proscribed but relatively innocent books that passed from hand to hand. These included the famous Frank Merriwell series and the Nick Carter detective stories. The library supplied me with fare ranging from the Rollo books, through Horatio Alger, G. A. Henty, and Oliver Optic to classics such as Dickens, Stevenson, and Charles Reade.

Later on in my life I was amazed to discover how much greater an impact reading had on me than on my friends. The common attitude was that reading was done merely to pass examinations, or for temporary amusement, and then promptly forgotten. Though I too have forgotten much that I learned and read in school, I also remember a great deal, especially in its broader outlines. I have always had the advantage of an excellent memory, but I was also very interested in what I studied, and from an early age I determined to make these things part of my culture, my mental equipment, and my future life.

My studies were for me a continuous process, and I always took a particular pleasure in recognizing in some later class a reference that I had first run across before. Recently (1957) I noticed my son Buz writing a report on Washington Irving's *Legend of Sleepy Hollow,* which I too had studied in school many years before. I remembered that the story quotes a line from Milton's "L'Allegro"—"Of linked sweetness long drawn out"— to describe the nasal echoes of Ichabod's voice raised in song. With a little difficulty I located the very passage that had intrigued me in 1904, and that I had not seen since. But that was not extraordinary; reading "L'Allegro" in high school, I was reminded of the "linked sweetness" phrase in Irving's *Legend*. The associations re-echoed each time, in later years, that I repeated long passages from Milton's poem to myself.

I constantly surprise myself and others with my literary memory. Yesterday I went to an ophthalmologist in Beverly Hills to have my eyes examined. He asked me to read a continuous text in descending sizes of type. I looked at a few words, and then asked innocently: "Isn't that from the *Autobiography of Benjamin Franklin?*" Dr. Hare answered "Yes," and seemed so amazed that—inadvertently, I am sure—he put the card down, and I never finished the test. He had never had a patient who recognized the text. I said nonchalantly that I had read the book only once, and that was in elementary school more than sixty years ago. Perhaps I should have added that that book made a special impression on my unconscious, because in my Walter Mitty daydreaming I had imagined myself a fetching mixture of Ulysses, Benjamin Franklin, and Victor Hugo. (How wonderful to be old enough to boast without giving a damn about modesty!)

One of the great heroes of my childhood reading was Odysseus. In spite of the great praise heaped on the *Iliad*, as the world's foremost poem, I must confess that I had never been able to read it through—until Robert Graves's ironical version came along—although some passages, such as Hector's farewell to Andromache, have long been my favorites. But the *Odyssey* has fascinated me from the beginning, nor has that fascination diminished through the years. The wiliness and the courage, the suffering and the triumphs of its protagonist carried an appeal for me which I never could quite understand. At first I thought it was the attraction of opposites—Ulysses enthralled me because his character and fate were so different from my own. Only after I had long passed maturity did I begin to realize there was quite a bit of the typically Odyssean faults and virtues in my own makeup.

As a youngster I rejoiced to think that Ulysses' wanderings

and trials had ended in his triumphant reunion with Penelope, and that they both were to live happily forever after. But a few years later Tennyson's great poem was to introduce me to the real Ulysses, for whom his island home and his wife's bed could never be more than a port-of-call. The concluding passage rang through my brain like a fiery challenge to a kind of life that seemed the very antithesis of my own values, ambitions, and expectations. How often did I repeat to myself "To strive, to seek, to find, and not to yield."[2] Still later, I read Dante's version of the dauntless expedition and the stormy death of Odysseus, as he is made to recount it in that brief unforgettable passage in the *Inferno*. And, finally, I now hold in my hands a tremendous epic on the same theme, newly written by the gifted Kazantzakis. Perhaps Ulysses is about my own age, as again he leaves his wife and his now married son. Perhaps he is ageless, as at times I feel myself. In any case, in his mind of many turns (*polytropon*), in the restless heart, in the dauntless body, all under his peaked sailor cap, I sense an iconoclastic ideal which has always attracted me, like an unseen magnetic pole of ever-growing intensity.

Such experiences may be something like those involuntary memories that lie at the heart of Proust's re-creation of his youth. But for him the moving cause was something quite unintellectual—the famous dipping of the madeleine in the tea, or the stooping down to unbutton boots—while in my case it is almost always literary words, especially poetry, that bring back the scenes and contexts.

No doubt the peculiarities of one's memory reveal the peculiarities of one's character. In both cases, no doubt, mine must appear a bundle of contradictions. The things that I cannot remember, despite repeated encounters, are legion. I have looked up the same telephone number in the directory fifty, a hundred times. I may have visited a friend's or relative's home a score of times without remembering the floor he lives on, or the direction to turn from the elevator. Many faces, too, I don't recognize even though I may have met and spoken to their

owners an embarrassing number of times. I forget many names
that the laws of politeness would require me to remember.

I have often been able to make my social forgetfulness a
cause of general laughter, instead of personal embarrassment,
by stealing a disarming remark made by Italo Svevo, author of
The Confessions of Zeno: "There are three things I always forget—names, faces, and — and — I can't remember the third."
On the other hand, I have often astonished a former student of
mine by recalling his name long years afterwards.

The key to the latter contradiction, and to the others in the
quality of my memory, lies in the sharp division that my mind
makes between persons and events on the one hand, and ideas
on the other. I remember the things I learn, rather than the
things I live. Thus, anything derived from my studies, my
leisure reading, my work and activities appears to make a special and often ineffaceable impression on my mind. But the
things that happen and the people I meet in other aspects of
my life—social, sports, travel—seem to leave but little mark.
Thus I can remember a student's name if I have identified him
in some way with the subject matter of the course, or his contribution to it; I would probably not remember him for other
reasons of contact, even though he had been especially agreeable or troublesome.

In the Metropolitan Museum of Art in New York I remember seeing a plaster replica of a Roman triumphal arch. The
plaque below it identifies it as the "Arch of Septimus Severus."
When I first read that inscription, I was truly shocked. They
dared to misspell the name of one of the Great Emperors! Nor
did they care enough about the man to correct the blatant
error, even in a center of scholarship! But my emotional reaction was no doubt stranger than that minor blunder. One might
well ask in Hamlet's phrase "What's Septimius Severus to him
or he to Septimius Severus?" The fact is, I must confess, that
Severus was my *friend*, in a way in which living men have not
succeeded in being my friends—more correctly stated, in
which I have not succeeded in making friends of living men.

When I was fifteen Septimius came to life for me in the grandiose pages of Edward Gibbon; I followed intently his struggles with internal and external foes; I gloried in his reassertion of the power of that splendid Roman Empire whose fall I knew to be inevitable, but which I was eager to postpone as long as possible. Septimius Severus crossed over to my native Britain and repaired Hadrian's Wall; he thus associated himself in my impressionable thoughts with that still greater and far more complicated emperor, whom I loved and admired in Gibbon's pages, and came many years later to understand completely— and almost to identify with—in Margaret Yourcenar's masterpiece, *The Memoirs of Hadrian.*

So it is true that the real friends and intimates of my life have been Hadrian and Severus and countless other characters of history—even Gustavus Adolphus and Oxenstierns of Sweden—together with those writers whose work and personalities had a special meaning for my developing youth. Among these were Virgil, more than Homer, Milton more than Shakespeare, Lessing more than Goethe. What these authors wrote had far more significance for me and left a greater impression on my memory than the living people around me.

My public school career closed on a successful note. I just nosed out my closest friend, Sydney Rogow, for the highest-average mark. This entitled me to the title of Valedictorian and to become editor of the *Wide-Awake*, the school magazine, for which, however, I don't recall having done anything but write a longish poem. But I was a proud boy when I made my Valedictorian's Address at the graduation exercises, and prouder still when my beloved teacher, Mr. Bayne, wrote in my green-covered autograph album, in a large, flowing hand, the following tribute:

> To the Poet, the President, and the Valedictorian,
>   With best Wishes,
>   Stephen F. Bayne

But my days at P.S. 10 ended in remorse. The graduating class was urged to buy school pins of solid gold, costing five dollars. That was more than I had any right to ask for, but my unwillingness to admit our poverty before my fellows led me to coax and wheedle Mother into giving me the money. In less than a month I had lost the pin and had nothing left of the incident but a lifelong regret at my lack of true character. I console myself with the thought that Mother must have sympathized with my weakness and false pride, for she herself had for years been a prey to the same emotions. In those days nearly every family wanted to appear richer than it was; for us it seemed even more essential not to appear as poor as we actually were. Mother tried hard not to talk too often and with too much regret of our former and vanished splendor. But there remained so much to remind her of it that she found it difficult to put it out of mind. No doubt the chief of her chagrins came from the best-meaning source—our old friends. They remained faithful and did not desert us. But the contrast between their financial state and ours was only too visible to Mother's eyes. More tangibly, their visits to us and ours to them imposed a constant pressure on Mother to disguise our poverty as much as possible, to cultivate all the stratagems of seedy respectability, to live always and precariously a little higher rather than a little lower than our means allowed.

We boys were steeped in that frustrating atmosphere, and on one of us at least it made a strong, unwholesome impression. My natural inclination, I believe, was always away from the material and towards the intellectual and even the spiritual side of life. But the difficult conditions of my childhood existence affected me no less than my brothers; I became too conscious and respectful of money. I took it for granted that the primary mark of success in life lay in large earning and large spending. Several decades were to pass, and many vicissitudes to be undergone, before I could master the simplest and most important of all the rules of material welfare: The most brilliant financial strategy consists of living well within one's means.

CHAPTER FOUR

High School Days: Brooklyn and the Bronx

U pon graduation from P.S. 10 I was recommended for admission to Townsend Harris Hall, the high school (or "subfreshman") division of the College of the City of New York. This institution had only a three-year curriculum compared to the others' four, but the students were expected to cover as much or more in the shorter time. The standards for admission and retention were comparatively high. Nonetheless, the school had what seemed to me a huge first-year class, some four hundred pupils distributed in about twenty sections. Since the entire student body was arranged in strict alphabetical order, the result was odd. One section was said to consist entirely of Cohens (and Cohns). That may or may not have been so, but I do know that all the names in my section began with G. On the first day of school I was privileged to meet a boy about my own age, Frederick F. Greenman, who became my immediate and lifelong friend. Also in my class of G's was little Morrie Gottshalk, destined to be the dean of that enormous college which he entered then with such a modest and apprehensive mien.

I have forgotten most of the teachers I had at Townsend Harris Hall, and some I remember are scarcely worth describing. But two stand out in my memory: one was Eduardo San Giovanni, a holy terror of a Latin teacher, who really taught me that complicated language. I can still hear him ask in his customary menacing tone: "Garten, what ess zee characteristic vowel of zee second declension?" A reply. Then his next question, "Mr. Garten, ess zee earth round? Yes? So ees your mark." No false modesty deterred him from boasting to his classes how he used to speak Latin to the Pope in the Vatican gardens.

The other was an extremely quiet and undistinguished-looking teacher of geometry, exactly opposite in temperament from the ebullient San Giovanni. His name was Morris Raphael Cohen—which meant nothing to the world in those days but was destined to shine lustrously in the annals of philosophy.[1] Teaching geometry was evidently not his forte. Townsend Harris Hall had its special curriculum, which emphasized hard work, and the course required us to cover all twelve books of plane and solid geometry in one academic year. Mr. Cohen didn't plan our assignments very well, and by early June we were very far from finished. So one day he announced to a thunderstruck class, "For tomorrow, gentlemen, we shall do the tenth book." His regular procedure was to have us go to the blackboard in platoons, each assigned a different proposition or problem. The aforementioned Garten was a tall, stout, jolly individual, more successful as a friend than as a student. So Gottshalk or I, having finished our work rapidly, would sometimes change places with Garten and do his assignment on the board. Mr. Cohen, deep in a volume of James or Royce, would be innocently unaware of what was going on.

About seven years later I met now Professor Cohen under different circumstances. I was a rather self-important senior at Columbia College, interested in philosophy and French, among other subjects. Professor Raymond Boutroux of the Sorbonne had come to the campus to deliver a lecture on the subject, "M. Bergson, est-il un pragmatiste?" ["Is Mr. Henri Bergson a pragmatist?"] Boutroux opened his lecture with the pronouncement "Oui, Mesdames et Messieurs, M. Bergson est certainement un pragmatiste" ["Yes, ladies and gentlemen, he is certainly a pragmatist"], and ended it, no less assertively, "Alors, M. Bergson n'est pas du tout un pragmatiste" ["So, Mr. Bergson is not a pragmatist at all"].

Leaving the lecture hall in a state of perplexity, I recognized the short curly hair and unprepossessing features of my old geometry instructor. He greeted me civilly, and I said to him in the somewhat patronizing tone that a Columbia man of those days adopted towards someone connected with CCNY: "Hello, Mr. Cohen, are you interested in philosophy too?" Mr. Morris Raphael Cohen smiled self-deprecatingly. "A little," he said, and went off. The student with me stared at me aghast. "You damn fool," he exclaimed, "Don't you know that Morris Cohen is universally accepted as the successor to William James?" No, I didn't know. But my ignorance taught me something for life: never patronize anyone.

When I was in high school, Mother decided to move out of Uncle Maurice's house and to start a boardinghouse. She rented a brownstone house on 129th Street in Harlem, furnishing it I know not how. Mother's business ability was so modest that only too late did we discover that the house faced onto a livery stable. As the summer grew older and hotter, the disadvantages of our situation became only too evident, to our tenants even more than to ourselves.

As an ambitious boy just turned twelve, I felt the need to seek gainful employment. Not far away was a Saxton's Dairy Shop which displayed the magic poster "Boy Wanted." When I applied for the job, the manager of Saxton's looked distrustful and said "You're not strong enough for this work." I assured him that I was and that he could count on my eagerness and reliability as well. The law permitted summer employment to workers of any age, and for any salary, so I was hired at $2 per week. Things went quite well at first. I would push a loaded delivery cart to different apartment houses in the neighborhood, then carry the merchandise down into the cellar, find the customer's bell and speaking tube, and establish contact. Then all I had to do was to pull up the loaded dumbwaiter, pull it down to get the money, and generally pull it up again to deliver the change. It was not unduly difficult, though everybody seemed to live on the sixth floor. But then the delivery wagon was given to someone else, and I had to carry a loaded basket. That I found exhausting, especially in the burning sun of early August. Once I set my heavy basket down to wipe my face and rest my aching arms. Next door were two boys playing stoopball. As I took up the basket and trudged away, one of them shouted after me, "Work, you horse." I was close to tears. Shortly thereafter, Victor—a much stronger youngster—took over the job and fared much better with it.

We gave up the fragrant 129th Street house at the end of the summer and moved our business to a similar brownstone house at 350 Manhattan Avenue, near 114th Street. There romance first touched my heart. I had divided women pretty much into two classes: (a) Mother and (b) inhabitants of another planet. This unwholesome attitude was due to the circumstances of my education. Except for the two unsuccessful weeks in kindergarten, I was never once in a coeducational classroom. Some unkind power deprived me of virtually any normal contact with girls my own age—with the sole exception of my cousin Helen, who made little impression on my thoughts or feelings.

The inspiration of my infatuation was a beautiful, brilliant, vivacious girl whom I adored and who was extraordinarily fond of me. Unfortunately, she was a glorious eighteen to my preadolescent twelve. Constance Fleischmann had come with her mother to board with us in order to be near Barnard College. No one could be kinder to a bashful boy than Constance was to me. She volunteered to give me lessons in French, to which I applied myself faithfully in spite of my numerous other studies. Long afterward my library contained a text-book edition of Prosper Merrimée's *Colomba*, complete with vocabulary, notes, and the following inscription on the title page, written in Constance's beautiful hand: "J'aime les marrons glacés" ["I love glazed chestnuts"].

We read French poems together as well. There was one by Victor Hugo, entitled "La Tombe et la Rose," which she called her favorite, and which she bade me learn by heart. I not only did that eagerly—and remember it to this day—but I translated it into English verse. This marked the beginning of one of the great diversions of my intellectual life. Like many romantic and thoughtful men, I have written a considerable amount of poetry of my own, which my critical sense tells me lacks the divine spark. But translating the masterpieces of others has given me the benefit of their inspiration. The task requires devotion plus a certain knack, and these I think I have been able to bring to the task. I have found much private satisfaction in making numerous translations from Greek, Latin, French, and German—plus one rendering of a poem of A. A. Housman into French.

I cannot forbear including here my translation of Hugo's little poem:

THE TOMB AND THE ROSE

The tomb said unto the rose,
'With those tears the dawn bestows
What does thou, flower of love?'
Said the rose unto the tomb,
'What dost thou with them whose doom
To thy maw sends from above?'

Said the rose, 'Home of the dead,
Of the tears the breezes shed

Amber-sweet perfume make I.'
The tomb said, 'O plaintive flower,
Of each soul that knows my power
I an angel make on high.'

Now I was nearly thirteen, and so was duly trained for the
bar mitzvah ceremony. Of this I shall say only that I dismayed
my preceptor by a stubborn refusal to deliver the usual speech
of gratitude to parents and solemn commitment to the glories
and observances of Judaism. Having listened to countless ora-
tions of this kind on Sabbath mornings in the synagogue, I had
conceived a violent antipathy towards their monotonous
sameness, their emotionalism, and their evident hypocrisy.

I lost my faith in short order. I found the overelaborate and
antiquated ritual, which I had previously accepted unques-
tioningly, to be the enemy of both reason and comfort. Whatever real meaning and appeal the great affirmations of religious faith might have had for a sensitive mind were suffocated
under a mass of repetitious jargon. Sunday school became a
nuisance and the synagogue a bore. For a short time, however,
during an impressionable period in my early teens, I found
myself stirred by the ethical ideas of our faith. I listened with
some emotion to the singing of the choir of young voices on
Friday nights and even responded inwardly to the earnest if
ineloquent exhortations of the rabbi. But that interest was
short-lived. As the years progressed, the once vise-like hold of
Jewish rituals and customs upon me became ever more
relaxed, until finally they all but disappeared from my horizon.

But this did not mean, as it had for so many others of my
acquaintance, that I lost all interest in religion itself. On the
contrary, religion *in general* has long been one of my chief
objects of inquiry and meditation. The varieties of religious
revelations, beliefs, and experiences have furnished me with a
limitless subject for study. The contrast between man's un-
doubted need for *religion* and the dubious character of his *religions* is striking. It is hard to deny the existence of the Divine

in the universe; but it is equally hard to accept any of the numerous and conflicting doctrinal ways in which the Divine is said to have revealed itself to man. Even monotheism—that gift of Judaism to the world—is suspect to my skeptical mind. The idea of one God is appealing in its magnificent simplicity, but whether it corresponds to the realities of the unseen world is another question. When in my college days I read William James's *A Pluralistic Universe* (1909), I was most impressed by his lucid speculations because they corresponded to the thoughts that had been germinating in my own mind.

As an inquiring citizen of the Western world, I found much fascination in the doctrines and the history of Christianity. Jesus became my hero quite early in life, and in a rather humorous way. Most of the bar mitzvah gifts I received were books. One of these was sent by a young rabbi, quite a close friend of the family: its title was *A Prince of the House of David*. When I read it some months later, I found to my surprise it consisted of a series of fictional letters describing the life and martyrdom of Jesus. I was not converted to Christianity by the rabbi's gift, but it did introduce me to a character who has never ceased to attract and intrigue me.

Naturally I wondered at the strange present from a Jewish rabbi. I met him a number of years later—he had become the prominent Dr. Rudolph I. Coffee. He told me how I had been the unwitting cause of great embarrassment and twinges of conscience. It seems he had asked a mutual friend to pick a suitable book for me. The lady, shopping hurriedly, saw the little volume and inferred, without bothering to look, that it was about one of our Jewish heroes. She told Dr. Coffee the book's title, which meant nothing to him at the time. But, as luck would have it, he became acquainted with the book and its contents some time afterwards, when it was too late to rectify the blunder and too awkward even to offer an explanation.

In *A Night in the Luxembourg* (1906), Rémy de Gourmont speaks of the Jews and comments: "Strange fate of a people, to have rejected a God which they gave to the world." None of the many ironies of history are equal to these two: That an obscure Eastern sect should have imposed its religious concepts on the entire Western world and on peoples so different from themselves in origin and character. And that the Jews have survived throughout the centuries *in spite* of their great creation, Christianity, rather than because of it.

When one reads the New Testament, one is struck by the contrast between its ethics and its theology. The ethical teaching of Jesus is a great step forward from the Old Testament— not in the novelty of its ideas, but in the imaginativeness of their expression. But in his expectation of the imminent end of the world, in his concern with devils and with the physical aspects of Heaven, Jesus seems to reflect a naive and even superstitious environment, intellectually inferior to the refined concepts of the Jewish prophets of old. And to a nonbeliever, the elaborate Christian doctrine constructed after his death is indeed an extraordinary demonstration of the supremacy of faith over reason.

It is startling to reflect on the change in religious orientation of segments of the Western world within a single lifetime. The ease with which some people have given up belief and even interest in religion seems amazing compared to the control which it used to have on the thinking of the multitude. Often I have told young people, "One must think a great deal about God before one has the right *not* to believe in Him." But religion appears to be like the earth's gravitational field to astronauts. Those who have broken away from the doctrinal traditions of their family establish without difficulty a way of life that ignores religion altogether. It is strange to contemplate the cohabitation on the planet of millions of people who find God, Heaven, and Hell supremely real, and millions of others who never even think about these notions.

After a lifetime of meditation on the great questions of religion, I have not been able to arrive at anything approaching religious faith. But I have attained a great respect and even envy for those who have preserved their faith and who employ it as a guide to right conduct in this world, a rock against adversity, and a promise of salvation and life eternal. If faith is such a wonderful possession, if it is free for anyone to take, why do I not gladly accept it? Alas! anyone of mental integrity cannot believe *merely* because belief will make him happy. Pascal, in his famous wager, may have convinced many readers of the mathematical advantage of believing in Christianity, as a protection or hedge against the infinitesimal chance that the unbeliever will go to Hell. But even he must have realized that he was proving too much and that his argument could not help one decide which, among the score of conflicting religions, was best. I am content to go to the end of my days still seeking the ever-elusive truth, still asking myself the old, unanswerable questions, still gently chiding God from time to time for concealing Himself so adroitly from those who would serve Him nobly if they could but find Him.

Let me set down briefly but frankly my attitude towards Judaism. I cannot help thinking that on the whole it has been a great misfortune for Jews to be born Jewish; Providence would have been kinder to them if it had permitted them to be born Christian. Yet in my own case I can say with equal candor that my Jewish birth has brought me only small disadvantages, and that these have been more than offset by certain gifts of mind and personality conferred on me by Judaism. The problems experienced by Jews during my early years, even in America, were all too manifest, and I personally experienced them in specific incidents (mostly of minor importance) and in a general atmosphere of malaise and apprehension surrounding our relations with Christians. I have lived to see most, though not all, of these problems disappear. Recently, in conducting a private Sunday School class for a group of eight Jewish children living in Beverly Hills I was amazed to find that not one had ever heard the word "anti-Semitism." They did not know what it meant. When I was their age, anti-Semitism was an important part of the air we breathed; it affected all our plans for dealing with the outside world; it played the leading part in our literature and in our humor. But my adult life has been most fortunate in this area. My business and academic careers have brought me in close contact with innumerable Christians, and I have rarely suffered rebuffs or embarrassments because of my religion. Of course, this freedom from unpleasantness has been helped not a little by a self-protective avoidance on my part of social contacts or ambitions that I suspected might be ill-received.

I must confess here that I feel little emotional loyalty to the Jewish people from whom I sprang. Loyalty itself is doubtless a great emotional virtue, but it can be an equally great intellectual fault. Loyalty is the shining front of a shield whose obverse side may be inscribed with prejudice, intolerance, and fanaticism. I believe I can be unreservedly loyal to ideals, to great causes, to whatever and whomever I admire. I can *act* loyally, too, out of a sense of duty, toward people and institutions to whom I owe such conduct by conventional, and no doubt inherently sound, standards. But I cannot give myself passionately to people and institutions merely because I happen to be a part of them. This is probably a fault of character, a manifestation of still wider deficiencies which grow out of my lifetime emphasis upon the intellectual as opposed to the emotional in human life.

Many Jews appear to have a low opinion of the Jewish people—at least of those born in the less-favored regions of the world. I am not one of these. It seems to me that the Jewish character has been both degraded and elevated, both coarsened and refined by long centuries of contumely and oppression. Yet—and this is a marvelous advantage—I am convinced that, under favorable conditions, the Jews can lay aside the narrowness and the shifty devices so long forced upon them by their misery without giving up the quickness of intellect and spirituality that arose as compensation. I have a theory which is anathema to most of my Jewish friends. It is that the real mission of Jews is to intermarry and thus to contribute their hard-won stock of talents and abilities to a much wider group. What a wonderful adventure in genetics that would be!

Mother's career as a boardinghouse keeper ended disastrously. The red flag appeared before our house and virtually all our possessions were sold at auction. I recall oscillating between shame at the disgrace of our being sold out publicly under the hammer and excitement at the crowd, the activity, and the strange goings-on. Each of us boys was given some little job to do on the day of the auction; since I was the mathematician of the family, mine was to add up the proceeds realized from the furniture of each room. How sad Mother looked as item after item was knocked down to ridiculously low prices. But our upright piano found two determined bidders, and was finally sold to one of them for a magnificent $150. That was the only time that day that I saw a smile light up poor Mother's face.

We had no other choice than to go back to living with Uncle Maurice in his frame house in Borough Park. At the time that neighborhood was considered pretty far from the center of things and particularly far from Townsend Harris Hall on Amsterdam Heights in Manhattan. To get there from my new home I had first to take a streetcar, then a BRT elevated train across Brooklyn Bridge, and finally the newly built subway line to 137th Street and Broadway. The ride took an hour and a half each way. However, the main difficulty was the double fares, which—at 5 cents each—amounted to $1 per week. But the long hours I spent on trains were far from wasted. I did nearly all my homework while being transported hither and yon. I remember studying first-year Greek while we rolled slowly over the Brooklyn Bridge and raising my eyes from time to time to see the red girders of Manhattan Bridge then under construction a little to the north.

I made small sums of money in whatever ways possible for a thirteen-year-old boy. I took care of the coal furnace, not too difficult a task except for the backbreaking job of hauling the barrels of heavy ashes up the cellar steps, and then dumping them in a sunken part of the road. I tutored a boy named Barondess, who lived a few doors away at the corner of our street, in mathematics. His father was the famous labor agitator, Joseph Barondess.[2] Our families quickly became friendly, and I listened to many an animated discussion between Barondess and Uncle Maurice—both brilliant men. One of my chief sources of income was typing the reports made by my uncle to his various clients. These were elaborate productions of many pages, which I transcribed on an Oliver typewriter. This machine had only three rows of keys, but made up for that by supplying three characters instead of two on each key. (It took me quite some time to unlearn my hard-won proficiency on the Oliver. Are there any still in use, I wonder?)

By adding part of my earnings to birthday money, I was able to buy a secondhand bicycle. Its acquisition was a red-letter day in my life. I pushed the bike over to a secluded street—not hard to find in those parts—and, after a half-hour of falls and unsteadiness, I taught myself to ride. When summer came, the bike proved a boon. Nearly every day I rode with my neighbor and chum, Claude Gassner, to the Public School Athletic League field in Flatbush, where we played tennis with great enthusiasm and creditable progress.

During my Borough Park summer I made a serious effort to learn French, building upon the slender foundations of my lessons with Constance. The only French book that remained in the Grossbaum library was *Etudes sur la Nature*, by Bernardin de St. Pierre. Like other books it had been acquired by Father at the sale of Sir Moses Montefiore's collection; it had once a nice binding, but now it was decaying. Our copy had been printed about 1800, in six volumes of small size. The pages were yellow, the type antique and not very legible, the French itself rather archaic; for example, the ending *-ait* was written *-oit*. This St. Pierre was a typical eighteenth-century French writer—a naturalist, a would-be general scientist, and a *romancier* all rolled into one. He wrote extensively about plants and animals, and about his various scientific theories—one being that the tides were caused by the melting of ice at the poles! He offered all sorts of philosophical speculations.

I would look up each word whose meaning was unknown or uncertain in my *Heath's French Dictionary*, and then copy it, together with its English equivalent, on a sheet of paper. I would conceal, in turn, the English and the French sections of these lists and try to give back the proper translations in both languages. By the end of the summer I had acquired an additional though rather special vocabulary of several thousand words. Since many of them had to do with exotic flora and fauna, they rather quickly disappeared from my memory through disuse, but a considerable number remained. Later, I sometimes astounded my French professors by using highly specialized or archaic words in my conversational efforts. Alas, much of this impressive French vocabulary was sadly mispronounced since I had acquired it all through reading, and my idea of how to pronounce a word was often as erroneous as the good St. Pierre's scientific theories.

When Uncle Maurice, having become more prosperous, moved into a rather swanky apartment on Washington Heights, we moved to a little place in the Bath Beach section, farther out in Brooklyn. Mother was very pleased to be once more on her own, and we all accepted the limitations of our modest flat in the best spirit.

However, because of the increased distance to Manhattan, it became virtually impossible for me to continue at Townsend Harris Hall, and with much reluctance I decided to transfer to Boys High School in Brooklyn, which had the standard four-year course instead of the Townsend Hall's three years. With childish vanity I had set my heart at entering college at the spectacular age of fifteen, and the change of high schools meant that I must give up that quite unsound ambition.

That year Boys High School had a new principal, Dr. Sullivan, who later became Historian of New York State. (He had taught history to my brother Leon at the High School of Commerce in Manhattan.) I came into his office with my report card from Townsend Hall and at first received a chilly reception. But when he saw my record, his round face became one

big smile. "Now that's a card I like to see," said he. "Nearly all
the boys that come to me from Townsend Hall have been
kicked out of there because they couldn't make the grade, and
I'm compelled to admit them, though they lower our average."
In fact, Boys High had long enjoyed one of the highest reputa-
tions in the country for scholastic excellence, and I was fortunate indeed in being able to go there.

I spent two fruitful years at Boys High. I was unable to continue my Greek because of scheduling difficulties, but I
devoted myself with special enthusiasm to the Latin courses.
Although I admired the eloquence of Cicero, I could never
accustom myself to his egotism and self-glorification. The real
love of my classical education was Virgil. In him I found a
genius perfectly suited to both the demands and the limitations of my own spirit. Granted, he is an imitator of Homer,
and his work falls short of the directness and powerful simplicity of his model. But he adds something that Homer lacks
and to which I respond fully—a sensitiveness to all the
nuances of his narrative, a supreme mastery of poetic expression, both its meaning and musical sound. There is no naivete
in Virgil, but neither is there oversophistication, nor unfath-
omable mystery, nor the least touch of obscurantism. For me
he is as Brahms in music. The composer of the four sym-
phonies was no doubt inferior in scope and power to the composer of nine; but Brahms somehow gives me more than
Beethoven.

The classical languages have given inestimable value to my
inner life, yet I do not favor the compulsory study of Latin—
much less, Greek—nor even great emphasis on these studies
as electives. The two languages are expensive mental luxuries, paid for by many hours of hard application. Work in itself
is not a bad thing; the tragedy, as I see it, is that for so many of
my fellow students all that time and effort proved practically
wasted in the end. After a few years they had forgotten every
idea and nearly every word. In the study of every language—
ancient or modern—there is a certain point of permanent

return which must be reached for the effort to prove worthwhile. If the student stops before reaching that point, practically all that he has learned will fade through the years, sometimes with incredible speed. But if he persists and passes to the other side of the borderline, the language will become a permanent possession, one that can readily extend and deepen throughout the rest of his life.

The idea of studying a foreign language for "mental training" or "discipline" without caring about the literature and culture it communicates does not appeal to me. There is plenty of mental discipline to be gained in a really intensive study of the English language—from learning the art of reading rapidly, of understanding what is read, of remembering for years to come the gist of the material and some of its salient details, and from the art of expressing one's own or others' thoughts in clear, succinct, and grammatical fashion. If I were to write my own *Emile*, the first eight years of my curriculum would include only two subjects: English and science, the latter, of course, including mathematics. But I would add history, geography, and civics to the continuous English course, and would not separate those subjects sharply from literature.

Although I have always been a good speller, reason tells me that the study of English spelling has very little intrinsic value, and its mastery is necessary only for reasons of tradition or convention. I should gladly let everyone spell as he pleases (as did the great men of Shakespeare's time) as long as his message is sound and well expressed! But I suppose I have always been a Utopian. Everyone wants to improve the current educational system. This is not the place to express my own ideas in all their detail. But I must argue for the encouragement and special treatment of gifted students from their earliest age. They should study foreign languages as a supplement to the standard curriculum, which moves too slowly to keep them interested and well occupied.

My achievements at Boys High were moderately impressive. I ranked third in my class. (In my defense, let me add that they were an especially brilliant lot.) I contributed a story, "The Great Pie-Plot," to the school's annual literary publication, a fat book, bound in our school colors red and black, and bearing as title *The Recorder*. I did some interclass debating. My chief recognition was election to Arista, the honor society for all New York high schools, a society founded in my graduating year. But the event that gave me the greatest satisfaction was winning the school tennis tournament. Earlier in the year I had gone out for the tennis team, but had been passed over. Thus it was a great personal triumph to win two sets out of three from Jennings, the team captain, who in turn had defeated Cedric Major. Major later won the Veteran's National Singles Championship at Forest Hills; his game must have improved a lot after our tournament. He also became president of the Lehigh Valley Railroad, but died on the tennis courts at sixty. Since I was regarded as something of a grind at Boys High, and presumably as worthless in athletics, my tennis victory could have added greatly to my prestige with my classmates if the timing had been less awkward. For the tournament finished *after* graduation, and so virtually no one heard the world-shaking news. In fact, I didn't get my medal until the following fall. It was handed to me by our athletic director with the words, "How did you do it?"

We moved again, this time from Brooklyn to Kelly Street in the Bronx. This absurdly reversed the situation of two years before. Then I lived a way out in Brooklyn and went to school in northern Manhattan; now I lived far up in the Bronx and went to high school in the heart of Brooklyn.

At fifteen, I thought up an invention—the first of several to have teased my brain at various times in my life but never amounted to anything. In flats like ours a visitor rang a bell below, which sounded in the kitchen; the resident would then press a button which controlled the latch at the lower door, permitting the visitor to enter. Since I was youngest, I had to leave my book when the bell rang. Irritation with this duty was the mother of invention. I figured out that wires could be run from the bell to the button, so that the movement of the bell clapper would close a circuit and open the latch below.

After a number of clumsy efforts I finally got the apparatus rigged and working. I even had a little switch cut into the wires, so that the gadget could be turned off when we all went out, and didn't want the door open. Sure enough, as soon as any one rang our bell in the vestibule the latch started ticking and one could open the door. In the meantime we had been alerted by the sound, just as before. I had visions of my invention being installed in every flat in the whole world. The cost would be very small, and by putting them in ourselves (to start), we could easily make a dollar on each one. Then, of course, there would be huge royalties paid by licensees in other cities. The impractical dreamer of the family was going to restore its fortunes, nay, raise it to new heights of affluence.

In a few days the bubble burst. What was wrong? In the first place there was a mechanical difficulty. The latch clicked only so long as one kept one's finger on the downstairs bell button. A visitor would ring, notice the immediate clicking of the door, leave the bell and grasp the doorknob. Alas! As his finger left the bell, the clicking would stop immediately, and the door be locked again. Frustrated, the visitor would repeat the maneuver—several times perhaps—always with the same result. By that time one of us upstairs would have to come to his rescue. We would offer lame explanations, followed by the visitor's remark that he didn't think much of our invention. But worse than the people who didn't know how to operate our gadget were some of those who did. It didn't take long for all the youngsters in the apartment house to catch on. They would nonchalantly ring our bell, skillfully keeping the other hand on the doorknob, press it open, and dash up to their own flats while we on the top floor were wondering why our visitor didn't show up. Soon Mother had had enough. She ordered the darned thing dismantled, which I did with an aching heart. Long thereafter I pondered various ways of solving the problem but never actually did anything about it.

CHAPTER FIVE

The Farmhand
and The Mechanic

It is 3:30 a.m. one morning in June 1910. The terminal of the Erie Railroad in Jersey City has the air of a huge, empty barn; only an eye accustomed to the gloom could distinguish the arched and raftered outline of its waiting room. In one corner there is a pinpoint of yellow light. It comes from a telephone booth, its door ajar.

In the narrow booth sits the only occupant of the great building, a youth just turned sixteen. He is hunched uncomfortably in the small seat near the instrument, which projects far out from the wall in the old-fashioned way. Under the green-shaded light attached to the wooden shelf he holds a heavy book, also green. It is Volume Forty-Four of the *Library of Universal Literature:* the *Magna Instauratio, or the Advancement of Learning,* by Francis Bacon, Baron Verulam.

I was terribly sleepy. Never before had I stayed awake so late, and the effort caused me acute physical pain. Everything impelled me towards slumber. The hour, the strain and exhaustion of the previous day, the surrounding darkness,

silence and solitude, the ponderous volume I was reading—all
battled against me like an army. But I was determined to stay
awake; almost by sheer willpower I kept my heavy eyelids
open. For I could not miss the train again. That would be too
ridiculous even to think about.

In the long hours still to go before the 5 a.m. departure I
relived my stupid blunder of the previous afternoon. How
could I have been so inept, so childishly bashful?

Shortly after lunch the day before I had bidden goodbye to
my mother. I was off to New Milford, New York, to work as a
summer hired hand, junior grade, on the farm of a Mr. Jacob
Barman. It had all been arranged by Dr. Weaver, the math
professor at Boys High. Beneath his skullcap and acid manner,
Weaver was intensely devoted to helping city lads experience
the wholesome discipline of life and labor in the country. I had
been easily convinced by his eloquence. With three others I
had signed up to be summer apprentice on a farm. The pay:
$10 per month and board.

It was the first time I would be away from my mother since
her widowhood seven years before. She had been visibly
moved at the farewell, but her moist eyes had smiled bravely
as she uttered the inevitable formula: "Take good care of yourself, darling, and *write!*" I ran quickly down the three flights of
stairs, carrying Mother's black suitcase, not too heavily
packed. I seemed almost instantaneously to turn into a man, or
nearly one. In my pocket was the ticket to New Milford, sent
me by Farmer Barman, and about $5 in cash.

Taking the subway to Cortland Street, and then the ferry
across to New Jersey, I arrived at the Erie Terminal a good
hour ahead of train time. I settled down on one of the uncomfortable long benches, opened my valise, and brought out
Bacon's treatise. I had packed other volumes, but they were
strictly for formal study: the *Anabasis* in Greek, and a standard Greek grammar—by Greenough and Kittredge—which I
had received as a graduation present from Dr. Reiss, head of
the Department of Classical Languages at Boys High. I had

done so well in his Virgil class that the good professor—quite in character with his Van Dyck beard and thick German accent—had urged me to take up Greek in the "long zommer eefenings" ahead of me. Together with this light provender I had brought a red paperbacked volume entitled *The Palmer Method for Perfect Penmanship.* This, too, had been a gift from a teacher, not as a tribute to my graphic prowess but to remedy my one academic weakness. My handwriting was atrocious. My family claimed, indulgently, that this flaw was only further proof that I was a genius. But Mr. Edwards, of the English Department, had taken five points off my composition for poor penmanship: "Little enough," said he, "to compensate for the damage done my eyesight and disposition." So, in an amiable gesture, Edwards had given me the Palmer exercises, extorting a promise that—again in the long summer evenings—I would faithfully practice, with stiff elbow and rotating shoulder, my lines and curves.

The work by Bacon was the only one left in the family's depleted library that I had not read at least once. (There had originally been a complete *Universal Literature* set, along with many other books, but alas! over the years nearly all had been converted into spending money by a light-fingered brother.)

Seated in the waiting room, I tussled with Bacon—it was heavy going—until a little before train time. Then I went to a ticket window to ask what track the New Milford train would leave on. "At 5:12 on Track 9," the man replied brusquely. This was surprising because Barman's letter had given the time as 4:30. But I was too bashful to question the agent—a not too agreeable fellow—and so returned to my seat to wait and read some more.

Just before 4:30 it occurred to me that the agent might have been wrong. I hurried to the window and asked again. Then my own stupidity, and the agent's, too, came to light. Because I had said only "New Milford," the man had given me the departure time of the train for New Milford, Pennsylvania.

That was a much more important town and station than its New York State namesake. Yes, the New Milford, N.Y. train did leave at 4:30 p.m.—in exactly ten seconds.

I rushed off only to see the gate shut in my face. The next train would leave at five o'clock the following morning. It was a kind of milk train in reverse, bringing back empty milk cans from the city to the dairy country. So now I had nearly thirteen hours to wait. What should I do? I thought of returning home, for dinner and some rest in my bed. But my pride said no. I could not confess my blunder to Mother, nor face the amused sympathy of my brothers, who would be returning from work.

It would be more manly, I thought, to wait it out by myself. So I spent an hour or more traveling across the Hudson on the Erie ferry. By remaining on the boat, I could ride indefinitely at no cost. At first the New York skyline, the river traffic, and the mild June air delighted my senses, and I was almost pleased by the delay. But by the tenth crossing I was bored to death. Then I ate an economical supper, took a long walk, dozed in the station, then tried another half-dozen ferry trips. At last I settled down once more on the wooden bench, Bacon in hand, to wait for the 5 a.m. train.

I had plenty of time to think about myself, my recent graduation from high-school, my hopes and plans for college. Although reminders of my silly mistake kept barging in— "How moronic can a man be?"—I was actually far from dissatisfied with my accomplishments. A born student, I had done well in every subject, and ranked close to the top of my class. My ambition, of course, was to go to college, preferably to Columbia, and I had high hopes of winning one of the twelve Pulitzer Scholarships—those fabulous prizes that paid full tuition plus living expenses away from home. For this purpose, I had competed in the notoriously difficult College Entrance Board Examinations. Having compared notes with some friendly rivals, I felt certain that I would rate high on the list, above the hundreds of other candidates.

Thus I had much to be happy about. The years of poverty since Father's death had touched me only lightly. They had developed in my character a serious concern for money, a willingness to work hard for small sums, and an extreme conservatism in all my spending habits.

At two o'clock in the morning I faced a new disaster. Suddenly all the lights in the waiting room went off, and I was left in utter darkness. Apparently no more trains were scheduled to leave until early morning, and there was no point in wasting electricity on an empty building. I wondered desperately how I could fight off the drowsiness that welled up around my eyes. I roamed aimlessly in the dark from one long wall to another. Then I discovered the single telephone booth in the waiting room. There was a small electric light in the cubicle, and to my joy the light worked: I had found salvation. I had already gotten pretty far along in the heavy, green book. I opened it at my place, propped it against the shelf, and bent to the double task of absorbing Bacon's grandiose outline of a new world of knowledge and keeping my sticky eyes open.

After a while I looked up and around. Across the room, where there had been only blackness before, I noted a faint tinge of gray. A long new summer day was knocking at the windows of the Erie Terminal. A few passengers came into the room. I was no longer alone, and I knew that I was not going to miss the train.

I spent two months on the farm as Mr. Barman's hired hand. That amounts to one-quarter of 1 percent of my life to date [1958], yet somehow this short stay left me with more lasting memories than have many year-long experiences. Not that I was tremendously happy at New Milford, for I found the work hard and unappealing, and grew terribly impatient for the day of liberation to arrive. Nor have I ever had the slightest inclination to return to a farm, even as a nonlaboring proprietor. Yet it was not suffering that etched so many scenes on my memory. For I was not at all mistreated, and in any case I had already acquired the faculty of disregarding the misdeeds of others. Rather, it was the complete change in my way of life, coming at an especially impressionable age that explains the sharpness and persistence of these recollections.

Mr. Barman was about sixty-three years old and seemed very ancient indeed with his white beard and wrinkled face. He had come to America with his parents from Germany after the political troubles of 1848. Towards the end of the Civil War, at the age of eighteen, he entered the Union Army. I am not sure whether he actually fought in any battles, but he was a full-fledged veteran, receiving a monthly pension that represented a good part of his cash income. Mr. Barman had a small farm, a few acres around the farmhouse, plus a meadow some distance down the road. He possessed two cows, both named Lucy, a few pigs, a lot of chickens—and the indispensable horse Charley, used both for farmwork and transportation. He grew numerous kinds of vegetables and fruits, plus hay and alfalfa for the stock. He sold some of his milk, and consumed the rest, partly as butter and cheese.

The Barman household consisted of himself, his second wife, and a schoolteacher daughter by his first wife. The ladies were pleasant enough to me, but they didn't get along together at all. Barman constantly needed to arbitrate their disputes. At meals we had the company of Mr. Snedecker, who kept the general store of the village. Snedecker was a crusty old bachelor with whom I exchanged no more than a few words throughout the summer. But his life, like others in the village, was tragicomic. It seemed he had been engaged for the past eighteen years to a young lady of New Milford. The marriage was to take place when the store paid enough to support a wife and children. But his little business never seemed to grow; the wedding was postponed year after year; and at last, when the unlucky lady had lost all chance of another match, the engagement became "permanent"—that is, hopeless.

Now and then some other men, doing special work in the village, put in an appearance for meals. They paid so much per day to the Barmans for their food. Their appetites were enormous. I can still see one looking contemptuously at me while I ate, and pronouncing his verdict: "D'ye call that eating eggs? Why I wouldn't dirty my plate with less than a dozen!"

The house also had authentic mystery: an unseen inhabitant! Who he or she was I was not to learn for a long time. But soon after my arrival I discovered that everyone avoided a wing of the house where someone was living.

I had a little attic room, furnished with bed, cupboard, washstand, and kerosene lamp. There was no electricity or running water. Like most farmhouses of the time, it had an outdoor privy, complete with last year's Sears Roebuck catalogue. Needless to say there was no automobile or telephone. The water for household uses was pumped—generally by me—from a well in the farmyard. On the few occasions when I wangled a bath, water was heated in a kettle on the coal stove, then mixed with a pail or two of cold water in a clothes pan, which I carried up and set on the floor of my room.

The workday was long: at 5:30 Mrs. Barman woke me up; I dressed quickly and stumbled, sleepy-eyed, to the barn for my first chore—milking Lucy Senior and Lucy Junior. Then I ate an ample breakfast, however puny my trencher-work might have appeared to a real farmhand. Then I fed the chickens and the hogs, harnessed the horse, and did the duties assigned for the day. The work finished at supper time, after more milking and feeding. Saturday was like any other, but on Sunday only indispensable chores were done. I put in between sixty and sixty-five hours of steady work each week.

I learned many things on that farm. Milking a cow is hard work. Fingers get mighty tired before twelve quarts are extracted from four udders, and the cow can deftly turn the pail over if you're not careful. A horse needs a lot of attention too. Putting on the harness is surprisingly complicated, and the horse has to be fed regularly, with oats in his nosebag as well as hay in his stall. He requires rather strenuous going-over frequently with a currycomb. And, of course, his stable needs to be cleaned from time to time, along with that of the cows. I found that job singularly distasteful; in my self-pity I compared myself to Hercules working for King Augeas, but without any flowing river to help him.

The chickens were kept in a large room above the toolshed. Access to their lair was by means of a fairly high ladder. Twice a day I would carry up a pail of chicken feed. The moment my foot touched the lowest rung of the ladder, one of them would start running around the room, followed immediately by all the rest. As I climbed the rungs, I could hear the noise of scampering feet, working faster and faster. By the time I pushed open the door the noise had become a roar, and I observed a strange spectacle. There was no longer any leader; each chicken followed the one ahead in an endless circle, racing about at bewildering speed. They paid not the slightest attention to me, evidently having forgotten what they were running for. There was no point in waiting for them to stop. I would fling handfuls of chicken feed over them as they dashed wildly past me. After quite a while an especially hungry hen would stop and gobble up a morsel; then another would follow suit. Gradually the runners in this crazy race would stop their shenanigans and settle down to eating. By the time I had emptied the pail and reached the bottom of the ladder, all was quiet again. But the noisy spectacle occurred at each feeding.

The pigs behaved unintelligently too, but in a different way. They got two large pails of slops at each session. As soon as I came near the trough, they would stick their big snouts into it. The only way to feed them was to pour the slops over their heads. They were not a pretty sight at any time, but after that porcine baptism they looked positively revolting.

Taking pride as a student of agriculture, Barman was the only one in the neighborhood to grow alfalfa, at that time relatively unknown in the East. Barman said it was wonderful; it added nitrogen to the soil and was beloved as a food by the animals. Unfortunately for best results alfalfa had to be planted on a hillside, so my boss had selected his steepest slope for the purpose. Came harvest time, we had to cut the alfalfa with a mowing machine, drawn by the obedient Charley. The mower had a natural tendency to slip down the hill, and that was where I came in. While Barman sat in comparative comfort behind the machine, I had to walk on the downhill side in the blazing sun and push with all my might against the mower to keep it from sliding.

Harvesting the hay in the big meadow was less punishing. I stood on the hay wagon to receive the pitchforkfuls thrown at me by the indefatigable farmer, and I had to stow them as evenly as possible. In those days there were no machines to package hay in neat parallelepipedons at geometric intervals on the field. It was pleasant to take off fifteen minutes in the morning and midafternoon, to drink some cool water out of a small milk can in the shade of a leafy tree. More pleasant still to drive home at the end of the day, lolling luxuriously on top of the hay wagon, munching on a straw. But then came another operation, by no means so pleasant. It was called "mowing away the hay"—the "mow" rhyming with "how." Our entire harvest had to be stored in an attic above the barn. This time Barman stood on the wagon with his pitchfork, and I in the small entrance to the hayloft. As the hay was thrown at me, I would catch it in my arms and carry it to some suitable spot in the loft. It was boiling hot; it was suffocatingly dusty; it seemed as if the job would never end. But it did at last, and I would be mighty happy when the last forkful had been crammed into the bursting loft.

Of course, a farm is the best place for a young man to learn all about sex. When you live among farm animals, there is no such thing as innocence. One day, the elder Lucy went into heat, and it was time to take her to a bull to "freshen" her. A date was made to use the services of a neighbor's animal. But Barman had to go to a country fair. "That's all right, Ben," said he. "You take Lucy over to the Jones' place by yourself. There's nothing much to it, and they'll help you." I had my doubts about all this, but orders were orders.

The next day Barman rode off behind Charley, and I started

down the road with Lucy, holding her by a short rope fastened round her neck. The cow was unusually skittish. I tugged determinedly, and at last got her to Jones' farm. On the porch of the farmhouse sat a girl of about fourteen in a rocking chair.

"What do you want?" she asked.

I was embarrassed; my face must have turned awful red.

"I'm from Mr. Barman. I-I-I've got this cow...."

"Oh, you're taking it to the bull," she remarked indifferently. "You'll find him around there by the barn."

"But where's Mr. Jones?" I asked desperately.

"Dad's way down in the south meadow. But that's all right. You can go ahead by yourself."

I just couldn't tell that self-possessed maiden that I hadn't the faintest notion about how to introduce a cow to a bull. Hoping for the best, I dragged Lucy round by the barn. I found the bull, all right, in a pen by himself. He seemed enormous, gigantic, titanic. He stamped in his stall, and I could swear that fire came out of his nostrils. I tied Lucy to a fence, and looked around desperately for help. There was none in sight. I don't know how long I stood there, contemplating the bull, feeling more scared and helpless every minute.

At last I was rescued, ignominiously enough, by Miss Jones and her ample-waisted mother. Said the latter, "Young man, I don't think you can handle that bull by yourself. I guess you'd better take your frisky cow back home and let Barman bring it here another day."

She hadn't finished the sentence before I was tugging at the reluctant Lucy and heading for home. I felt the scornful eyes of that knowing girl on the back of my head, but I was too happy to feel much shame. Barman listened to my story with more amusement than reproach. "I guess I made a little mistake in sending you down alone to that there bull," he admitted. A few days later we went over to the Jones' place as a threesome; by this time Lucy was trying to leap every fence we passed. Once we arrived, Lucy was inexplicably coy and had to be dragged towards matrimony. The bull, *au contraire*, was all passion and fury. It took both Mr. Barman and Mr. Jones to hang on to his halter, while I had things to do as bridesmaid to Lucy. I am sorry to say that these duties, whatever they were, rather obstructed my view of the proceedings.

After supper and final chores, I would carry a lamp up to my bedroom, and set to work at self-instruction. There I would read the *Anabasis*, helped by the Greek grammar. I never finished the *Anabasis*, but I did get through a fair part of it. It did not arouse my enthusiasm as a work of literature, though I know it's considered a classic. One incident in the plot I shall never forget. It is when Apollo flays Marsyas alive after he has beaten him in a song contest. The edition contained an illustration of this gruesome act, copied from some ancient frieze or jug. In a single flash of enlightenment and despair I saw a vista of the depravity and cruelty of man. The classic Greeks, who sought truth and loved beauty, who governed themselves by the great philosophical motto "Nothing in excess," could still revel in the image of pain, could ascribe to their Phoebus Apollo—God of light and song and joy—a sadistic satisfaction in scraping the skin off a living human body! For me history drew a straight line from the myth of Marsyas to the too-authentic lampshades of Bergen-Belsen. Baudelaire felt this tidal pull of savagery beneath all our civilization when he wrote of "the blood that seasons and perfumes the feast" (from "Le Voyage").

One of my chores was to sift all the ashes that had accumulated in the large coal stove. Behind the farmhouse was an enormous ash pile. My boss set up his galvanized-iron sifter next to the heap, and showed me how to turn the crank. The ash was chopped up and fell through a sieve, while the coal remained in the barrel. I spent a long day at the task, most of it in the broiling sun. To make things more interesting, my ash sifter stood in the direct line of flight of several beehives. As I shoveled, I could hear countless busy bees whizzing past my face. I wasn't as charmed by them as Tennyson who wrote of

The moan of doves in immemorial elms,
And murmuring of innumerable bees.

Yet, I passed from an initial inquietude, through a state of sto-ical acceptance, to a sense of companionship with these inde-fatigable workers, obeying so blindly the stern orders of their own Mr(s). Barman.

I met some lads my own age in New Milford and spent a little time with them. I recall one characteristically ridicu-lous incident. Walking along the road, I was holding forth grandly on the wonders of New York City, bragging that there were so many automobiles there that one no longer paid any attention to them. An auto appeared up the road, coming at us lickety-split. My companions immediately dashed into the adjacent field. But I continued to saunter non-chalantly along the roadside. The car blew its horn madly and careened past me within touching distance. The driver must have thought I was crazy—which I was. But my comrades were much impressed.

Barman's apple trees produced excellent fruit, and I found the largest and reddest apple I'd ever seen. I decided to send it to Mother. I wrapped it up, addressed it, and took it to the post office, which occupied a corner in the general store. Old Snedecker, also the postmaster, asked me:

'How d'ye want to send it, boy?'
'I dunno. What's the best way. It's an apple.'
'An apple!' (These city fellers sure were daffy.) 'If you send it at all, you'll have to make it first class. Otherwise it'd spoil, for sure. But you'd pay five times what it's worth in postage.'

My intelligence, my filial devotion, my liberality were all being challenged. "I'll send it first class," I said firmly. That 89 cents was a small fortune. Mother wrote that she appreciated my loving thoughts, but hadn't it been very imprudent to spend all that money on postage—since the apple was in somewhat dubious condition when it arrived?

Not long afterwards Mother actually came to see me. She nearly always managed to take a little summer vacation, and this time she had the brilliant idea of staying at the Barmans' for one week as a paying guest. They were pleased to have her, and the $8. She came early in August, and it was a happy reunion. Mother soon became friendly with the three Barmans, and in a couple of days learned much more about them than I had in a month.

Indeed, she solved the mystery of the secluded wing of the house. It was inhabited by Mr. Barman's sister, an epileptic. I can only conjecture about why her illness should condemn her to the life of a prisoner. Perhaps in those days that was the approved method of dealing with the "falling sickness." You can imagine my amazement to see Mother over there conversing with an old lady in a rocking chair. All that Mother would tell me about the interview was that the invalid spoke quite lucidly.

One day I received a letter from brother Victor, written in verse; it contained exciting news about the results of the examinations for the Pulitzer Scholarships. "Hurrah, Hurrah! You've won, you've won! You're seventh on the list!"

There were about twenty of these precious scholarships to be awarded to contestants from all the public high schools in greater New York. I would have felt really thrilled if I had ranked first, second, or even third; but my position seemed eminently comfortable, and everyone assured me that I had nothing to worry about. I was in. The Pulitzer people duly visited my home, and Mother had a pleasant interview with them. Then an appointment was made for my own interview, to take place as soon as I returned to New York.

At last August 28 arrived. I bade a friendly, but by no means tearful, farewell to the Barmans. I did not miss the train home; the old farmer put me aboard himself.

As soon as I returned to New York, I went down to the

World Building in Park Place for my Pulitzer Scholarship interview. My examiner was no less than the editor-in-chief of Pulitzer dailies, Mr. [Alfred] H[armsworth], who was also chairman of the Scholarship Committee set up under the will of the great newspaperman. Though I was nervous, Mr. H. soon put me at my ease, and I found myself talking with some animation about my interests and ambitions. When he asked me what was my favorite book, I replied with enthusiasm, *The Decline and Fall of the Roman Empire*, which I had read from beginning to end with unflagging interest. Mr. H. seemed greatly impressed, remarking that I was the first boy he had met who had performed that literary feat. The interview went off very well, I thought, and I found it hard not to appear cock-sure of the result when I reported to my family.

A week later, following instructions, I phoned Mr. H.'s secretary to learn my fate. "I'm sorry," came the businesslike answer, "but you were not chosen." For a few seconds I was too overcome to speak. Then in a weaker voice I asked, "Can you tell me whether Fred Greenman got a scholarship?" "Greenman? Yes, he got a scholarship." "That's good. Thank you." The conversation was over.

This was worse than a disappointment; it came as a devastating blow. All splendor and hope suddenly went out of my life. Not that the Pulitzer Scholarships would seem overly generous today. They paid the recipient $150 per year, for four years, to cover his tuition costs at college. In addition, if he went to college away from his home, he was allowed another $250 per annum for living expenses. In those days one could make one's way through a first-class institution for such trifling sums. Mother had not been able to bear the idea of my leaving her for so long a time, and though I had a powerful yearning to emulate Fred Greenman, who had without hesitation chosen haughty Harvard, I had dutifully agreed to go to Columbia, which I could attend while living at home. But now all plans were canceled; neither Harvard nor Columbia were to be my lot.

My mother and brothers seemed just as dejected as I by my misfortune and a great deal more indignant. How could their Benny—number 7 on the list—have been passed over, while others far below his standing—including several of his friends—were chosen? Strange as it sounds, Mother ended up by blaming the catastrophe on our furniture! Through all our various removals, we had retained the Louis XVI chairs and sofas and some other elegant pieces. Badly worn as they were by this time, they still exuded at least a slight aura of luxury. The Pulitzer Scholarships were awarded on the basis of need, as well as on scholastic excellence and good character. The investigator must have concluded, said Mother, that despite our protestations of poverty, I could really afford to pay my way through college without a scholarship. (If so, he couldn't have been more wrong!)

I had my own theory about my rejection. I thought it was due to my weakness of character. For years I had been struggling against something the French call *mauvaises habitudes*, and which a combination of innate puritanism on my part and the hair-raising health tracts prevalent in those days had raised to a moral and physical issue of enormous proportions. I told myself that the perspicacious Mr. H. must have detected this secret deformity of my soul and awarded my scholarship to someone purer and better than myself. This explanation was even more fanciful than Mother's furniture theory. Still, after intensive wrestling with my problem, I found myself on February 12, 1911, reflecting on the strength of character of Abraham Lincoln whose birthday we were celebrating. I would take Lincoln as my inspiration and call on him to help me keep the new, inflexible resolution I was that day embracing. The idea worked, and my bad habits were at an end.

The first shock over, Mother quickly became her grave and practical self. If I couldn't go to Columbia, then I must go to the College of the City of New York, where—thank goodness—the tuition was free. And I would find some job after hours to earn my needed pocket money. So I duly enrolled at City College,

but with a heavy heart. Why? Out of pure, unadulterated snobbishness. City College did not have as many brilliant professors as Harvard, Yale, and Columbia, it is true. But it had a
good, stiff curriculum and turned out well-trained graduates.
Its alumni included many eminent men. But it was a free college, attended for the most part by poor students with rather
low social standing and often lacking in polish. Also, they were
preponderantly Jewish. To go there, instead of to Columbia,
meant the acceptance of inferiority, the admission of defeat.
Viewing the matter as objectively as I can, I must admit there
was some practical justification for this invidious conclusion. A
CCNY boy would be at some disadvantage in his professional
and social career compared to a graduate of a first-rate college.
This attitude reflected the general snobbishness of America in
1911; my own acceptance of these same distorted values intensified my feeling of humiliation.

I was quite unhappy at CCNY. In my morbid state, everything about the place was unappetizing and unsatisfactory. I
left my locker open one day, and two books disappeared from
it. They had to be paid for. I was dejected and disgusted, and I
had no source of pocket money. In my desperation I made an
extreme decision. I would give up college and get a job.

My first job consisted of assembling push buttons for electric doorbells. About six boys were gathered around a table,
on which sat baskets containing the various parts to be put
together. After a little instruction I learned the simple
motions involved and became a full-fledged member of the
group. We started at 7:00 in the morning and worked until 5:30
p.m., with forty-five minutes for lunch. I suppose I must have
put in a fifty-five-hour week; how many times I repeated the
same elementary manual operations in the course of such a
week I'd hate to calculate.

To while away the endless hours, I took to reciting poetry to
myself while I worked. Fortunately, I had a large repertory,
including Gray's "Elegy," all of the *Rubáiyát*, and even the first
four hundred lines of the *Aeneid*. There I sat, isolated from the

rest, communing with great poets while my fingers worked busily and expertly at their comparatively simple task.

After a short time—perhaps two weeks—I was fed up with the monotony of those push buttons and looked again through the "Boy Wanted" section of the Sunday *Times*. One ad offered a position in a telephone machine shop at 95 Fulton Street, far downtown in New York. It paid $5 a week, and thus seemed very attractive. I presented myself at the dingy telephone shop very early on Monday morning. There was quite a crowd of us after the job. Soon the boss, Mr. L. J. Loeffler, came in and interviewed us all. He asked about my education and was impressed to hear I was a high school graduate. Then he inquired about my experience and especially whether I could operate a drill press. When I answered yes, he told me I was hired, beginning the next day. The hours were from 7:30 a.m. to 6 p.m. It was a much longer subway journey to my new job, but I could get up at about the same time as before. What hurt was that I got home at seven o'clock, only just in time for supper.

Loeffler took on four other boys at the same time as myself, and we filled his little shop to overflowing. It was evident that he was not going to keep us all. As one of the three older employees promptly explained to us, this was an annual maneuver of the old man's. He was about to make up a number of parts for stock and would keep most of us on only until these jobs were finished—if that long.

The L. J. Loeffler Telephone Co. occupied only one floor in a rather small building, but the shop contained a lot of machinery and busied itself with an extraordinary number of manufacturing operations. The final product was telephone systems for private users. Most of these were installed in large apartment houses then being constructed on Park Avenue, Fifth Avenue, West End Avenue, and Riverside Drive. An installation included a switchboard for the lobby and phones for each apartment, along with the elaborate wiring needed to connect them. For many years after my apprenticeship, when I visited friends who lived on these avenues, I would often note the

Loeffler nameplate on the switchboard and wonder if my own hands had helped put those instruments together.

Loeffler's rule was "Never pay anyone else to make something you can make yourself." Hence he bought all his components in the cheapest and hence crudest state, and then cut, drilled, ground, shaped, assembled, and finished them. For the bells which rang in his telephones, he bought long iron rods, which we cut to size for the bell cores. Then we stamped out cardboard rings to fit at each end to make a spool; then we wound covered copper wire around the spools, using a special winding machine. All the other parts of the bell were made similarly in the shop, including the little round ball at the end of the clapper, which we fitted to the wire arm. We shaped the heavier metal parts on lathes; tempered and formed other pieces in fire; polished hard-rubber push buttons on buffing machines; assembled elaborate wiring systems; stamped all sorts of designations on black-lacquered nameplates; and brought out the letters with some kind of white plaster. We even painted the thin film of gold on the vibrating diaphragm of the transmitters.

I can say with some pride that I did these tasks well. When I came there I was clumsy with my fingers and quite ignorant about hand tools and power-driven machinery. But I learned countless tricks of the trade; my fingers gradually grew more supple, my hands and eyes more sure. I became interested in the mechanical and electrical problems involved in the operation of a telephone system. Fairly soon I was studying the elaborate blueprints that were used in the installations. My great day came when an electrical contractor called up, during Loeffler's absence, hurriedly asking to have some intricate difficulty in the wiring system cleared up—and I was able to explain it to him by looking at our copy of the blueprints. From that time on I was Loeffler's fair-haired boy.

True to my promise to Mother, I had written to Columbia the previous autumn, asking whether I could apply for a scholarship to begin in the February term. The answer was that no scholarships were given in the middle of the year, but I could write again in the spring for the year beginning September 1911. This I did early in April. In a few days I received a rather strange note from Frederick F. Keppel, Dean of Columbia College. It stated that the scholarship I wished to apply for was not available, but he had a matter he would like to discuss with me at some convenient time. Would I make an appointment with his secretary? I explained over the phone that I worked daily until 6 p.m. but could probably arrange to leave an hour earlier. In that case Dean Keppel would be pleased to see me at his house the next day, a little before six o'clock. What on earth could all this mean?

The next afternoon I cleaned my grimy hands as well as I could with grease solvent, took the West Side subway from Fulton Street to 116th Street, and walked over to the dean's residence not far away. With a thumping heart I rang the bell. Mrs. Keppel opened the door, ushered me upstairs to a study where some logs were burning in the fireplace, and said that the dean would be with me directly. In a few minutes he entered, a tall, handsome, well-tailored man, who combined a businesslike manner with a charming smile. Tea was brought in. I was painfully conscious of my shabby working clothes and the remnants of dirt around my fingernails. Keppel spoke to me pleasantly about my work for a few minutes while we drank our tea. Then he got down to cases.

"You know, we're frightfully embarrassed about you in the Registrar's Office. And I share this embarrassment, because I was registrar of the University before I became dean, and I put in the system that has misfired."

I was too mystified and tenterhooky to offer any comment.

"The fact is, Grossbaum," he continued, "you won a scholarship here last year, but we didn't give it to you."

"How—how did that happen?" I blurted.

"You have a brother or a cousin, Louis Grossbaum, who has been here for three years on a Pulitzer Scholarship. When we awarded yours the Registrar's Office got the names mixed up.

They couldn't give a scholarship to a boy who already had one, so they gave yours to the next fellow in line."

He told me further that the prize I had won was the Columbia Alumni Scholarship, providing for full tuition, and awarded annually to the candidate for admission to Columbia who had scored the highest average grade in the College Entrance Board Examinations. This I had done—for the six boys ahead of me in the Pulitzer ratings had all received that stipend or applied for admission elsewhere. If I still wanted to come to Columbia College, they could arrange to award me the Alumni Scholarship beginning next fall. That would be just as good financially as the Pulitzer Scholarship of my departed dreams.

"This is very interesting," was all I could manage to say. Then I added, "But I've lost a whole year."

"True, true," replied Keppel. "And we're genuinely sorry about our mistake. But how old are you?"

I told him I was just turning seventeen.

"Well, now, I'm not sorry at all. You would have been much too young to get the most out of college if you had started a year ago. This machine-shop training of yours is the best thing for you. You'll have much more savoir faire and maturity than the other boys of your age. Anyway, you can probably get your degree in three years if you work hard enough."

The interview was over. I returned home in great excitement. There was boundless rejoicing in our Kelly Street household. But Mother repeated over and over as she wiped away her tears, "I'll never be able to forgive them for causing so much heartache to my Benny."

CHAPTER SIX

The College Student

In September 1911 I entered Columbia College as an Alumni Scholar. Because I had covered so much material in my two high schools—equivalent to more than a semester's work at college—and because extra study enabled me to pass placement exams, I began at the highest possible advanced standing. To graduate I needed a total of 120 points—each the equivalent of a one-semester, one-hour-a-week course. I set my sights at graduating in three years. In fact, I was actually to receive my diploma after only two and a half.

My ideas of college life had formed many years before in avid perusal of the Frank Merriwell books. Of course, I realized that Merriwell stayed at Yale for an inordinately long time—has anyone ever counted *his* semesters?—and that he engaged in every possible undergraduate activity except study. (Perhaps that was the reason his college career lasted so long.) Nonetheless, I had always dreamed of college life as the halcyon period of youth, a wonderful combination of education, friendship, romance, athletics, and all-around fun. Alas! Looking back at my own college career, I recall no such happy interlude. In fact, I can remember comparatively little.

My most definite impression of college days is *un*conscious:
it recurs in my dreams. Normally, few dreams have been vivid
enough to remain in my mind after I wake, but during the
fifty-three years that have elapsed since I left Columbia College, one dream recurs with significant frequency. I am a college boy. I am heading for a class, or "recitation." But I have
mislaid my schedule of courses, and I do not know just where
to go. I wander from floor to floor, classroom to classroom, trying to recognize where I belong. In another variant I am actually in a classroom, but I have not prepared my work. In my
dream, I wonder anxiously how I shall be able to bluff my way
through if called on to recite. The two dilemmas never get
resolved in the dream, for I invariably wake up at some especially trying moment. No doubt a psychoanalyst could tell me
what is signified by these messages from my unconscious. But
they have little connection with the actual events of my college career.

I did not begin too brilliantly. One of the required freshman
courses was History A, covering Western Europe. Unlike
most of the students, I had been over this ground at Townsend
Harris Hall and was disinclined to apply myself to it again. But
my midterm grade of C− brought me up sharply; I recovered
pretty well in the second half, and I received no worse than a
B in that (or any other) course at Columbia. Now that I think
of it in perspective, my accomplishments seem better to me
than they did at the time. I finished with the second-highest
academic record in my class, earning an honorable mention
(but no prize) on the graduation day program. Now I wonder
how I did that well—in view of my heavy weekly schedule of
courses and the extraordinary number of jobs I held.

I studied French with Professor Jourdain, a Gallic combination of unbounded culture, religious skepticism, and a liking
for the ribald. This was a new phenomenon: a teacher who fascinated my intellect while he shocked my Victorian scruples.
Jourdain was one of the first to befriend me. As secretary of
L'Alliance des Professeurs Français en Amérique, he had to

send out program announcements several times a year. He gave me the job of running the Addressograph, folding the announcements, and inserting them into envelopes at the good pay of a dollar per hour. I also received a free ticket of admission to the meetings. At one such evening, shortly after the outbreak of the war in 1914, the famous Yvette Guilbert recited a war poem by Edmond Rostand. She was old then, but her hair was bright red and her voice just as fiery. I was deeply moved. Years later, I read in James Huneker's *Painted Veils* an account of an evening in Greenwich Village when he heard Yvette Guilbert reciting Baudelaire's "Le Balcon"—an imperishable poem rendered by an incomparable *diseuse*. That was the Guilbert known by Toulouse-Lautrec and Proust. And I, too, heard her once!

One evening Professor Jourdain invited me to his house for dinner, after which he entertained his wife and me by reading aloud a chapter from the *Gargantua* of Rabelais, the one in which the mountainous young prince seeks the perfect toilet tissue. The professor roared as he read, Mme. Jourdain smiled rather painfully from time to time, and I listened in acute embarrassment. Somehow I have never been able to see the amusing side of the scatological; filth has no comic dimension for me. On the other hand, a really good bawdy joke has much to recommend it. Sex is important, many sided, thrilling; thus it lends itself perfectly to those anomalous, absurd, and witty provocations which make us laugh without feeling ashamed of ourselves.

Another French professor, Camille Fontaine, persuaded me to compete in the annual national contest given by the French Professors' Alliance. The tests for the Eastern seaboard were held at Barnard College. That was the first and only time that I entered the portals of our sister institution—and the first and only time that I ever found myself in a classroom with females. Indeed, on this occasion, most of the contestants were women. The examination was divided between composition and translation, or "version." I don't recall the subject assigned for our essay in French, but I can never forget the text to be translated, Renan's celebrated "Prayer on the Acropolis," because I made a mistake in rendering the first few words. Nonetheless, to my surprise, I won third prize in version and honorable mention in composition.

Professor Fontaine said he was very proud of me. Some time later the prizes arrived—two rather nondescript French books, bound in second-quality leather, but duly inscribed. He presented them to me with proper flourish before our French class, and I responded with feigned enthusiasm. After class, Professor Fontaine motioned to me to stay. From a drawer in his desk he took out a very fine fountain pen, said with embarrassment that the books were not quite an adequate reward for the noble efforts I had made, that he received many more pens as presents from students than he could ever use, and asked whether I would accept this one as a little personal prize from him? I was touched by his gentle consideration; but I fear that I soon lost that precious pen, as I lost most of my small possessions.

I read quite a lot of German literature in college and in fact became something of a connoisseur. I took a course with Professor William Addison Hervey on Goethe, Schiller, and Lessing, finishing in a blaze of glory with an unprecedented A+. My magnum opus compared and contrasted the *Iphigenia at Tauris* of Goethe with that of Euripides. I also took a course with Frederick Heuser on Hebbel, Kleist, and Grillparzer. I visited him after I graduated, in 1915, and he told me of his difficulties in giving his course because the blockade of Germany had made it impossible to import the three authors' works. Accordingly, I donated my complete sets of Hebbel and Lessing to the college library—not without some tugging at the heartstrings, for the elegant volumes were among my prized possessions.

But eventually I lost my interest in German literature. Before the world war, I greatly admired the German spirit. Its combination of scientific efficiency with poetic sentimentality

appealed to my immature judgment and led me to overlook, or
rather to forgive, its bluster, its toadying to superiors, and its
bullying of inferiors. But in the period of 1914 to 1918 I conceived a violent dislike for the German "Volkspsychologie,"
and I turned my back almost entirely upon a language and a
literature which had once claimed my deepest interest. Perhaps, in some obscure way, I sensed the shadow of Hitler and
his concentration camps behind the fiery illogic of Fichte and
the sugary "Alt Heidelberg" sentimentality of *The Student
Prince.*

What happened to Latin? Precisely because it was one of
my best subjects I decided *not* to continue it at Columbia.
What need to take courses in Horace, Catullus, Lucretius, Tacitus when I could read them at home, in my spare time? I did
manage to make the acquaintance of these and other Latin
writers; Horace, in fact, became a rather close friend. My decision not to pursue Latin at college produced a rather absurd
situation. I could not receive the degree of Bachelor of Arts,
which in those days required college Latin. I therefore became
a Bachelor of Science, but with the odd twist that I hadn't
taken a single scientific course. The little physics and chem-
istry I had covered in high school met the B.S. requirements in
those subjects, while mathematics was quite acceptable as my
scientific major. When I ran into Dean Keppel, he scolded me
for having broken a well-established College tradition. "Up to
now," he remarked, "we had the saying around here that there
was only one thing certain about a Columbia Bachelor of Science degree—that the owner didn't know Latin. Because of
you, that's no longer so."

Since mathematics was my major, I took a lot of courses.
The professor I remember best was Herbert E. Hawkes, who
became college dean after Keppel was made Assistant Secretary of War. I presented two papers to the Mathematical Colloquium. Neither was a great contribution, and the first cost
me some money. It concerned geometric axioms. We had been
taught that axioms were self-evident but unprovable. Think-

ing of myself as a minor Descartes, I worked out what I considered a rigorous proof of the axiom that a straight line is the shortest distance between two points. Professor Hawkes was properly impressed and asked me to present my proof before the colloquium. It belatedly occurred to me to see what Euclid himself had said about that axiom. In the large annotated edition of Euclid kept in reserve at the university library, I found appended to the axiom *four* separate proofs devised by later mathematicians that a straight line is the shortest distance between two points. So one more of my youthful dreams of greatness dissolved into a sorry mist. However, I had one consolation: my proof was different from the four given in the book. Hawkes felt it would still be worthwhile presenting it to our group.

The library gave me special permission to check out the first volume of the precious set of Euclid. I presented my paper, responsibly reporting the competing proofs, and started home with the book. But I forgot it in the subway, and it was never recovered. The library settled with me for $15, much less than the value of the entire set, which was now irretrievably spoiled. That was a major financial blow to me; "The paths of glory lead but to the poorhouse," I sadly muttered.

I was also very interested in philosophy. I took the first year's course, in formal logic, required of all freshmen. Later I took Professor Frederick A. Woodbridge's History of Philosophy course. For one hour a week, Woodbridge lectured to an enormous audience. In the second hour we broke up into small quiz sections, handled by young assistants. Woodbridge was a wonderful lecturer, listened to almost breathlessly by the huge audience. I can still remember his beginning a discourse on Kant in something like the following words:

> Immanuel Kant was one of the greatest of all the philosophers, with a wider influence on his successors than almost any other. But sometimes I wish that he had never been born.

Once Woodbridge began a lecture with a reference that was personally thrilling. The subject was Descartes, and in particular his famous dualism separating the mind and the body of man into separate universes. Then he quoted me: "In preparing to speak to you about Descartes," he said, "I find it difficult to get out of my mind a phrase which one of you students included in his paper on dualism. It goes: 'What Descartes has put asunder let no man join together.'"

As for English, I took the famous course on the novel by Brander Matthews, then almost at the end of his fabulous teaching career. Immortalized by the Brander Matthews Theatre on the Columbia campus, he had an unforgettable leonine face, beautifully adorned with beard and whiskers. I also studied under John Erskine, the enormously popular teacher, writer (*The Private Life of Helen of Troy*), and musician. (He later became head of the Juilliard School of Music.) Erskine once paid me a compliment about an observation I made in a paper on *Wuthering Heights*. I had suggested that one of the reasons for the eerie impression created by that novel of violence is the strange, un-British fact that no constable or other representative of the law ever appears on the scene. Erskine told me that this was a new and important contribution to the study of that masterpiece.

I also studied with Carl Van Doren, another fine professor and writer. To him I showed my first, brief romantic poems, poems that entered my world as inevitably as (and along with) shaving. He toiled with me to improve some of the lines: they sorely needed his skill. After I graduated, in the summer of 1914, Van Doren was appointed headmaster of the Brierly School, one of the top prep schools for girls. He sent for me, asking whether I would consider joining his staff as an instructor in English. Pleasant surroundings, good pay, excellent chance for advancement. I considered the proposition and said no—for reasons I cannot quite piece together at this distance. A few times since then I have had a puckish vision of myself, a bashful twenty-year-old, teaching—or trying to teach—

English to a bevy of socialite girls very close to my own age. What might have come of that? In 1937 I would meet a much older looking Carl Van Doren once again. His daughter was graduating with mine from the original Lincoln School. Now, in 1967, I think once more about the Van Dorens when a nephew of Carl's wins a fabulous sum on a TV quiz program and then is shockingly revealed to have conspired to do so. So people appear, disappear, and reappear in one's life.

My closest and most meaningful friend on the Columbia faculty was an English professor of no special importance in campus life. His name was Algernon Duvivier Tassin. He graduated from Harvard, became interested in acting, and for years toured in the company of the celebrated Julia Marlowe. He wrote a number of plays which were never commercially produced. I took Oral English from Tassin: it required students to read a passage, explain it clearly, and argue about it intelligently. His other course, which I took the following year, was known as "Daily Theme." Every schoolday, rain or shine, we were required to turn in a one-page composition, on a subject announced the day before. This was grueling work, but it certainly taught us how to write English.

Tassin generally liked my themes. About the middle of the term he asked for a series of one-page character studies. I wrote about people I knew well—my mother, my brothers, my Cousin Lou, my then girlfriend, Alda. One day he called me into his office; he had a serious question to ask me: "Were all these character sketches my own work?" In amazement I answered, "Of course." "In that case," said he, "I must tell you that you have a great gift. I have never encountered so much insight and such power of precise, succinct expression in anyone your age." This was head-turning stuff. However, I never developed the art of character portrayal beyond those brief papers. In later years, Tassin remained a close personal friend, and afterwards a financial associate through lean years and fat.

The high point of my academic career was something called the English-History-Philosophy Seminar. A small group of honor students assembled once every two weeks to discuss some subject under the guidance of Erskine, Woodbridge, and the famous historian, James Harvey Robinson. Those were really inspiring sessions.

I made no close friends at Columbia. Was it because I was too busy studying and working, or had something happened to my emotional life that precluded male chums or cronies? No doubt the latter, for this same deficiency was to mar all the years to come. Not that I have ever had trouble making acquaintances—in fact, they come perhaps a little too easily. At Columbia a group of such friends did me the honor of inviting me to join the leading Jewish fraternity—Zeta Beta Tau. I declined, saying I could afford neither the time nor the money involved. I should have made the time and borrowed the money.

During my college years—September 1911 through June 1914—I worked at a great variety of jobs. Since my brothers were contributing towards the family budget, the least I could do was to earn enough for my personal and college expenses. In my freshman year I worked as cashier in a movie theater in Park Row, near the Bowery and Chinatown from 5 p.m. to 10:30 p.m. every weekday, plus a twelve-hour stretch on alternate Sundays. My pay was $6 per week, of which 60 cents went to carfare. This was my second job in a theater: the first was as usher at a vaudeville house, the Prospect Theatre, in the summer of 1910.

Since I am trying to make this narrative totally truthful, I must report incidents which are somewhat painful to my pride to recall. They had to do with peculation. In my long business career I have gained a reputation for scrupulous honesty; not the least of my satisfactions is that that reputation was fairly earned. I have only deviated from the path of strict rectitude on three occasions. When I was a very little boy I craved more sweets than were doled out to me by my strict mademoiselle. Every now and then I would filch a penny from Mother's purse and exchange it for candy in a slot machine. One day the shiny

penny didn't fit in the slot, and I brought it home in puzzle-
ment. It was a $5 gold piece—which Mother had been much
upset at missing and no less mystified to find returned to her
purse. (In 1900 there was nothing strange about carrying gold
pieces in one's wallet.) I was so shaken by the thought that I
had stolen $5 instead of a penny that I never filched again.

Then there was a week at the Prospect Theatre when I
accepted a few small bribes to give people better seats than
they were entitled to. This was small stuff, too, but it has
always bothered me. I also discovered a way to make ten tickets admit eleven people, and during some weeks of financial
stringency I used this device to misappropriate a few dollars.
I felt so uncomfortable about it, however, that I quickly
stopped the practice.

The last of my peculations was the only action in my business career proper about which I have serious ethical regrets.
A company in which my investment firm was interested had
some land taken over by the state for road-building purposes,
and we were entitled to fair compensation for it. The state in
question was run by a party machine, and we were told that in
order to get results both quick and satisfactory, it was necessary to hire the "right" firm of lawyers at a substantial fee.
Acting like most business firms in such circumstances, we followed this practical advice. My partner, who was a member of
the bar, later received part of the fee as a "forwarder." Since
we had a general agreement for dividing earnings, he offered
me half his share. I should not have accepted that money, but I
did—and I have regretted it ever since.

My own weakness has led me to practice a measure of tolerance about embezzlements by relatives, friends, fellow workers, or my own employees. I have always disapproved the
deed, but never permitted myself a holier-than-thou attitude
towards the embezzler. Where (as often happened) their theft
was inspired by heavy financial pressure, I was more inclined
to pity than reproach. However, I feel only contempt for rich
people who do dishonest things from habit, greed, or sheer

perversity, as well as for those who abuse positions of trust and honor. For example, in my eyes, Jimmy Walker's behavior as mayor of New York City [1925 to 1932] was disgraceful. His enormous popularity after his downfall, and his virtual canonization after death, make me despair of my fellow man.

At the end of my first college year, in early June, a friend passed the theater and stopped to chat. He had just started a wonderful job, paying $40 per month for regular day hours, and $50 per month on the night shift. They needed more college men, and he thought he could swing it for me. Of course I was interested. After a brief interview I signed up for the night shift, running from 4 p.m. to midnight, six days a week. My employer was the U.S. Express Company; my boss was M. A. Fisher, an efficiency expert.

This job was to mark an important stage in my development. The Interstate Commerce Commission had fixed a completely new basis for express rates throughout the country— by a so-called block method, to replace the complex station-to-station rates. The companies had protested, asserting that the new system would ruin them. To support their protest they were preparing an elaborate exhibit which would take all the business done in a single day, apply the proposed new rates to each individual shipment, and thus show how much the new methods would lower their revenues.

The four other large express companies—Adams, American, Southern, and Wells Fargo—were preparing their exhibits by hand, in the conventional way. But Mr. Fisher had sold U.S. Express on the new punched-card, or Hollerith, method for rapidly sorting and tabulating complicated data. Hollerith machines were leased by a weakly financed and poorly regarded company called Computing-Tabulating-Recording Corporation. Its stock was said to represent nothing but water, and may have been worth, say, $3 million in the market. Little did I suspect that some day I would see the stock of that company, renamed International Business Machines, sell on the New York Stock Exchange for billions of dollars.

The U.S. Express project was set up in rented quarters at 76 Washington Street. Our crews were trained to punch cards on the old-basis data, then to run the cards through the sorting machines to prepare them for the new-basis rates and revenues, then to run them through the tabulators to get various sorts of totals. There were many complicating factors, such as the difference between inter- and intra-state shipments.

Although the actual physical labors were essentially monotonous, I found broader aspects of our work very interesting. One of my associates, and a Columbia classmate, a lively chap named Lou Bernstein, was equally intrigued by the project. Bernstein and I discussed the work with Mr. Fisher, who was so pleased with our interest in his ideas that he invited us to his home one Sunday afternoon for a long bull session. Our discussions were to have quite unexpected results for him and us.

September 1912 came and with it the beginning of my sophomore year at Columbia. I continued my U.S. Express job from 4 p.m. to midnight, while carrying about twenty-one hours per week of classes plus homework. Bernstein had also changed over to the night shift, and we worked closely together. One evening a surprising rumor reached us: Fisher had resigned after an altercation with the chief auditor regarding some infraction of company rules by his assistant. We wondered what was going to happen to this highly specialized project. We had not long to wait: Mr. Tait, the general auditor, came into our workroom, somewhat the worse for liquor—no new phenomenon in his case. He asked to see Bernstein and Grossbaum. We presented ourselves. He had been informed, he told us, that we two had a very good understanding of what was being done; was that true? Without undue modesty we said it was. In that case, would we please come to his office when the shift was over at midnight?

There, a short and exciting colloquy took place. Did we think we could take Fisher's place and boss the job? Yes. Could we prepare immediately—and have ready by the next evening—a complete outline of every step in the process? Yes. Would I—Benny Grossbaum—arrange to apply for a leave of absence from college, take over the day shift, and assume primary responsibility for the job? I replied that I would have to consult Dean Keppel about that, and also that the compensation would have to be adequate. We agreed to return to his office at 10 p.m. the next evening with the outline completed, the dean's decision on my leaving college, and also my salary demands.

The next day passed like a fantastic dream. When I told my story to Dean Keppel, he was enthusiastic. He was an early apostle of the college man in business, and this was grist for his mill. "By all means, Ben, take this leave of absence. If you can manage to prepare your work enough to pass the semester exams, I'll see that you get credit for your present courses." So that hurdle was easily cleared. We then set to work on the outline. In its final state it appeared on a large piece of cardboard, properly ruled, with each step written out in Lou's copperplate handwriting. (Lord knows what would have happened if he had a scrawl like mine.) At the bottom of the chart we wrote the following sentence, doubly underlined: "ALL STEPS ARE TO BE CHECKED AND DOUBLE-CHECKED FOR ACCURACY."

Promptly at ten o'clock we were in Tait's office with our chart. He looked it over without much comprehension, for he had never mastered the intricacies of the project. But our crisp and logical arrangement of the steps impressed him, especially the part about checking and double-checking. He seemed visibly relieved. (Very likely his own job hung in the balance.) He repeated his questions of the night before, and we presented our answers. Then he asked me, "What salary do you want to take charge of the job?" I looked him steadily in the eye and said: "You'll have to double my pay, sir." "Done," said he in a flash. I realized that my request for $100 per month had been overly modest—but it was too late to change anything. Bernstein settled for a 50 percent raise, or $75 per month. But he did not have to take a leave of absence from college.

When these arrangements were concluded, Tait appeared even more relieved. In fact, he was overflowing with maudlin gratitude. He put his arms around me and said, "Ben, I'll never forget what you're doing for me. Don't you worry about anything. I'll personally guarantee that you get through college when you go back." As we turned to leave, he asked, "Tell me, Ben, how old are you?" I just couldn't bring myself to confess that I had just turned eighteen. So I lied—rather rare for me then and since—and said that I was nineteen going on twenty. He shook his head and muttered that I was going to get a mighty fancy salary for a kid. His gratitude was five minutes old and already wearing a little thin.

Did we speak to Mr. Fisher before definitely accepting the job? I don't remember, but we did meet with him some time later, concerning a matter he had left hanging, and he was most cordial to us. But how did he really feel?

I held my high position for four and a half months. I doubt if I did a very efficient job, though Bernstein and I understood the technical problems well. I did receive praise for a new arrangement for punching and sorting subblocks for certain shipments which had not been organized in the original card design. But as managers of a large staff of employees, we undoubtedly lacked maturity and savoir faire. The day after we took over, two new faces made their appearance. They were bright men named Greiner and Ryan, from the accounting staff; they had been assigned to learn the project thoroughly and prepare themselves to take over. A most sensible move by Tait, though Bernstein and I rather resented it.

Then something crazy happened. In response to Vice-President Platt's dissatisfaction with our rate of progress, Tait decided that we must run three shifts and that I would have to run two of them—not only the one from eight to four but also the graveyard shift from midnight to eight. This would leave me all of eight hours a day for dinner, sleep, and recreation. After all, I was young and could take it. It was clearly out of the question for me to travel up to the Bronx each day to sleep, so I arranged to spend the night at an old and famous hostelry on Cortland Street known as Smith and McNeill's.

After finishing the day shift at 4 p.m. I would eat some kind of a meal and crawl into bed about 5:00, leaving word to be awakened at 11:30. Then my workday would start in pitch darkness, running on for sixteen hours, with two forty-minute breaks. The company rules provided for time-and-a-half pay for overtime. My first semimonthly check came in at the rate of $250 per month—a princely salary for those pre-1914 days. This bothered Tait. He said it would cause dissatisfaction among important employees earning less than I did, and he asked me to accept regular pay for the second shift. I agreed. But the whole arrangement lasted only another two weeks. The graveyard shift workers were so inefficient, and probably my own supervision was so imperfect, that much of our labor was offset by mistakes. So the experiment was soon dropped. I went back to my $100 a month and normal way of life. Mother was happy.

As the work progressed, the team of Greiner and Ryan began to assert more and more authority. Towards the end they had taken over the actual direction of the task, and Bernstein and I were restricted to keeping track of a few operations and giving advice about some technical question now and then. By the end of January the collation work was finished; there remained only the final marshalling of figures and drawing of conclusions. I duly received my last paycheck, accompanied by a rather frosty set of goodbyes. There will be more to say later about my relations with the U.S. Express Company.

During the last month of my job I had plenty of time to prepare for my return to college. Mindful of Dean Keppel's offer, I determined to take several of the current semester examinations, in English, French, German, and mathematics. I had begun elementary economics before leaving college; but the few weeks of exposure to "the dismal science" had failed to arouse my interest, and I decided not to pursue it when I returned. As things turned out, I was to make my lifetime career in that branch of economics called "finance" and to become a professor of the subject in two of our larger universities.

Another financial disaster suddenly struck our family. Leon had long been anxious to rise above his position as chinaware salesman in Wanamaker's, and he was attracted by the possibilities of the fast-growing movie industry. He wanted to buy a small theater in Jamaica, Long Island—then not much more than a village—for $1,500. Mother borrowed $1,000 from her rich sister in Warsaw, and I turned over all my savings from the U.S. Express job to pay the balance. As might have been expected from Leon's youth and total inexperience, the enterprise proved a complete flop, and all the money was lost in a couple of months.

Now I had no funds and no job. I immediately wrote to Mr. Tait, telling him of my predicament, recalling his promise to see me through college, and asking for a part-time job. His secretary replied that Mr. Tait was sorry but it was against the policy of the company to hire part-time workers and so he could do nothing for me. It was a bitter lesson, and I never again relied on anyone's open-ended promise to help me. I looked for work everywhere, but could find nothing. At last, in desperation, I accepted a door-to-door job selling coupons for cut-rate photographs. No job could have been more humiliating and heartbreaking. To ring a doorbell, to be greeted by a disheveled woman with a harassed or ugly expression, to try (usually in vain) to present the attractive proposition, to have countless doors slammed shut in your face in the middle of a sentence, to return home often without a single sale for a long afternoon's work—this would take the courage out of a hardened drummer, and I was far from that.

I remember coming home one day from this fruitless job, throwing myself on my bed and bursting into tears—a luxury all but unknown to me. Mother came in quietly, put her arms around me and said she was sure things would soon take a turn for the better. Her support helped me get clarity. I thought over Tait's refusal to live up to his promise, and then wrote directly to Mr. Sereno Platt, acting president of the U.S. Express Company, telling him my story in the most dignified and poignant language I could muster. The move proved successful. Mr. Platt wrote me that in view of the special circumstances he would make an exception to the company's rule; I could work half-time, as a checker of waybills, at $25 per month, and during the summer vacation I could do the same work full time. I felt as if my life had been saved.

The work was terribly monotonous, but I soon found an antidote against boredom. It was writing sonnets. I tried to compose a different one each day, completing the first draft in the morning, and slowly polishing it throughout the afternoon. Most were love sonnets inspired by my particular Laura of the period—whose name was Alda. The sheaf of poems have all vanished completely, except for a single line which sticks in my memory because I was so inordinately proud of it the day it came to me: "Hope writes the epitaph of buried hope."

One day while I was busy with my waybills and my *abbaabba* rhyme scheme, there was a stir in the large room where I worked. A group of corporate officers entered, including a small, stern-looking man we did not recognize. Soon the story was passed along: it was Mr. Roberts, recently elected president of the company. The directors had decided to liquidate the business, and he had been brought in to do so. I saw him look at the long line of cuspidors that had long been as essential to the business as the ledgers. Practically all the clerical workers chewed tobacco. "Disgusting," I heard him say. The next day the order went out: no more tobacco-chewing and no more cuspidors. Roberts's hand was indeed heavy on the personnel.

Three years after Roberts's election as president, the company was in active liquidation; I was out of college, making my way as an employee of a New York Stock Exchange firm. My boss said to me: "Ben, I understand U.S. Express still owns $100,000 of Lehigh Valley Railroad perpetual 6s. Run over and see the president, and ask what he will take for them." This new relation with Roberts appealed to my vanity. I clapped on my hat and was soon in his office, enjoying the consideration given me as an emissary of a Wall Street brokerage. When I spoke to him of the Lehigh Valley 6s, he said he might be willing to sell them and asked for a quotation. Shame on me! In my haste to show off, I had neglected the elementary precaution of checking the market for the bond prices before I left. I mumbled some awkward coverup about the need for a special survey of the market by our Philadelphia office and left in confusion. I don't remember whether we bought the bonds from Roberts; but I do know that from that day forward I never went to a business interview without making sure I was adequately prepared.

I met Mr. Roberts about seven years later. By that time I had developed a business of my own in the field of undervalued securities, particularly those of companies in liquidation which were likely to pay out considerably more for their shares than the market price. The stock of U.S. Express was precisely one such opportunity; its final dissolution had been long delayed, but it seemed to offer a sure profit. Thus I became one of the principal stockholders of the company—quite a change from the lowly waybill checker of 1913. I went over to ask the president about the date and amount of the next cash distribution, which I felt was about due. Mr. Roberts had changed greatly too. He was now a wizened old man, much given to reminiscing. He insisted on telling me at length just how he had sold the U.S. Express Building at 2 Rector Street—for $3,500,000 in cash—years earlier. He included details about who was sitting in this chair and who in that as the checks passed from one hand to another. Was this senile chatterbox the little tyrant before whom we cowered as he strode around the room that summer's day in 1913? I was to see many such changes in men and institutions during my career in Wall Street. And I was to learn that there is a great difference between the life histories of companies and of those who run them. Both can grow antiquated and lose their ascendancy, but many a doddering enterprise has received a new infusion of lifeblood and regained its place in the sun, whereas once an executive has grown too old, he is usually finished.

I also had a job tutoring the children of army officers, including one of the sons of the famous General Leonard Wood, who lived on Governors Island with his family. In 1920 Leonard Wood was to be a leading candidate for the Republican presidential nomination at Chicago. He came within a few votes of the required majority after which the choice and ultimate victory went to a very dark horse—Senator Warren Harding. I met General Wood once in his fine library and was much impressed by his demeanor and conversation. But unfortunately his children were far less interesting than their distinguished father or dignified mother.

Four times a week I made the trip in a special ferry boat which left Manhattan from a berth in South Ferry. The officers and their invitees (including me) had relatively luxurious accommodations on the upper deck, while the enlisted men sat on wooden benches below. One day, being alone above and rather bored, I wandered down the stairs and struck up a conversation with a couple of the men. The next day Colonel Mitchum came into the study room where I was tutoring his son to tell me that I had been seen talking to the enlisted men on the lower deck of the ferry. This was strictly against regulations, and I was not to let it happen again. Such were the ironclad mores of the U.S. Army in 1913.

One of my less successful jobs was what I may call "Operation Shirtboard." Sometime in my last year, the Columbia Employment Office put me in touch with a Mr. Buchman, who had the idea of selling advertising space on the oblong cardboards which laundries inserted in men's shirts. Before he could approach possible advertisers, he had to sign up a sufficient number of laundries to use his boards—the bait being a reduction in price from the usual $1.40 per thousand to $1. I was hired to persuade as many local laundries as possible to sign our contracts; for each signed contract I was to receive 15 cents. As samples, Mr. Buchman supplied me with beautiful Arrow collar streetcar ads in three colors: these happened to have the same dimensions as the shirtboards, which were not yet cut. I dutifully told the laundrymen that these would be the kind of boards they would receive if they signed up with us for the important cash saving. But when Mr. Buchman's boards finally made their appearance, they were of poor-quality carton disfigured with a host of small local advertisements in black ink.

There was something in my earnestness and innocent enthusiasm that won over the laundrymen, for a large proportion of those I visited signed on. Or maybe it was because they weren't being asked to hand over any money. But not all were persuaded: the third laundry I visited was run by a Chinaman who listened impassively to my long speech, examined the Arrow collar card with interest, duly studied the two-page contract, and then handed it back to me with the remark "Chinese laundry no use shirtboard."

After a while, Mr. Buchman called me down to his office. I had done so well with these contracts he wanted to give me a much more important assignment, a chance to make real money. I was now to go after potential advertisers and get them to sign up for space on our shirtboards. I first tackled a rather large retail store, Blumstein's, on 125th Street. It was with some difficulty that I got into the office of young Blumstein, who handled their advertising. Hardly had I begun my story when he snapped "Not interested." I continued, and he repeated "Not interested. Get out." I felt it my duty to say something in remonstrance, whereupon he said "Will you get out, or shall I have you thrown out?" I got out. My enthusiasm diminished, I approached several others on the list, but with no success. It was a discouraged salesman who reported to Buchman the next day. He took it philosophically. Evidently I was a little too young to sell advertising, but I could still do a good job with the laundrymen. I went back to my bicycle.

Then there was the little matter of sex. Although precocious in intellect, I was considered retarded when it came to girls and love. At thirteen, while reading Fielding's *Tom Jones*, I overheard my French tutor, Constance Fleischmann, remark to Mother, "Isn't that a rather risqué book for Benny to be reading?" To which Maman replied confidently, "Oh, he wouldn't understand those parts." Of course, it was only a parent's obtuseness that led her to imagine that her Benjamin was quick to learn about everything *except* sex. But, of course, I had the same curiosity as any other youngster, and since I read more than other children, I had an ample share of book learning about the subject. But it was true that in actual experience I was behind other boys.

For one thing, I had inherited or acquired, Lord knows where, a linguistic prudishness. The vulgarity of my comrades always made me uncomfortable; I would as soon have put a hot coal to my lips as use such words myself. This modesty about language has held me in its grip all my life. For another, I was bashful with girls. My school career never brought me into a classroom with them. Up to college days my contact with them was limited to a puppy's devotion to Constance and to an unexpressed, wraith-like interest in a girl named Violet Gassner. This unnatural state of affairs could not last forever. The moving spirit in my transformation was my older brother, Leon, who had quite a way with the young ladies. He was self-assured and a good talker, given to quoting romantic poetry. From time to time he had more girls than he could handle, so naturally he turned some over to me. Indeed, I became part of Leon's conversational stock-in-trade with his girlfriends. If he was to be believed, I was not only a genius, but *the* genius. They demanded to see this prodigy plain, and Leon graciously acceded.

Through my cousin Helen, I met a girl named Rose, but didn't dare put my arm around her waist, even as we floated through Ye Olde Mill at Coney Island. Rose married another, but I wrote a juvenile poem to her memory, which can be found in my looseleaf collection of "Versions and Verse." Leon also took me along to visit a pretty girl who sold phonograph records at Abraham and Strauss in Brooklyn. He had acquired an enthusiasm for opera (which he communicated to me) and having sufficiently captured this girl's affection, he spent free Saturday afternoons in the record booth, sampling virtually the entire collection of operatic masterpieces without ever buying a record. The young lady was attractive, wistful, and rather unceremoniously neglected by my discophile brother.

These meetings were only warmups for a more serious one. Leon had become interested in Sylvia Mazur, who lived in Bath Beach, Brooklyn. When Sylvia got engaged to one Armand, Leon started paying his visits to her younger sister, Hazel, then only sixteen. Hazel had everything to recommend her. She was pretty, intelligent, with remarkable poise and practical knowledge of all sorts. She was energetic and ambitious, and earned a fair amount of money teaching dancing and elocution to the children of the neighborhood, as well as to some adults. She was charitable, helpful to others, and in every way a fine person. If she had a fault, it grew out of her manifold virtues: she was convinced of her own infallibility.

Soon Leon needed to show off his famous younger brother to Hazel, and vice-versa. Besides, the journey from the Bronx to outer Brooklyn was long and tedious; he could use company on these expeditions. One Sunday I went along with him and found myself in the parlor of a small frame house. Hazel came in to greet us. She was plump, but pleasingly so, and the deep brown hair falling over her shoulders gave her a deceptively childish appearance. We found each other most interesting. I became a frequent visitor to the Mazurs, sometimes with Leon, sometimes alone. This double courting of the same girl did not escape the notice of Cousin Lou, who made many a jest at our expense. Some months later, Hazel was busy arranging an entertainment to display the talents and progress of her young pupils. For that purpose I composed a masque, in the genre of Milton's "Comus," entitled "A Fairy Festival," which

Hazel set to music from various sources. The piece began with a female Prologue, aged seven:

> Far from the rural haunts of Bensonhurst,
> And old Bath Beach, in slumber deep immersed,
> There lies the joyous land of Faerie...

To assist in this grand undertaking, Hazel had assembled all her beaux, past, present and even future. They made up a numerous team of ushers, ticket sellers, and scene shifters. Hazel even enlisted my other brother Victor into service. She knew everything, including his talents as an amateur stage performer. The high spot of the evening was a duet in which long, lanky Victor and a microscopic six-year-old boy sang Al Jolson's current hit, "When the grown-up ladies act like babies, I've got to love'm—that's all." The applause was terrific. But Cousin Lou, who somehow had been persuaded to attend the event, waxed cynical. What? All three of us in the clutches of a girl scarcely more than a child? It was disgraceful, a blot on the Grossbaum escutcheon. But soon he too was part of Hazel's entourage.

When I was nineteen, I had a more concentrated romance. Through Lou Bernstein I met Alda Miller. Alda was not as pretty as Hazel, but she had an animated, interesting face. She worked as secretary-typist for a firm of patent attorneys, and the constant stream of technical material passing her desk served to widen her horizons. I shall always remember Alda with deep affection and some compunction. Our romance budded very quickly. Soon I was meeting her every day at the El station on our return from work. The Millers had a backyard, with a swing hanging from a tree—just wide enough for two young people. I remember one lilac-scented evening when I sat next to her in the swing and talked some nonsense—I think about Kant's philosophy. I felt her hand against my cheek, and then it seemed to be turning my face more and more imperiously toward hers. It took me much too long to fathom that she wanted me to kiss her, but even the dullest wits catch on at last.

After that, we were definitely in love. It was a delicious and disturbing period. Every time we met, Nature urged our bodies to unite; but they never did, because that wouldn't have been respectable, and we were both highly respectable. There were, however, some experiences in the Miller hammock whose details the reader must imagine, though we remained virgins. But I, at least, felt ashamed. In some irrational way, I resented Alda's physical power over me.

One Sunday afternoon amid a gathering of young people at the Millers', Alda sat on my lap—an act which I adored in private, but which made me feel ridiculous before all those friends. She asked, and not in a whisper: "Ben, don't you love me?" "Of course I do, dear," I whispered. "But tell me that you love me more than anyone else in the world. Tell everybody," she insisted, her voice almost strident. "Yes, yes, Alda, I love you more than anyone else."

The next evening I sent Alda a long sensible letter. I argued that I was still in college, and after I graduated, I would probably be spending three years in law school. How could we think seriously of love, if marriage would have to be deferred until I could support her in proper fashion? But in the meantime we were becoming more and more involved with each other. Desires were sharpening that we had no hope of satisfying. I wrote that she was so much in my thoughts and blood that I could not do justice to my college work. After much argument and excuse, I announced my sad decision: we must end our romance immediately by a complete break. It was best for both of us not to meet again.

At this distance in time and experience it is hard for me to recapture the premises on which that letter was based. It never occurred to me then that Alda and I could become lovers in the flesh. To sleep with a respectable girl, or even to marry one before you could provide for her suitably—such things were like stealing or drunkenness. For a decent, ambitious young man they were quite unthinkable. Alda sent me her reply, accepting my decision with no word of rancor and wishing me all success and happiness in the future.

My relationship with Alda, and a later, shallower one with a less interesting girl, paved the way for the main romantic chapter of my youth, the one that led to marriage to Hazel, to five children, and to a close sharing of many successes and sorrows. But also to an ultimate divorce. This very morning I happened to be reading Conrad's *Heart of Darkness* and was haunted by Marlow's profound observation:

> Droll thing life is—that mysterious arrangement of merciless logic for a futile purpose. The most you can hope from it is some knowledge of yourself—that comes too late—and a crop of inextinguishable regrets.

Hazel and I had almost everything to give each other, yet we lacked the necessary knowledge of ourselves, and that was to prove fatal to our marriage.

Hazel returned to Bath Beach after spending a year at Emerson School in Boston and took up at once with all her old beaux, including me. Gradually and carefully Hazel made up her mind that I was the boy she wanted, and having done so, she set about convincing me to like effect. All this took time and skill. There were no embarrassing professions of love in public, Alda-fashion, nor even enthralling confessions to me in private. It was best for both of us to wait until the proper time.

I graduated from Columbia in the spring of 1914 and was making a start in my career, though the summer of 1914 hardly looked a propitious time to begin. World War I had started, and the New York Stock Exchange was closed tight, but I was able to get and hang on to a job in Wall Street.[1] I was earning only $10 per week, but I supplemented that with tutoring army officers' sons on Governors Island and teaching English to foreigners in a night school. The latter was my first teaching experience: we used the Gouin method, by which the action had invariably to be suited to the word. For example, in the first lesson the teacher intoned: "I open the window," and straightaway did so. One by one the pupils repeated the sentence—generally with an approximation like: "I oopen ze vindow"—and simultaneously walked to the window to let in a brief blast of cold air. It was somewhat better than the teaching method at Dotheboys Hall in *Nicholas Nickleby*. There, if I remember correctly, the schoolmaster Wackford Squeers taught spelling somewhat after this fashion: "Winder—w-i-n-d-e-r-. Johnson, you wash the classroom winders this afternoon, or I'll thrash the living daylights out of ye."

We experienced an unexpected taste of luxury in 1914, moving into a rather exclusive apartment complex called the Hunt's Point Palace. How could such a fairy story have come to pass? Quite simply. It turned out that one of the less desirable five-room apartments could be had for a mere $45 per month, only $10 more than our rent on Kelly Street. My three jobs were bringing in about $28 per week, which, added to my brothers' contribution, amply provided for that modest rent. Imagine with what pride the Grossbaum family took up their abode in this huge and glistening palace, complete with marquee, gorgeously attired doormen, numerous elevators, and five unequaled tennis courts. That was a golden day in our history. No blasé experience of the past could dull our enthusiasm for this new world of luxury—nor could any deeper wisdom tell our triumphant hearts that all these things were only baubles.

I received an official letter from Columbia University Law School informing me that I had been awarded a tuition scholarship and that I had to send in my acceptance within a week. This was good news, but it plunged me into perplexity. Should I go forward into a professional career, as I had always anticipated? I could give up my Wall Street job with little enough material sacrifice, and as yet I had no indications whatever that I was cut out for finance. But, weighing heavily in the balance was the prospect of three years' delay before I could make a real start in life—and correspondingly more years before I could think about marriage. I discussed the matter with Hazel. In subtle fashion she gave me to understand that those extra three years would be very long ones for her as well as for me, whereas, with my great abilities, if I stuck to my present job... She didn't tell me what to do, but I did what I knew she wanted, and what—after all—I wanted too. I wrote to the Law School declining the scholarship with thanks. I communicated my decision to Dean Keppel as well (without mention of Hazel). He wrote back an approving note, saying that with the closing of the Exchange, many of the light-weights would undoubtedly drop out of Wall Street, thus leaving better chances for the good men.

Hazel and I soon made our promises to each other. I recall not the date but the scene. I was taking her home from the theater, and we had to wait quite a time at one of the BMT stations to change for the Bensonhurst train. I must first have declared how much I cared for her, *mein Sehnen und Verlangen.* She said that she greatly cared for me and had definitely decided to wait for me. We were very happy but equally solemn about it all. Hazel warned me that our mutual pledge must remain a complete secret to everybody, since her mother (whom Leon called the "dragon") and her important Uncle Max would be scandalized at the idea of their precious Hazel tying herself down to a mere stripling just out of school. (Her father—a Pop Miller type—didn't count.) But Hazel assured me that she could handle all the problems that would arise, and I believed her.

We kept our engagement secret for about a year and a half, until the summer of 1916. The delay taxed all of Hazel's ingenuity and resourcefulness in dealing with her numerous admirers—including a passionately devoted, hot-blooded South American named Caicedo—plus a strong-minded mother always on the lookout for a good match. Her mother's zeal led to various incidents, one of which was somewhat humiliating. It seems that Mrs. Mazur had spotted an eminently eligible young man. His name was Nathan Gutman, and his father and he had a flourishing business in ladies' sweaters. She and Hazel had plans to spend Easter Week, 1915, at Lakewood, New Jersey. When I asked Hazel if I could come up too for the weekend, she said that would cause her great difficulties. But it could be arranged if I agreed to pass as her cousin—and please don't ask her any questions about it. I consented, in all innocence. When I got to Lakewood, I found Gutman cozily settled at Hazel's hotel, being treated with the utmost amiability by Mrs. Mazur, who greeted "Cousin Ben" with undisguised displeasure.

Of course I was unhappy with this comedy, but I realized Hazel's difficult position sufficiently not to be nasty about it. This was not an easy interval for two young people strongly attracted to one another, meeting nearly every day or so, restrained from following their sexual instincts by the mores of the time, and having temperaments that did not always accord too well. Hazel was very sweet, but she was also as strong as steel, certain of herself, and possessive in even more than the usual feminine fashion. I was easygoing and pliable on the surface, but deep down I resented possessiveness and domination of all sorts. Besides, I was given to absentmindedness, disregard of small attentions, and a certain British undemonstrativeness.

We had many misunderstandings of lesser and greater magnitude. We agreed to call it quits more than once, but such rifts were only momentary. But one incident was extraordinary: I had taken Hazel out for a row on the lake. Suddenly she announced that she was sure I did not love her enough, that our romance was doomed, that she had nothing more to live for, and was determined to drown herself. Whereupon she plunged, clothes and all, into the lake. She was a good swimmer and had no difficulty in keeping afloat, while I rowed as close to her as possible and pleaded with her to be sensible, to have more confidence in me, and so on. After some minutes of this divertissement, Hazel climbed back into the boat and announced that she had decided to give our love another chance.

Late that summer I formally requested Hazel's hand. I presented my case to the triumvirate of Father, Mother, and Uncle Max. Hazel had ostensibly retired to her room, in proper Victorian fashion, but was actually sitting at the top of the stairs, listening intently. I spoke briefly of our mutual devotion and at greater length about my financial prospects—which by that time were considerable. Mother Mazur admitted that she had been expecting this for some little time, but could hardly reconcile herself to my extreme youth. In fact, she actually inquired whether I shaved regularly. I satisfied her on that point, and no further objections were raised. We celebrated the occasion with a bottle of champagne, held in reserve for such an emergency. That November we had a regulation engagement party, and the following June we were married—but not before I faced an agonizing personal problem raised by America's entrance into the war.

CHAPTER SEVEN

My Career Begins

My last month at college involved a flurry of activity. First came an invitation from Professor Woodbridge, chairman of the Philosophy Department, to lunch with him at the Faculty Club. He proposed that I stay on at Columbia as a member of the Department of Philosophy. Soon thereafter came a corresponding offer from Professor Hawkes on behalf of the Mathematics Department. Then, to my surprise, the great Professor Erskine invited me to his office for a chat. He felt that I would make a valuable addition to the Department of English and that I would find a university career most congenial. True, the starting salary was low and advancement less than rapid, but the offsetting satisfactions were enormous. The better to convince me, he gave me a fascinating account of his own beginnings as a college instructor, of his early marriage and consequent financial problems.

Needless to say, I felt both complimented and bewildered by this wealth of offers. When I talked them over with Dean Keppel, however, he advised me to delay my decision. He had a strong predilection for sending bright college graduates into business, instead of shutting them up in the ivory tower of academic life. Perhaps he would be able to steer something interesting my way.

A few days later, when we met on campus, Keppel told me: "I tried to reach you on the phone yesterday, without success. Too bad. There was a most interesting opportunity for you."

"What was it, sir?"

"Sir Norman Angell—you know him, author of *The Great Illusion*—was in my office. He was leaving this morning on a new peace campaign, to be carried on all over Europe. He wanted a young assistant, and I recommended you. But he had to leave without you."

I felt really downcast at this missed occasion to make a most unusual tour in the company of a distinguished writer and speaker. Later I was to reflect on the quirk of fortune involved in that telephone call gone wrong. About two months later World War I broke out. I might well have been in England with Angell at that time. As a British subject, I would have been subject to military call and might have found myself before long fighting in Flanders fields. What an ironic conclusion that would have been to my peace mission!

One of my friends, Freddy Sweyd, ran a small advertising agency. He thought I might make a success as a writer of advertising copy and suggested that I come to his office on a trial basis, at a nominal salary. Since I had some time between the end of classes and Graduation Day, I was happy to take a fling at it. His chief account was Carbona, the well-known non-flammable cleaning fluid. I was set to work dreaming up slogans and other advertising ideas. My first effort, I think, was: "Carbona—Knocks the Spots out of Everything." After a few others in like vein, I produced my masterpiece—a limerick which I remember only too well:

> There was a young girl from Winona
> Who never had heard of Carbona,
> She started to clean
> With a can of benzene,
> And now her poor parents bemoan her.

When I showed this to Sweyd, he waxed enthusiastic as only an advertising man can. He clapped on his hat and rushed over to the Carbona offices to show my gem to the president, Mr. Weinstein. I waited, on tenterhooks. In half an hour he returned—dejected.

"What's wrong, Fred? Didn't Weinstein like the limerick?"

"Sure, he nearly died laughing over it. Then he told me it wouldn't do."

"But why?"

"Because he says their whole campaign is directed towards scaring people into buying Carbona. This would make them laugh and would tend to nullify the rest of their copy. Too bad, Ben. It did look awfully good to me."

I don't know whether Weinstein's judgment about my limerick was better than Sweyd's. I do know I felt pretty discouraged and ready to consider a more dependable occupation than writing advertising copy.

I had competed for the Mathematical Prize at Columbia, which paid $150 each year—no small sum in those days. I think there were five contestants. Cousin Lou had won it in his graduating year, and somehow it was taken for granted in the family that I would do likewise, so much so, that I remember that Lou's elder brother, Wilfred, actually offered me $100 in cash for my chance to win. I told him he overestimated my prowess, or underestimated that of my competitors. (We had a group of real math sharks that year.) As it happened, the money was won by my friend, J. J. Tanzola, who ate and slept mathematics and went on to become a math professor. I was disappointed, but far from surprised, about coming in second.

In the Commencement Day Program, I read that I was also runner-up for the prize given to the graduating student with the best average marks in his entire college career. My only consolation was honorable mention beneath the winner's name.

Despite these setbacks I had the pleasure of being elected to Phi Beta Kappa. This was a highly coveted honor, which in one way or another was to serve me advantageously in later life. But another distinction eluded me in the accidental or mixed-up fashion to which I was growing rather accustomed. It seems that the mathematics faculty planned to nominate me also for Sigma Xi, which is the honorary society in the technical—chiefly engineering—fields, corresponding to Phi Beta Kappa in the humanities. Such nomination would have assured my election. But they didn't know I had been around Columbia long enough to be graduating and so put off my nomination to the next year. That proved to be too late since the rules prohibited elections after graduation. (I learned of this slip-up only later from Professor Hawkes.)

Just before Commencement Day I received another summons to Dean Keppel's office. It seemed that a member of the New York Stock Exchange had been in to see him about his son's rather woeful grades and in the course of the interview had asked the Dean to recommend one of his best students for employment as a bond salesman. Keppel had given this Mr. Newburger my name, with a rousing recommendation. He was convinced that Wall Street presented fine opportunities for college men and that I ought seriously to consider this career rather than college teaching. I agreed to see Mr. Newburger, and an appointment was made for the next day at 3:15, when he would return from 'Change. The firm's name was Newburger, Henderson, and Loeb, and its office address was 100 Broadway.

I well remember arriving early and walking up and down in front of Trinity Church clock, waiting for the hands to reach 3:10. Then I crossed the street and entered rather cramped quarters on the ground floor of the American Surety Building. I was ushered into Mr. Samuel Newburger's—"Mr. S. N.'s"—office. I found a handsome, corpulent man with imposing white hair. He seemed terribly old to me, though he was actually not much over fifty. After a few general remarks, he turned me over to the next brother in line, Mr. Alfred H. Newburger, for my real interview.

Mr. A. N., whom I soon found to be the de facto senior member and guiding spirit of the firm, proved to be tall, handsome like his elder brother, but grey- instead of white-haired. He spoke with great earnestness and authority. He asked me about my studies in economics, and I had to admit that I had skipped the subject completely—largely because of my job with U.S. Express Company. However, I satisfied him that I knew the difference between a stock and a bond. He said that despite my lack of specific training, he would take me on because of Dean Keppel's sponsorship. What was my general financial situation? I replied that it was weak and I had to depend on my salary to support myself. "Well," he said, "we always start our young men at $10 a week, but in view of your necessities we'll stretch a point and make it $12. You know it will be some time before you're able to earn your salt with us by selling bonds." He spoke of the great opportunities in Wall Street for the right kind of man. I knew it only by hearsay and in novels as a place of drama and excitement. I felt the urge to participate in its mysterious rites and momentous events. I accepted the terms and agreed to start the next week. As I rose to leave, he said to me, with ministerial solemnity, holding a long finger in the air: "One last warning, young man. If you speculate, you'll lose your money. Always remember that." With these somewhat forbidding words, the interview was over, the bargain was closed, and my lifetime career was determined.

Our arrangement was that I would spend a few weeks in the back office as runner and general helper, to learn the business from the bottom up. After that I would move to the bond department and learn how to sell bonds. Wall Street in those days was not nearly as streamlined as it is today, and there was a great deal more exchanging of bought-and-sold slips ("comparisons"), deliveries of securities, check certifications, and similar messenger work. I learned many things, first in the delivery department, then in the order room, and later in the bookkeeping department.

In my first week as runner, our cashier gave me a check to be certified at the National City Bank. "You know where that is, don't you?" I saw the address as 55 Wall Street on the check, so I answered "Sure," and out I went. After 49 Wall Street I came to an enormous building that evidently must have been my bank, but to make certain, I started looking for the name or address on the walls. I walked twice around the building, which occupied a square block, before I finally gave up and asked someone. It was the National City Bank, of course; they were so reputation-conscious that they didn't think it necessary to put their name on their portals.

I was astonished at the financial industry's easygoing ways of dealing with large sums. When a check was certified and ready to be returned, the clerk at the window would call out "Newburger," or "Content," or whatever. A runner would go up to the window, say "Check for Newburger," and a piece of paper calling for maybe half a million dollars would be handed to him, with no identification asked. Even more striking was the offhand treatment of stock certificates. I would be leaving an elevator to make a delivery. At that point another runner would say to me: "You going to Sartorius?" "Yes." "Then deliver these for me. Thanks." And he would thrust a sheaf of stock certificates into my hands and run off. Strange to say, very few checks or securities went astray under that apparently crazy system. But I understand that delivery methods have greatly changed since my day.

Despite the casual dealing in large sums in the brokerage business, I discovered to my surprise how parsimonious the rich can be. Sometimes when I came into Mr. A. N.'s office, I would find him sending out checks to pay personal bills. For this purpose he used stamped self-addressed envelopes received from corporations for their annual meeting proxies. A. N. would cross out the corporation's address, write in the new addressee, and thus save a 2-cent stamp. He remarked with quiet satisfaction that there was no point in letting the envelopes and stamps go to waste. This exhibition of parsimony by a very rich man shocked and offended me, especially so since I had a great admiration for A. N.'s intelligence and acumen. I asked myself, "How could someone who signs 'day-notes' to our bank for a million dollars scrounge to save a 2-cent stamp?" It was something I might do because pennies were important. But then I'd be darned careful not to let anybody know about it.

Nearly half a century has marched by since those reflections. After some serious financial reverses along the way I have attained considerable wealth—far exceeding, in fact, that of my Wall Street employers. The passage of time has brought me a better understanding of the monetary psychology of rich people. It is a subject about which little has been written. The basic fact is that our attitude towards money is determined in early life, by innate disposition, the conditions of existence, and certain key experiences. A person born extravagant is likely to remain so, subject only to force majeure of various kinds that restrains his expenditures. If such a man passes from poverty to wealth, he easily throws off the shackles of early compulsions and becomes a genial free spender. He is completely at home with his wealth.

Most children, however, come into the world without a strong predisposition in matters of finance. Their attitudes and their future behavior are determined in good part by early environment. Even if their family is well-to-do, they can be trained to careful and even parsimonious money habits by example, precept, and discipline. Being young, they learn these habits when handling small sums, typically their weekly allowance. When they later inherit great wealth, their attitude is unbalanced. They tend to be overcareful and picayune in small things, yet careless, generous, and even personally extravagant in larger matters. Of course, those born to wealth and reared in an atmosphere of liberality follow without difficulty the gracious pattern of behavior appropriate to their circumstances.

It is useful to distinguish between (a) the true miser, (b) the bargain hunter, and (c) the victim of conditioned parsimony.

The true miser is almost always avaricious—i.e., eager to amass unneeded wealth, and he has a neurotic block against expenditure at all levels. The second group, which includes a large number of successful businessmen, continue beyond reason to work hard and pile up additional wealth through momentum and force of habit. They tend to carry over into their private expenditure their business stance of seeking the "best buys" and driving hard bargains. Such men are not miserly at all, for they like high living, deriving a triumphant pleasure from owning a Rolls-Royce, a large yacht, or fabulous jewels. But they buy both their rolls and their Rolls at a discount.

It is the third class of rich men, however, which is most interesting because it presents the greatest complexities and puzzling contradictions. These are men born poor, or who knew poverty in early life—as I did. Necessity compelled them to count every penny. (I can still remember a cylindrical tube, which once contained Van Houten's chocolate chips. My pennies just fitted into the bore, and I often counted them to find out the sum of my present wealth.) In later life these strongly imprinted habits pass into the subconscious, where they influence behavior in a hundred irrational and rather shameful ways. But this behavior is always around small sums, not large expenditures or gifts. Their childhood conditioning concerned items under a dollar, or a few dollars at most. A thousand dollars or even a hundred were so far outside the child's experience that he developed no habits about handling such sums.

As a consequence, a typical poor boy–rich man, such as myself, becomes ridiculously inconsistent in the field of expenditure. He can be easy-going, even extravagant in all the larger outlays, and at the same time must wage a constant war against an ingrained cheapness in all his smaller ones. In my own case the drive towards such stinginess is checked by two countervailing factors. First, I have become aware of the problem and determined to use my intelligence and willpower to surmount it as best I can. Secondly, I am highly sensitive to the reaction of others to my conduct—in everyday life, at least. Whether on the whole this is a bad trait, I do not know. But with respect to small change, its effect is good. I am much too "ashamed before the neighbors" to yield to my parsimonious instincts if I think anyone is watching me.

It is when I am quite alone that I sometimes relax and do the silly, stingy things prompted by my childhood conditioning. Naturally, there has to be "rationalization" even here. For example, in New York I invariably use taxis when I am with anyone but often take the subway when I am alone. For this I give myself two stock excuses. The first is that the streets are so crowded that the subway will be much quicker than a cab. The second is that I can read in the underground while I can't in a taxi. Yet—believe it or not—I may even forbear to buy a newspaper on the grounds that it is a nuisance to carry around. Perhaps this disinclination to spend small sums accounts for the fact that I have never smoked or developed a taste for liquor.

Like all newcomers to Wall Street, I was greatly intrigued by the Curb Market. It was then located, as it had been for years, right out on Broad Street, occupying a roped-off area about twenty yards square. Here the curb brokers assembled in all kinds of weather to carry on their trading in the open air. In heavy rain they were all attired in oilskins; on a cold winter's day earmuffs were in evidence. Many wore gaily colored hats to facilitate their location by the order clerks, who were ensconced in windows overlooking the market and sent down instructions and received responses through elaborate hand signals. Although the Curb Market was far less important than the New York Stock Exchange, it listed many corporations of first importance—in addition to numerous cats and dogs of all descriptions. Often the trading grew to large volume, involving many millions of dollars in a single day. Somehow it was handled with reasonable efficiency, despite the outlandish physical arrangements. About ten years later the

Curb Market went indoors, occupying a large new building west of Trinity Churchyard. It took another twenty years for these conservatives to change their name from the overly modest "New York Curb Market" to the overly pretentious "American Stock Exchange." But old-timers will always speak of it as the "Curb," recalling somewhat nostalgically those funny red hats on Broad Street.

After about four weeks as a runner, I moved into the bond department, lodged in a single exposed room separated by a narrow corridor from the customers' room and its quotation board. Before my arrival the personnel consisted of two young but relatively experienced bond salesmen, a few years out of college. One was Daniel Loeb, nephew of the firm partner Jake Loeb. He was dark, with rather bowed shoulders, hard-working, and always serious. The other was Harold Rouse—quite the opposite type. He was tall, well built, handsome, blondish, a crack swimmer, and quite a playboy. His motto, which he soon confided to me unblushingly, was "Never do yourself what you can get someone else to do for you," and he was able to apply it successfully to nearly everything resembling work. He could always get someone else to do his work. The Fates, with their usual irony, were to spin far different futures for these two young buddies. The intense, almost dedicated Dan Loeb was to marry the firm's Irish telephone girl, and later to lose everything in a speculative venture during the 1920s. Harold Rouse, always imperturbable and never known to be really busy at anything, inherited his father's wealth, became a partner in an important stock exchange firm, and put all the copybook maxims to shame.

My twin assignment was, first, to learn all I could about bonds and, secondly, to make myself as useful as possible in the department. My chief job was to supply the thumbnail descriptions of each bond in the lists of recommendations which Dan and Harold sent out almost daily to their prospects. Even in my spare time I took my job of self-education very seriously. I got myself a small looseleaf notebook, and on each page I wrote the salient data about a given bond issue in convenient form to be memorized. After all these years I can still remember the appearance of that black notebook and some of the entries in it. The first was: "Atchison, Topeka, & Santa Fe, General 4s, due 1995: 150 mil." There must have been a hundred different issues entered; I memorized their size, interest rate, maturity date, and order of lien. Why I wanted to memorize facts that could be readily obtained from manuals or my notebook I am at a loss to explain. No doubt it was another manifestation of my vanity. After making what I thought was wonderful progress with these studies, I found all the different issues hopelessly mixed up in my mind, and I gave up the exercise as a bad job. But I was surprised to realize some months later that the figures had somehow straightened themselves out. I had become something of a walking Railroad Bond Manual.

In July 1914, the heir-apparent to the throne of Austria was assassinated in Sarajevo, Bosnia, leading to sharp exchanges between Vienna and little Serbia. The New York stock market paid only slight attention to this European tension; it would probably blow over, as did the Agadir incident[1] a few years previously. My Phi Beta Kappa key arrived, and I wore it proudly dangling from a watch chain spread across my vest. Lester Newburger, youngest member of the firm, a cigar salesman not long before, was much impressed by this honor to one of the firm's employees. An hour later he said to me: "Ben, can I ask a Phi Beta Kappa man to run out and get me a pack of cigarettes? You know the kind." And out I ran, my key flopping about.

One of my silliest jobs was as market letter writer. Samuel Newburger, the floor member, had to dictate a daily account of the market's doings after the close. This was sent over to the office in Philadelphia, where the firm had originated, to remind the local customers that our man was right in the middle of things at Broad and Wall Street, New York. S. N. disliked this chore sufficiently to turn it over to me. He suggested

I read some of his back numbers and continue in like vein. For a while thereafter our Philadelphia clientele was edified each day by the stock market observations of the new expert, who could boast all of six weeks' acquaintance with finance.

I have an imperishable memory of that quiet period just before the Victorian world was to disappear in flames, and the nineteenth century—which had its real beginning in 1815—was to come to its equally belated close. The Australian tennis team was challenging the Americans for the Davis Cup. One of the Newberger partners had two tickets for the third day's matches; he couldn't use them and kindly made a gift of them to me. I invited Fred Greenman, a sedentary tennis enthusiast, and we went off to Forest Hills Stadium, which had just been dedicated that very week. The Australians were leading, having split the first-day singles and won the doubles. Now the veteran Norman Brooks of the Aussies was to meet young Norris Williams, just out of Harvard, where he was Greenman's classmate. It was that match which, by its overwhelming drama, took tennis out of its tea party, kid-gloved, polite-applause past and hurled it into a new era of enthusiasm, excitement, and unrestrained emotion. Williams, just missing the sidelines, lost the first two sets, and our cause looked hopeless. Then he found himself; with wonderful power and control, he forced the match, won the third set and then the fourth. Spectators lost all sense of decorum; each point won by the slim American seemed to be greeted by increasingly uproarious applause. After one such rally was won by Williams, the noise grew so terrific that Brooks threw his racket down and stood in the court with both fingers pressed tightly in his ears—a sight forever rooted in my memory. The officials begged the crowd to restrain itself, but with little success. Nevertheless, battling with heart, head, and ancient skill, the Australian finally retrieved the fifth set. The stands moaned in despair. As he walked off the field, still wearing his strange-looking ocean-voyage cap, Norman Brooks passed the shiny silver Davis Cup, displayed on its table, and gave it a triumphant spin. The crowd, its sportsmanship returning, applauded this gesture.

Then the American Maury MacLaughlin, the fabulous redhead, won a beautiful but meaningless five-set match from appealing Anthony Wilding. Too short a time later, Tony Wilding died fighting in France.

Early in August 1914 the fateful conflagration ignited. Would it lead to the disappearance of Western civilization? Was it the result of a lack of sound leadership or diplomatic skill in the chancelleries of Europe? Or was it simply another in the endless series of wars among nations, which ultimately seem to leave no major historical scars but are catastrophic to those who fight them and portentous for those who survive? My own meditations on these questions are hardly worth noting here; others have thought more deeply and soundly than I about these problems. So I shall write now only from the narrow viewpoint of a young New Yorker who, as the early stages of the drama unfolded, experienced the same bewilderment and excitement as his neighbors

A few days before August 3 the stock market was showing considerable nervousness, but nothing approaching panic. The actual outbreak of hostilities caught the financial community by surprise, both here and in Europe. Our market was swamped by a terrific wave of selling, and very quickly the governors decided to close the New York Stock Exchange. All other exchanges followed suit immediately. This flood of selling may seem peculiar and quite illogical to those who, at this distance, are familiar only with the war boom that was soon to follow. But the explanation is at once technical yet simple. European investors held large amounts of American securities. When war broke out, their first concern was to take their money home. They felt instinctively, but wrongly as it turned out, that in time of conflict they were safer with their funds close at hand than in a distant country. This sudden and massive reaction of foreign holders put an intolerable strain on our local markets—which in those days took their psychological

cue from the daily behavior of the London Exchange—and our
stockbrokers quickly threw in the sponge. It is interesting,
perhaps, to compare this performance with our markets'
action just twenty-five years later, when World War II
erupted. On the second occasion, there was again some pan-
icky selling, in natural reaction to the new catastrophe. But in
a few days the American public began to see prospects of large
war orders, and in the same month of September 1939 the
markets recovered significantly. But this, too, proved delu-
sory to the public, for the fall of France in 1940 was to cause
discouragement and a serious decline.

In my mind's eye, I still see the glaring headlines: Austria
declares war on Serbia; Russia declares war on Austria; Germany on Russia; France on Germany; England on Germany. It
was all so hard to believe, and yet so dreadfully true. But how
quickly we all accustomed ourselves to this world catastrophe;
how soon we transferred our major interest to its effect on us.
When the exchanges closed, I wondered what would happen
to our business and my job. There was really nothing going on
in Wall Street, but all the firms retained their staffs on a
reduced-salary basis. I was glad I still had a job, if only at $10
per week.

After some months, trading was resumed on a limited basis,
with transactions being permitted at no less than the low
prices before the market closed. Before long, war orders
started coming in from the French and British, and the economic picture changed quickly from gloom to boom. Trading
restrictions were removed, and the stock market began its big
wartime rise. We were caught rather shorthanded by this sudden reversal, since a number of our employees had drifted
away. As a result, I was called into service on many fronts. On
some active days I would help our boardboy put up the stock
quotations. For this job I wore a heavy leather belt, with com-
partments containing each of the fractions from 1/8 to 7/8. On
other days I would be operating the telephone switchboard or
helping the various clerks in the back office, or even rushing

out now and then to make an important delivery of securities. My salary returned to $12 per week.

After a while I resumed my activities in the bond department, and it was soon time for me to go out and call on customers. This was a much pleasanter occupation than my previous efforts as salesman of cut-rate photo coupons or shirt-board advertising. It seems that being called on by a bond salesman rather flattered the vanity of the average businessman, and his "No" was invariably polite.

One of these calls—fruitless like the rest—was interrupted by the arrival of a customer of my customer. The latter, pointing to me, said in an important tone: "Excuse me just a minute, Mr. Zilch, I'm talking to my banker." Some banker! The fact is, however, that all the Wall Street houses then called themselves "Bankers and Brokers." Our letterheads and checks carried that rubric. I always liked the story of the man going into the stock and bond business who asked the sign painter to paint "John Smith, Broker" on his door, and asked how much it would cost. The painter said $5, but added that for $7 he would make it "John Smith, Banker and Broker." Whereupon Smith replied, "Go ahead. Who wouldn't be a banker for $2?" (A few years later a state law made us take "banker" off our stationery.)

During these early months I had made the acquaintance of Mr. Richard Willstatter, a floor member of the New York Stock Exchange, who rented a desk in our bond department. He would come over from 'Change every afternoon when the market closed and spend a little time at his desk, and he soon took an interest in me. He was a confirmed bachelor, myopic, with reddish hair, a Van Dyck beard, and a pronounced German accent. In fact, he was the brother of a famous German chemist who had won the Nobel Prize. Nonetheless, he was strongly pro-Ally in his sympathies. On a few occasions he took me to luncheons of the Republican Club, which were addressed by prominent people. On one such occasion, Ambassador von Bernstorff tried to present the case for Germany, but without much success; on another the Japanese ambassador told us why his country had entered the war on the side of the Allies. A great treat for me was to hear the then mayor of New York, John Purroy Mitchell, young and slim, tell of his successful battle against Tammany Hall. Alas, some three years later I was to be a part of the guard of honor at his funeral!

In connection with my bond work I had begun to study railroad reports in some detail. I had also applied myself diligently to reading the standard textbook on the subject, *The Principles of Bond Investment*, by Lawrence Chamberlain, a ponderous tome in every sense. (How could I have suspected then that a textbook of mine would one day supplant Chamberlain's throughout the country?) On the basis of these studies I conceived the idea of writing an analysis of the Missouri Pacific Railroad. Its report for the year ending June 1914 had convinced me that it was in poor physical and financially dangerous condition and that its bonds should not be held by investors. When my report was finished, I showed it to my friend Willstatter. He liked it and in turn showed it to a partner of J.S. Bache and Company. The Bache people told him that if I was interested in doing that kind of work, they would like to take me into their statistical department. By that time I was certain that I would rather be a "statistician"—as security analysts were then called—than a bond salesman, so I went over to see Mr. Morton Stern, who was later to become an important partner in the Bache firm. After some palaver he offered me $18 a week to come and work under him, turning out reports and answering inquiries—provided my firm made no objection.

This was all very wonderful! I was quite sure that N.H.&L. would be glad to get rid of me, since I had brought in absolutely no bond sale commissions to offset my $12 per week emolument. But when I rather airily announced to Mr. Samuel Newburger my decision to change jobs, the result was quite contrary to what I had expected. How could I be so disloyal as to think of leaving them after all they had done for me? How could that other firm have the gall to steal one of their employees—it was contrary to stock exchange regulations! "But I thought I was not earning my salt here." "That's for us to decide, not you." "But I'm not cut out for a bond salesman; I'm sure I'd do better at statistical work." "That's fine. It's time we had a statistical department here. You can be it." "Well, Mr. Newberger, if you really want me to stay, of course I'll be happy to stay." "That's fine—and we'll talk over the salary matter, and let you know later."

After a firm meeting, it was decided to raise my wage to $15 per week—it was unreasonable for me to expect them to pay more, considering their previous unproductive investment in me, and so on. I was glad to settle at their price and especially to begin my real and definitive career as security analyst. Some months later, when business was booming, S. N. summoned me to say that I was now to get $18 a week so that I shouldn't think I was losing anything by staying with them. This ended the Bache incident in my career—except that some months later, when I got another raise, S. N. told me with great feeling that if I had taken the other offer, the firm was resolved never to hire another college man!

Some time afterwards, my benefactor Willstatter changed quarters, and we saw much less of each other. Though he asked me to visit him, I was too busy to do so. Once I saw him in the street, and feeling guilty about neglecting him, I turned the other way. The next time our paths crossed, he reproached me for gross discourtesy in failing even to bow to him on the previous occasion. I felt heartily ashamed of myself and confessed it freely; which he took in good part. I think that little incident taught me something. If you have failed in your duty towards someone, there is a natural tendency to disassociate yourself from him—which hurts him still more. Fair and friendly dealing requires you to confess and repair your fault at the very first opportunity.

CHAPTER EIGHT

Early Years in Wall Street

I was destined to spend forty-two years—my entire business life—in Wall Street, beginning as a brokerage-house runner and ending as one of the heads of a substantial investment fund and chairman of two major business enterprises. Over the years I learned a lot from the teaching and example of others, though what I learned never prevented me from making my own blunders, large and small, nor did it contribute very much to whatever success I have achieved. (This judgment probably reflects that unconscious vanity which makes even a veracious and reasonably modest autobiographer conveniently forget what he owes to others.)

What I brought into Wall Street was a central academic viewpoint which was self-adjusting to practical considerations. My school training had made me searching, reflective, and critical. I was able to add to these qualities two others which generally do not accompany the theoretical bent: first, a good instinct for what was important in a problem or a situation and the ability to avoid wasting time on inessentials; and second, a drive towards the practical, towards getting things done, towards finding solutions, and especially towards devising new approaches and techniques.

If I was fortunate in the assortment of talents I brought to financial analysis, I was equally fortunate in the epoch in which I entered Wall Street. When I started, investment was almost entirely limited to bonds. Common stocks, with relatively few exceptions, were viewed primarily as vehicles for speculation. Nonetheless, a considerable amount of window dressing began to be arrayed around common stocks, to impart some aura of respectability to what was previously considered a near relative of the gambling casino. Detailed information on operations and finances was beginning to be supplied by corporations, either voluntarily or to conform with stock exchange requirements. The financial services had begun to present this material in convenient forms in their manuals and current publications. In addition, regulatory bodies, such as the Interstate Commerce Commission and various state public utility commissions, were gathering enormous quantities of data regarding the railroads and gas and electric companies, all of which was open for inspection and study.

But in 1914 this mass of financial information was largely going to waste in the area of common-stock analysis. The figures were not ignored, but they were studied superficially and with little interest. What counted most was inside information of various kinds—some of it relating to business operations, new orders, anticipated profits and the like, but more of it to the current activities and plans of the market manipulators—the famous "they" who were held responsible for all the significant moves, up and down, in every important stock. To old Wall Street hands it seemed silly to pore over dry statistics when the determiners of price change were thought to be an entirely different set of factors—all of them very human.

But for a variety of reasons—not the least being the improvement in the financial strength of large industrial companies resulting from World War I—intrinsic value and investment merit were destined to assume increasing importance in common-stock analysis after 1914. As a newcomer—uninfluenced by the distorting traditions of the old regime—I could respond readily to the new forces that were beginning to enter the financial scene. I learned to distinguish between what was important and unimportant, dependable and undependable, even what was honest and dishonest, with a clearer eye and better judgment than many of my seniors, whose intelligence had been corrupted by their experience. To a large degree, therefore, I found Wall Street virgin territory for examination by a genuine, penetrating analysis of security values. With my double good fortune—of internal equipment and a favorable tide—I could hardly miss being successful. Nevertheless, my career has had more than one setback.

A small example at the outset: among the customers' men of Newburger, Henderson, and Loeb was old Mr. Werner, who had been forced by bad business to give up his own stock exchange firm and take a job with us. He was white-haired, aristocratic, benevolent. He bore a heavy cross in the person of his son, Arthur, a brilliant boy, but a heavy drinker. Still, he seemed to know infallibly the last quotation on any stock and every piece of information or gossip then current in the street. He was never seen without his cane, and he once persuaded me to acquire a proper walking stick and parade through the streets with it. I did so, but only for a very short time.

In 1915 I was helping out as board-boy in the customers' room where I would exchange remarks with Mr. Werner about financial developments, corporate earnings, and the like. Missouri, Kansas and Texas Railroad was then showing some improvement in its profits, but the stock (familiarly called "Kitty") was selling at the seemingly low price of $12 per share. I must have been helpful to Werner in some fashion, and in return he suggested that we jointly buy a hundred shares of Kitty common stock. He would put up his money and would carry my half. This I was happy to agree to. Some time later Mr. A. N. got wind of the affair—he seemed to know everything about everybody in the office. He called me to his office and gave me a good dressing-down. He reminded me of his advice against speculating and then added, in an especially reproachful tone, "At least, Ben, if you are going to speculate in something, you should have more sense than to pick a run-down, no-good railroad like M.K.T." Of course, I ended the matter straightway by selling out my position at a tiny profit. I can imagine the rebuke that A. N. must have given to the venerable Mr. Werner.

But later it would be my advice that the firm would follow, rather than the other way around. Ironically, it was the same Missouri, Kansas and Texas common stock which lent itself to an unusual financial operation which I persuaded my firm to pursue, an operation exemplifying the kind of calculation that I was to become good at. The Kitty railroad was now in bankruptcy (a fact which bore out A. N.'s criticism of my earlier, neophyte's flyer). A reorganization plan had been promulgated, which gave the common stockholders only the right to buy shares of stock in the new, reorganized company. The stock was regarded as practically worthless, and was selling at about 50 cents per share. I pointed out to the partners that it would take at least a year for the plan to be consummated. In the meantime the old Kitty stock would constitute a cheap call on the same number of new shares.[1] In other words, if the new stock advanced only $1 from its current indicated price, the old stock would also rise $1 in value—which would mean a profit of 200 percent on an investment in the old stock. In fact, one could easily make 3 or 4 points during any strong period in the railroad market, while the maximum loss could only be a half-point. The N.H.&L. partners were opposed in principle to any-thing resembling speculation for the firm (although they were happy enough to see their customers indulge and even over-indulge in it). But in this case, my logic prevailed over their scruples. We bought 5,000 shares. During the next year we made a profit of around six times that amount.

The real beginning of my career as a distinctive type of Wall

Street operator dates back to 1915, with the dissolution plan of the Guggenheim Exploration Company. This concern held large interests in several important copper mines—namely, Nevada, Chino, Ray Consolidated, and Utah—all of which were actively traded on the New York Stock Exchange. When Guggenheim proposed to dissolve and to distribute its various holdings pro rata to its shareholders, I calculated that the current market value of the various pieces together would be appreciably higher than the price of Guggenheim shares. Thus, there was a practically assured arbitrage profit by buying shares of Guggenheim and simultaneously selling shares of Chino, Nevada, Ray, and Utah. The possible risks lay (1) in failure of stockholders to approve the dissolution, (2) litigation or other trouble occasioning a protracted delay, (3) difficulty in maintaining a short position in the shares sold until they were actually distributed to the Guggenheim stockholders.

None of these risks appeared substantial to me. I recommended the operation to the firm, who arbitraged a fair number of shares. I also recommended it to others in the office. I recall that Harold Rouse proposed that I handle the entire operation for him in return for a 20 percent share of the profits. In that way I effected my first arbitrage, an operation which was to prove one of my special fields of study and action. The dissolution plan went through without a hitch; the profit was realized exactly as calculated; and everyone was happy, not least myself.

The years 1915–1916 witnessed the big bull market of World War I; the United States was not yet involved as a participant but benefited hugely from war orders for munitions and supplies from England and France. Common-stock prices—which had collapsed at the outbreak of the war—advanced to unprecedented levels. The firm's business grew. I found myself performing a wide variety of duties, not only as statistician or security analyst and financial-letter writer but also as aide to the cashier in the busy days when he was swamped with work. The cashier in a Wall Street firm was then the head of the back office, in charge of security deliveries, call-loan and term-loan borrowings, and all bookkeeping and records. Our cashier was a Mr. Herd, whom we all regarded as sour, sarcastic, and rather tyrannical. However, I worked smoothly enough with him, and he seemed to appreciate my help. In fact, one day when the firm had granted me one of a succession of $5 and $10 weekly raises—perhaps this time from $25 to $30 per week—he said to me gruffly as he handed me the higher pay, "It's about time you got wise to yourself."

By September 1916 my salary had advanced to $50 per week; I took the plunge and formally asked for Hazel's hand—which was accorded without too much hesitation. In November we had an engagement party, complete with champagne and telegrams. One of these telegrams was not congratulatory but related to my draft status. This became a deeply troubling subject for me, and one which I must set forth as frankly and honestly as I can.

In April 1917 we declared war on Germany. Immediately an officer-candidate training camp was set up at Plattsburg, New York to prepare junior officers for the large armies soon to be created. I decided to apply for admission to the camp, in hopes of achieving a second lieutenant's rank. I armed myself with a formidable array of recommendations—including letters from General Leonard Wood, Colonel Mitchum, the CO of Governors Island, and an especially enthusiastic one from my old dean, Frederick Keppel, now Assistant Secretary of War. With such backing, I felt I was practically assured of admission to the camp, and I made my plans accordingly—much to the dismay of Mother and Hazel. But I was to be disappointed. I soon received a curt note stating that it was army policy to admit only American citizens as officer candidates. Since I was a British subject, they could not consider my application. My sheaf of recommendations was returned therewith.

This presented my family and myself with a serious problem. My two brothers were earning comparatively small sums at the time; I was the big contributor to the family budget. On an officer's salary I could have continued to take care of my mother; on a private's allowance it would have been most difficult to do so. The logical course was for my two brothers to go into the army when the time came, and for me to remain in my job, claiming exemption from the draft as my mother's support. I agreed to this with real reluctance, for I strongly felt the sense of patriotism which makes young men fight for their country. (I considered the United States to be three-quarters my country then, and England to represent the other quarter; both needed my services, and I was loath to fail them.)

Hazel and I had long planned a June wedding. At the time of my application to the officers' training camp, I had indicated to her that the marriage would have to be indefinitely postponed. But when I was not accepted, and it appeared unlikely that I would be drafted, we decided to proceed with the wedding, despite all the uncertainties. It duly took place on June 3, 1917, at the apartment of my bride. That morning I had played some hot tennis matches with Sey Cohn and Archie London on the Hunt's Point Apartment courts, and I took my tennis racket with me as Hazel and I set out for a honeymoon sojourn at Old Point Comfort, Virginia. As we left the house, my mother-in-law remarked that I looked very unbridegroom-like with my slight figure, my ultrasmooth face, and the tennis racket under my arm. There may have been something prophetic in that observation. Many a Sunday morning was to see me, bright and early, on the tennis courts, instead of being better engaged at home in bed.

My brother Leon married his Nellie a few days before my wedding because his bride's family was very Orthodox: they felt that it was improper for a younger brother to take a wife before the older one did. Leon went into the army shortly thereafter, and because of his years of training in the National Guard, he was sent to officers' training camp—his lack of American citizenship being remedied in summary fashion— becoming a second lieutenant in the Quartermaster's Corps. He fought most of the war at the Deaf and Dumb Asylum in

Indianapolis, which had been taken over as an army base. Victor, too, was taken into the army in due course, but the war's end found him also still in America.

Around the end of 1917, I appeared before the draft board in connection with my application for exemption. At that time we were expecting our first child. The board inquired about the circumstances of my marriage and were duly impressed by the telegrams of congratulations on our engagement the previous November. Despite the courtesy shown me by all the board members, I felt myself in a humiliating position. I stated with some fervor that family obligations had led me to claim this embarrassing exemption and that if the board ruled that I was subject to the first or a later draft, I would accept that verdict with some personal sense of relief. However, the exemption was granted.

In the meantime I had commenced a very watered-down military career. A new organization, called the New York State Guard, had been formed to take the place of the National Guard units, all of which had gone off to war. I became a member of Company M of the Twenty-Second Engineers. We drilled in the armory at 168th Street near Broadway, which was the home of the real Twenty-Second Engineers. We had weekly drills, monthly regimental reviews, various special assignments—including acting as Guard of Honor at Mayor Mitchell's funeral. Our colonel was Cornelius Vanderbilt, our honorary bandmaster none other than the famous Victor Herbert. I can still recall the very special lift I experienced as our company marched onto the huge regimental drill floor on the night of our first general review. There was the band blaring full force, while the rotund conductor waved his arms energetically; and there was our colonel, tall, thin and Van Dyck-bearded, watching with a critical eye as each formation marched past him in turn and responded to the command "Eyes Right."

Our company had been organized by a Lieutenant Leisenring, who expected to be promoted to its captaincy as soon as our master roll reached the required minimum of forty men.

This task proved difficult to accomplish, but Leisenring toiled
unceasingly to recruit new members and to encourage those
who had joined. We all grew very fond of him. At last our goal
was reached, and we became a full-fledged company in the
regiment. A few weeks later Leisenring was dead, a victim of
pneumonia. A captain was assigned us from some other regiment. He lacked Leisenring's spark, and our enthusiasm faded
rapidly. It disappeared entirely when the Armistice came in
November 1918, and none of us had any practical reason to
continue our soldiering. Still, I remained for about a year as an
acting corporal, in charge of a squad. I was only "acting"
because I was much too busy getting ahead in the world to be
willing to devote the one evening per week at the armory
required of noncommissioned officers. When my two-year en-
listment expired in 1919, I was glad to receive my honorable
discharge.

That is the inglorious story of my wartime experience. My
failure to join the real army and to risk my neck along with
millions of other youths remained a source of regret and inner
discomfort to me throughout my life. A highly disagreeable
scene comes back to me as I write this. Sometime in 1918,
chiefly because of a financial problem to which I shall refer
later, my mother gave up her apartment and came to live with
us. Hazel and she did not get along at all. Mother was used to
complete independence and unaccountability to anyone; my
wife was energetic, conscientious, and dictatorial. There was
constant tension and a certain number of vocal differences, in
which each sought my support against the other. In the course
of one of these quarrels, I recall seriously announcing my
intention of leaving home and enlisting in the army. Things
quieted down immediately, and my threat was forgotten.
Today my reason tells me that it was better for me and, I hope,
for my country that I wasn't killed fighting in France. But
nonetheless I have an unbanishable feeling that the part I
played in World War I was far from credible.

1916 was the year of the Wilson-Hughes presidential race,

one of the closest in American political history. In those days
the center of election betting was Wall Street itself. Nearly all
those who traded in stocks frankly called themselves "speculators" (whereas today everyone is an "investor"). They did
not draw too fine a distinction between their financial operations and racetrack or other betting. The reader may be surprised to learn that one of the services provided by the New
York Stock Exchange houses was to act as stakeholder for
their customers' election wagers. (This genial practice was
outlawed some years later when the stock exchange went all-
out for respectability.) The fact that I was elected to take
charge of the election bet department of Newburger, Henderson, and Loeb in 1916 will give some hint of the factotum character of my activities with the firm. Nearly all these bets were
made at even money. I had a strongbox full of cash and signed
memoranda. There was plenty of excitement the day after
election, when nobody was sure who had won. In fact, it was
not until the third day that Wilson's reelection was made official in Wall Street, and I was allowed to pay off our clamorous
Democratic bettors.

I come now to the first of two serious setbacks in my financial career. My good friend Algernon Tassin, professor of
English at Columbia College—a confirmed bachelor and, let us
say, a supereconomical person—had saved up a fair-sized sum,
most of which he had invested in a very high-priced and gilt-
edged public-utility stock named American Light & Traction
common. My initial success with the Guggenheim Exploration
dissolution had given me a strong interest in specialized operations of this kind—arbitrages and hedges—and also in the
wider field of undervalued securities, which I staked out as my
own particular domain in Wall Street. Among other things, I
concluded that money could be made both conservatively and
plentifully by buying common stock which analysis showed to
be selling too low and selling against the other common stocks
which a similar analysis indicated to be overpriced.

When I described my ideas to Tassin, and recounted some

successes obtained in minor operations along these lines, he was greatly interested. We worked out an arrangement under which he would supply $10,000 of capital in the form of twenty-five shares of American Light and Traction, then selling at about 400; I would operate the account; and the profits and losses were to be evenly divided between us.

The account prospered famously during the first year or so, and I was able to withdraw several thousand dollars as my share of the profits. With this money I became coproprietor of The Broadway Phonograph Shop, situated at Broadway and 98th Street. My brother Leon had long been anxious to move out of the undistinguished ranks of John Wanamaker clerks. His interest in music, chiefly operatic, and in phonographs had developed through the years. Somehow he learned that a Mr. Irving Zion was prepared to sell out the Broadway business at what seemed a reasonable price. Leon thought this an excellent opportunity, especially since he had an exclusive arrangement to sell Aeolian Vocalion, a record then rather new to the market. Remembering our ill-fated venture into the moving-picture business several years before, I lacked some of my brother's enthusiasm, but nonetheless I was happy to make it possible for him to realize his dream. If I remember rightly, we paid Zion $3,500 for the fixtures and goodwill of the store, and took over the merchandise at its wholesale value. The total investment was about $7,000. For the legal formalities, we called in our old family friend, Alexander Rosenthal—the same who, thirteen years before, had pronounced the oration at the unveiling of Father's monument. When the papers were ready, Alex addressed the gray and hollow-cheeked Irving Zion somewhat as follows: "Now, Mr. Zion, I want you to do something special for these two young men, who evidently have more enthusiasm than business experience. They accepted your selling terms without haggling the way older men would have done. Can't you see your way clear to take $500 off your price, so as to leave them that much badly needed capital in their struggle for success?" Mr. Zion smiled benignly and complimented Mr. Rosenthal on his solicitude for his young clients' interest. But he had made a rock-bottom price, and any reduction now would mean unnecessarily taking bread out of his children's mouths. Alex sighed, and the deal went through as previously arranged.

Our phonograph venture was far from a prodigious success, but we did keep it going for several years before selling out— at a reduced price, of course—to an ex-opera impresario who knew much more about the music business than we did. As far as Aeolian Records was concerned, I found myself in an ironic position, of the sort that was to recur several times in my career. The Aeolian Company had a palace on 42nd Street which we visited in humble awe—either to ask some favor or to defend ourselves against their criticism that we were neglecting their merchandise for the benefit of other labels. Fifteen years later the Aeolian Company itself was in financial straits. My investment fund was then the largest holder of Aeolian's guaranteed 7 percent preferred stock, and I had become chairman of a protective committee to work out the best readjustment plan for our holdings. (We eventually got out of the situation without loss.) I was able to express some sharp words about the way the Aeolian management was running the business—quite a reversal of roles from the one I played in 1917.

World War I naturally played havoc with our phonograph business. When Leon went into the army, his place was taken by Victor, who stayed on until he too was drafted. I used to help out some evenings and Saturdays. Sometimes we had amusing requests. A customer once asked Leon if we had the records of Lucy Gates,[2] and he replied winsomely, "No, but we do have the records of Lucy Marsh." (That moment reminded me of Farmer Barman's farm: two cows—both named Lucy.) Another time, a German fellow came in and asked me for "Games from *Cavalleria Rusticana*." I assured him, most seriously, that they did not play games in that tragic opera. He was understandably miffed at my explanation because what he wanted, of course, was "gems" from the masterpiece.

When Victor left the shop, he was replaced by the brother of one of our closest friends. I knew the young man very slightly, but I had often heard him referred to, and always as a "prince." He was indeed good looking, amiable, and as unbrilliant as most princes are allowed to be. Alas, after only a few months of his incumbency as manager, he managed to embezzle a considerable sum by selling a fair part of our inventory to other shops and pocketing the proceeds. When the inevitable showdown came, he appeared at a conference flanked by a young lady and her father. The girl took me aside and whispered, "Don't worry about that measly thousand dollars. I've made up my mind to marry him, and I'll make my father do whatever is necessary to keep him out of jail." I don't recall how much of our lost capital we recovered, but I'm sure that the "prince" got off easier than he deserved.

Beyond the vicissitudes of Broadway and 98th Street, I was learning the hard way about the pitfalls of Wall Street. Beginning with a so-called peace scare in the fall of 1916, and continuing for a year after we entered the war in 1917, security prices suffered a persistent decline. My operations in the Tassin account were generally in rather obscure issues—such as certain bonds of my old friend, the Missouri, Kansas & Texas railroad, which I had calculated would be worth much more than their market price when the road was reorganized. But their quotation, together with other things we owned, went down in the general weakness; what was worse, the bids tended to disappear. The Tassin account was called on for more margin, but I couldn't replace the money I had withdrawn, since it was all tied up in phonographs, records, and fixtures. It was finally necessary to sell some of the professor's beloved American Light & Traction stock, and that too at a considerable loss. The account remained under margin and was frozen. I had a debt to the account which I could not repay; what was worse was that my management of Tassin's capital had failed abjectly.

I recall spending one of my lunch hours walking around the

financial district in bleak despair. At that moment I thought,
more or less seriously, of suicide. But I returned determined to
tell the facts immediately to my old friend and to work out of
my predicament in the best way possible. Needless to say, the
unsuspecting Algernon was shocked by my recital, but he
proved most understanding and sympathetic. He suggested
that I agree to pay monthly into the account whatever sum I
could afford, until my deficiency was made up. The amount
was fixed at $60 per month. I made these payments for some
two years until an improvement in the general market and in
our own portfolio made further contributions unnecessary.
Fortunately, Tassin retained his confidence in me—though it
would seem undeservedly. In later years I was able to build his
fortune to quite a respectable figure.

It was during this period of relative financial stringency
that Mother came to live with us, and the quarrels with Hazel
began. But my material situation began to improve quite
rapidly, even before my debt to Tassin was fully discharged, so
that before long I was again able to pay for a separate apartment for Mother. She kept her solitary way of life for more
than a quarter-century, until her tragic death. No proposals
from family or cronies that she share living space with others,
no urgings for reasons of health or psychology were able to
budge her from her determination to live alone. Could those
few months of living with a daughter-in-law have really made
such an indelible impression upon her, or did her choice arise
rather from the wellsprings of her character?

During the early years of my marriage, as before, I had sup-
plementary sources of income in addition to my weekly salary.
There was the annual Christmas bonus from my firm. In
December 1914 the stock exchanges had just reopened after
the long shutdown that followed the outbreak of World War I.
No one expected much in the way of Christmas bonuses, and
everywhere they were indeed meager or omitted entirely. As
I left the office that Christmas Eve, an old-time employee who
was with me pointed to an almost deserted bar next to 100

Broadway and said sadly: "You should have seen that joint last Christmas and all the ones before. It was crowded three-deep with us guys spending most of our bonus." I forbore to tell my friend something that A. N. had strictly enjoined me not to communicate to others. He had given me an envelope containing a $100 bill, as a special reward for the great variety of services I had been performing for the firm.

I recall that hundred for a special reason. I used about $20 to buy Mother a small GE electric-grid broiler that she had always wanted to own; the gift surprised and overjoyed her. She used that broiler nearly every day to prepare her little meal of lamb chop or fish, and she was still using it the day she died, thirty years later. Each year thereafter my bonus grew larger, until it ran into the thousands, but I doubt if any of those fat checks brought me quite the thrill I experienced in opening that first envelope.

I gave up my night-school teaching job in 1915, but I continued for some time to tutor the officers' sons on Governors Island—plus other more-or-less successful pedagogy, such as the instruction of a Miss Koues in punctuation. Moreover, my contact with that lady's sister, an editor at *Vogue Magazine*, gave me an opportunity which I mistakenly interpreted as the beginning of a belles lettres career. I was asked to submit a short essay on some literary or humanistic theme, for publication on their editorial page. With great care I produced something called "Saints and Sinners" which raised (once again) the question of why bad people were always so much more interesting in books, and perhaps in life, than good. I drew on my much-prized erudition to refer to the notion of "cher criminel" in Corneille's *Le Cid*—assuming jauntily that all readers of *Vogue* would place the allusion without difficulty. The piece was accepted, and I received a check for $15. I promptly went to work and composed two or three more such gems, but my buoyant hopes were dashed by the announcement that *Vogue* had engaged a literary editor who henceforth would write that monthly piece. For some reason I never tried elsewhere with my stuff, and abandoned literature until my playwright efforts many years later.

Perhaps one reason for this surrender was that I had just embarked on a different sort of composition. With some misgivings, I had submitted to *The Magazine of Wall Street* an article entitled "Bargains in Bonds." This reflected a pretty thorough study of the entire bond list, calling attention to a number of disparities between the prices of comparable issues. Barnard Powers, editor of the magazine, promptly accepted the article—the cash proceeds being $25, I think—and asked for more. From then on I became a frequent, almost regular, contributor to *The Magazine of Wall Street.* I got to know its founder, Richard D. Wyckoff, and its publisher, his wife, the redoubtable Carrie G. Wyckoff. Mrs. Wyckoff had a fascinating career. She started it, I believe, as Mr. Wyckoff's secretary, then became in turn his wife, his business associate, his successor as manager of the magazine, and finally its sole owner. This last stage was the outcome of the breakup of their marriage, accompanied by much legal wrangling and bitter enmity.

Throughout the Wyckoffs' imbroglio I had no difficulty in remaining on the best of terms with both parties. When I think it over, it occurs to me, again, that I was cut out to be everybody's friend but no one's bosom pal or crony. The reasons I have remained in (virtually) everyone's good graces is quite simple, and by no means entirely praiseworthy. I have rarely asked a favor of anyone; I have been most loath to refuse a favor asked by others; and in any exchange or bargain, I have always wanted to feel, and the other to feel also, that I gave more than I got. This may sound like a very altruistic formula, but the truth is that it has been most profitable for me, all things considered. Firstly, I have run my life needing a minimum of help or favors from others. Secondly, I have genuinely enjoyed doing favors for others, short, at least, of being exploited. Lastly, I have been in the fortunate position of never *having* to drive a hard bargain with the other man in order to get what I wanted. I have little capacity for moral indignation over the conduct of others—a trait much to my discredit, I am sure—for I address my critical faculty almost exclusively to my own conduct. Again I have the most selective memory imaginable, the principle of selectivity being to forget as quickly and as completely as possible all disagreeable events, especially how others may have mistreated me.

With these traits, amiable or flabby as the reader may judge, I have acquired friends easily and lost them with the greatest difficulty. The latter has applied not only to men with whom I have found myself at times in fairly serious disagreement over matters of business but also to women with whom I have formed and terminated a romantic attachment. Somehow or other, even that usually fatal denouement has produced at most no more than a temporary estrangement, followed by resumption of friendliness if not amour. A few days ago, for example, my wife Estelle said something to me about one of my former loves and then asked me to guess who it was. Seeking a clue, I innocently inquired, "Is it someone with whom I am on friendly terms?" Estey greeted that question with a burst of laughter: "And with which one of them, may I ask are you *not* on friendly terms?"

The other side of the easy-friendship coin is the lack of what most people would call "depth," but which I prefer to call "total commitment." I'm afraid I have heeded only too well Kipling's counsel: "Let all men count with you but none too much." Naturally, some of my friends are closer than others; but since my high school days I have not had a real pal—one with whom I would readily share all my thoughts, one whose enemies would ipso facto become my enemies, and whose friends would become half-friends and half-rivals of mine. Something within me rebels at the idea of exclusiveness or monopoly in human relations. This makes me, if not a bad friend, at least an impossible crony—and, I must add, a fundamentally unsatisfactory lover.

After the Wyckoffs' split-up, I found myself contributing

both to her magazine and to his investment service. In the latter case, I wrote up a monthly suggestion of a "special situation" or bargain issue. Twice Mrs. Wyckoff endeavored to persuade me to leave my firm and join her staff. The first offer I refused without much internal struggle. The second offer, however, was that of the chief editorship of *The Magazine of Wall Street*, with a large salary and a good share of the profits. I was strongly tempted to accept this flattering offer, but A. N. talked me out of it. It was then, I think, that he promised me a junior partnership in the firm, which took effect in 1920.

My connection with the Wyckoffs had a cardinal bearing on the career of my brother Victor. By 1920, he had been at loose ends for quite a while; though an excellent salesman almost from birth, the companies he had worked for always seemed to fail. I asked Mrs. Wyckoff to give him something to do. She took him on a trial basis and had him peddle some sort of dividend calculator advertising the magazine to the brokerage houses. He did so well at that unpromising assignment that he was taken into the advertising department. There his career was nothing short of spectacular. He soon became advertising manager, replacing the former head—who became his assistant. With the bull market of the 1920s the circulation of *The Magazine of Wall Street* multiplied, and its advertising revenues—having expanded rapidly under Victor's energetic and resourceful handling—built up the department's revenue to a fabulous figure, and earned a great deal of money for himself. But alas! troubles developed. I think that Mrs. W. either had amorous designs upon my brother or she wanted him to marry her younger sister (or both). But Victor, after some complicated romances of his own, developed a chaste passion for a beautiful and lively eighteen-year-old named Sylvia Goodman, whom he very promptly married. That was in 1928. It appears that Mrs. W. never forgave him that heinous crime. He quit his lucrative and otherwise congenial post with the magazine and entered the investment banking business. That move came at the worst of all possible times, and it embarked my brother on a career not at all suited to his genuine but quite special talents of resourceful salesmanship. It took Victor nearly twenty years, and much frustration and heartbreak, to get back on the right track. His final decade of employment was not nearly as remunerative as his job of the 1920s, but it gave him the right kind of challenge and security.

My sources of income included special operations of the arbitrage type, as well as the general sharing of the Tassin account results. Until the disastrous fall in the latter, in 1918, I considered myself quite a financial success and developed a taste for the enjoyments it made possible. As early as 1915 I became the owner of an automobile, jointly with my cousin Lou. It was the new Model A Ford, just succeeding Ford's ubiquitous and changeless Model T. In the early months of ownership a crowd used to collect about the car to admire its handsome new lines—no small source of pride to the young driver. Louie, very engineering-minded, had prepared both of us for the responsibilities of ownership by buying an instruction kit, explaining the mechanical principles of the engine, transmission and so on, together with a cardboard model with moving parts. We thus became automobile experts before ever laying hand on throttle. (Yes, the autos of those days were accelerated by a hand throttle, like a locomotive, instead of a pedal control.)

Learning to drive was quite a different matter in the New York of 1915 than it is today. Ford offered free instruction to those who bought his cars. So I went down to the sales office, somewhere in the Fifties on Broadway, plunked down my $395 for a shiny new touring car, and was promptly driven over to West Street for my driving lesson. First I had to learn how to crank the car, no easy task for the beginner. Then the salesman showed me how to deal, more or less simultaneously, with the three pedals (clutch, brake, and emergency brake), the four positions of the gear shift, the spark advancer and retarder near the steering column, and the hand throttle. I had also to be ready to blow the little horn by squeezing the rubber bulb behind it. Each time I stalled the car during my first lesson—

say six times—he would say disgustedly, "Take all your feet off the pedals," and I would try again. These operations took place within about ten blocks up and down West Street, which then boasted no West Side Highway above it, nor any large amount of traffic. At the end of half an hour, he said I would do. I drove him back to his salesroom, and then proceeded, with no little trepidation, to negotiate the perilous passage from the center of Manhattan to my Hunt's Point Apartments home in the Bronx. Somehow I got safely home.

"How about your examination for a driver's license?" you may ask. Believe it or not, in those days just owning a car was enough. The law assumed that once you owned a car, you knew how to drive, as a matter of course. Only nonowners, therefore, needed a special driver's license, for which they took a test.

My joint ownership of the car with Louis worked out very smoothly, despite numerous warnings I had received against so rash a project. Our arrangement was the height of simplicity; each of us controlled the machine on alternate days; expenses of all kinds—which did not include the luxury of insurance—were divided equally. A few times we traded days, but as far as I can recall we never had a dispute over the car.

It is a tradition in our family that I am, and always have been, a poor driver. The fault is generously laid to my incorrigible absentmindedness, rather than to any lack of basic competence. Yet in my defense I protest that, in forty-five years of driving, I have never caused the smallest injury to anyone, never damaged another car beyond a fender scratch, and caused no greater damage to my own car than a broken windshield—which in those remote and happier days cost all of $8 to replace.

But you, my critics, so near and dear to me by blood or marriage, what have you done to my cars? Leon and Victor, do you recall the day when you slunk into my office—one of you carrying a small valise—and glumly informed me that my car had accidentally hit a telegraph pole, that both of you had miracu-

Ben's father, Isaac Grossbaum, 1896.

Ben's mother, Dora Grossbaum (later, Dorothy Graham) with her three sons — Victor, Leon, and Ben — circa 1896.

Ben at age two, with his older brothers Leon and Victor, circa 1898.

Ben with son Newton, and holding infant son Benjamin Jr., 1945.

Ben, son Benjamin Jr. ("Buz"), and third wife Estelle, Central Park, New York City, 1947.

Farewell dinner for Ben's son Newton, about to leave for the army, 1953. Left to right, daughter Marjorie, her husband Irving Janis, daughter Winni, daughter Elaine, her husband Daniel Bell, wife Estelle, son Newton, Ben, Walton's wife, nephew Walton Graham, first wife Hazel, her husband Arthur Greenwald, Rose Kraus, Empire Room, Waldorf Astoria, New York City.

Daughter Winni and Ben at Winni's wedding, 1956.

Ben and wife Estelle in Greece, at the Acropolis, 1960.

Ben and Benjamin Jr., Stratford, England, 1960.

Ben and brother Victor with Rev. and Mrs. William Barber at dedication of the Dorothy Graham Memorial Building of the Mount Sinai Baptist Church, Bridgeport, CT, 1965. The Graham brothers donated money for the building as a memorial to their mother.

Ben with son-in-law Irving Janis, daughter Marjorie's husband, in Cezanne's studio, Aix-en-Provence, France, 1969.

Ben at his desk in La Jolla, CA, 1976.

Portrait of Ben in his eighties.

lously escaped injury, but that the auto had been smashed to bits? As I recall it, my only reply was to ask whether you had brought me the bits in your valise. And, Estey, you paragon of drivers and my severest critic, was it not you who blithely turned up Park Avenue in the wrong direction and ran into a taxicab transporting a pregnant woman to the hospital? (Our Government Employees Insurance Company policy gamely took care of the whole matter, so I never knew the ultimate cost.) And Hazel, remember that dreadful day in 1919 in Hewlett, Long Island, when you ran our Ford smack into the Maxwell, propelling Mother through the door with our infant Newton in her arms? (Most luckily again, no bodily damage.) The owner of the Maxwell sent me a bill for $150 for repairs. You insisted that was an outrage; all you had done was to smash his running board, and the car was a jalopy of most ancient vintage. I duly wrote the man offering him a generous $75. He came to our summer place in Hewlett, one rainy night, breathing fire and refusing to accept a dollar less than $150. I raised my offer to $100 to end the matter. He rushed out into the pouring rain, brandishing his umbrella and shouting that we would have to deal with his lawyer. But we never saw or heard from him again. A far as we were concerned, he vanished into thin air—and we never bothered to solve the mystery.

Our own car suffered a damaged front axle—which damage mutely but irrefutably fixed the blame for the accident. Our ambitions leaned towards a new Chevrolet, then selling at the astronomical price of $720 because of post-World-War-I inflation. To make his sale, the local dealer undertook to have our car repaired and to sell it for $250, less his repair costs, provided we paid in full for the Chevrolet now. I had enough business sense to reduce the agreement to writing, which he signed. He fixed up our car, but couldn't find a buyer for it. Just before we returned to New York, I marched determinedly into his place, flourishing the document and demanding either the cash or at least the return of my car. He threw

up his hands and let me drive the Ford home. When we got it
to Washington Heights, we promptly found a neighbor who
bought it gladly for $300. We thus emerged scot-free, and bet-
ter, from what seemed like a nasty situation.

But the real reason I recount this story is because of the
love affair that developed between our buyer and his—once
our late-lamented—automobile. Like most owners of the day,
he parked the machine in the street at our corner. He was a
dentist, and between patients he would dash down and dust off
the car with a chamois rag, polish it spick and span, wash the
windshield and whatnot. As we passed this touching scene, it
was hard to repress a chuckle as we recalled the sorry estate
of his Rosinante in a Hewlett garage not so many weeks
before.

CHAPTER NINE

The Beginnings of Real Success

B etween 1919 and 1929 my upward progress in Wall Street was rapid, even spectacular. It was an exhilarating period, marked by many financial triumphs, a continuous advance in my standard of living, a widening and deepening of my knowledge of life's material and intellectual enjoyments, and a feeling of great satisfaction about my position in the world and the esteem of my fellow men. But there were developments also on the debit side. The loss of my first-born son in 1927 was a bitter blow, the more staggering perhaps because it came so suddenly in the midst of dazzling prosperity. There were also strains developing in my marriage, which neither Hazel nor I—as brilliant as we considered ourselves—had enough insight to recognize and act upon in time. I was too ready to accept materialistic success as the aim and goal of life and to forget about idealistic achievements.

At the beginning of 1920, I was made a junior partner in the firm of Newburger, Henderson, and Loeb, members of the New York Stock Exchange, a fact which was duly announced in newspaper advertisements. The new arrangement gave me—in addition to my salary—an interest of 2½ percent in the annual profits, without liability for any losses. The same promotion was conferred on Dan Loeb and Harold Rouse, who were my seniors in employment by two years. Mr. A. N. informed me that my divvy was a half-percent higher than Loeb's and Rouse's but added that I was not to divulge this fact to them. My share in the profits ran about $5,000 per annum during the four years that I enjoyed it.

That year I had my Japanese bond experience, a venture which assigned me a rather special position in Wall Street. One of my young friends, Lou Berall, had given up schoolteaching for a financial career and was working for Bonright & Company, an important bond house. We went to lunch from time to time, and on one occasion he brought along an exceedingly young Japanese named Junkichi Miki. This lively fellow had come to America as representative of a large Japanese banking firm which had thought of selling American bond issues in Japan. Bonright & Company had undertaken to train him in American investment methods, hoping thus to find an outlet in Japan for some of their merchandise.

But things developed in an entirely different direction. Miki or his superiors soon discovered that large profits could be made by buying up various issues of Japanese government bonds which had been placed in various countries abroad during the Russo-Japanese War of 1906 and reselling them to investors in Japan. Their attractiveness to Japanese buyers grew out of postwar discrepancies in foreign exchange rates, on the one hand, and the right of investors to demand payment of principal and interest in fixed amounts of yen, on the other. The Japanese asked Bonright to cooperate with them in acquiring and importing these bonds in quantities into Japan, but the American firm was too busy with its own underwriting operations to take much interest.

At my luncheon with Berall and Miki, the young Japanese asked me whether our firm had European connections and other facilities to do this reacquisition business on a large scale. Fortunately, I could say we had and could offer him comprehensive and energetic service. After we had carried out one or two trial orders to his satisfaction, Miki was ready to make the big deal. He agreed to use our services exclusively for large-scale purchases, and we agreed to buy for no one but his firm, the Fujimoto Bill Broker Bank of Osaka. Bonds were to be shipped to Japan, draft attached. We were to receive a commission of 2 percent of each purchase, out of which we paid all expenses, including cable and shipping charges.

The business ran into the millions. We established good contacts with brokerage firms in London, Paris, and Amsterdam, which had been centers for the original distribution of the bonds. Because of the discounts of the franc against the yen, the bonds sold in Paris at enormous premiums over their par value and at the same time could be bought by the Japanese investor at a large discount, even after allowing for big brokerage expenses.

One aspect of this business made me rather unpopular in our back office. For some reason (which I have forgotten), a large portion of these bonds were first sold in America in $100 denominations, instead of the customary $1,000 or less frequent $500 pieces. The same had been true of the issues placed in Paris and London. These small pieces were considered a nuisance and sold at a substantial discount in the Western markets, but there was no prejudice against them in Japan. Miki was glad to buy them up at the cheaper price. As a result our office was constantly inundated with reams and reams of these bulky documents of small unit value. Our typical single purchase would be for $100,000 face amount, which would usually entail 1,000 separate bonds, each of which had not only to be counted but also inspected for possibly missing interest coupons.

Since we usually had a quantity of these bonds on hand waiting to be made up into a large shipment, we acquired a special safe deposit box for them. To our runners, who had to carry this heavy box to and from safe deposit vaults each day,

it was known, not too favorably, as the Ben Graham box. However, the business made millions and proved extremely profitable to the firm; our commissions must certainly have
exceeded $100,000. After about two years Miki set up his own
office, acquiring the bonds directly himself—a move which we
had regarded as inevitable and did not resent. In the meantime we had become extremely well known in Japanese financial circles. Two of their stock exchanges sent a delegation to
study our brokerage methods and techniques, with the view to
imitating them in Tokyo and Osaka. Miki brought them in to
see me; they picked my brains for a long time and departed
with a complete set of our numerous printed forms. Not long
thereafter they published a long report in Japanese on the
New York stock market, a copy of which was sent to me. I was
both startled and gratified to observe that after every few
pages there was inserted a reproduction of one of our forms
each bearing the name Newburger, Henderson, and Loeb in
our conspicuous type.

As we wound up business with the Fujimoto Bank, we
relaxed the exclusive clause of the arrangement, and each side
did business with other houses. We bought bonds on cabled
instruction from two other Japanese banking firms. These
cables used a five-letter code, which economized greatly on toll
charges. Despite many possibilities of ambiguity and error in
code messages, especially when one of the parties thinks in
Japanese, this business ran with remarkable smoothness for a
two-year period. We did, however, have one untoward incident
which illustrates the special efforts made by the Japanese to
build confidence in their business honesty and reliability. (Ori-
ental nations were then suspected of being crafty and double-
dealing.)

On a large order from a Tokyo banking firm, we bought several hundred thousand bonds, which we duly reported. But
they sent us a cable that read "Cancel order. Confirm." We
canceled the balance of the order, cabled back "Order canceled," and proceeded to ship the bonds they had bought.

When the bonds arrived in Tokyo a month later—there was no airmail in those days—our Tokyo friends were most unpleasantly surprised. They insisted that this purchase had been canceled and they were not responsible for it. We, of course, claimed that in Wall Street a "cancel order" refers only to an unexecuted order, and they should have cabled us "cancel purchase" (though it was too late to do that). It was stupid of me not to have made the point clearly in my cable.

The market had had a sinking spell during the shipment period, and a loss of several thousands had accrued. We took the matter up with the Yokohama Specie Bank in New York, which was a Japanese government agency and the official representative of their financial community. After a relatively short delay, they paid us in full for the bonds—although they could very well have suggested that, under the somewhat ambiguous circumstances, both parties divide the loss.

Miki and I became good friends. From time to time he came to our house and seemed to enjoy our Jewish cooking. In return he took me to a sumptuous dinner at the Nippon Club near Columbia University, where I had my first taste of Japanese food. To my own amazement, I found myself swallowing varieties of raw fish dipped in numerous sauces. But sitting on the floor for two hours proved an uncomfortable experience.

Miki introduced me to various Japanese VIPs from time to time, most of them figures in the financial world. One day he asked me if he could bring his friend, Mr. Kwagai, to lunch. Mr. Kwagai proved to be a handsome, stocky, amiable young man. During the meal we talked about Wall Street and miscellaneous matters. When we were leaving, Miki said with his invariable smile, "Mr. Graham, perhaps you would like to see Mr. Kwagai play at Forest Hills some day next week. If so I shall be glad to get you a ticket." Only then did I realize that I had been lunching with the famous Japanese tennis player who had a good chance to win the American singles championship. And we hadn't spoken a word about tennis, my favorite sport! How dumb or unlucky can a fellow be?

Thirty-five years later I visited Japan and renewed my friendship with Junkichi Miki. After his return to Japan, he had become an official of the Osaka Stock Exchange, and then a professor of finance at Kobe University. He took me to visit the Osaka Exchange and its officials. I was ushered into their directors' room where a large group were seated. The introductions completed, Miki said blandly to me, "And now, Mr. Graham, will you kindly give this assemblage a forty-minute talk on the principles of security analysis? I shall be glad to translate what you say." This was certainly more than I had bargained for, but I did the best I could under the circumstances. At the end of each sentence or two, Professor Miki unhesitatingly translated my highly technical language into Japanese, and there would be a nodding of comprehending heads around the room.

During this renewal of friendship with Miki, I was taken to the best Osaka restaurants and introduced to that wonderful institution, the Geisha girl. In consideration of its numerous American guests, one of the restaurants had a sort of well dug under the low table. In this way one could sit on the floor with one's legs hanging down, a much more comfortable arrangement for Westerners than the other. The Geishas were beautiful, gorgeously dressed, highly accomplished in song and dance and on the tamisen and continuously attentive to their patrons during the long meal. They had a rather limited knowledge of American dances, but mine graciously allowed me to teach her an additional step or two. We played a few harmless games and altogether had a delightful time. Will it ever be possible for us to introduce this completely moral institution into America for the delectation of the tired or not-so-tired businessman and bon vivant by persuading oversuspicious wives that such an amenity would actually contribute to happiness in marriage?

Back to 1920: Miki came to our house one evening asking to be taught how to play poker. I instructed him according to Hoyle, and he carefully wrote down the values of the various hands in a little notebook. After some rounds of play, during which he sedulously compared his hands with his notebook, he declared himself satisfied and ready to play with his friends. A few days later I asked him how he had made out. "Ah, Mr. Graham," shaking his head sadly, "You were a very imperfect instructor. I lost a lot of money to my friends." "My goodness," I replied, "what did I tell you that was wrong?" "You didn't tell me anything wrong. You just forgot to tell me about bluff. They bluffed me all night long, and when the game was over, they never stopped teasing me about it." I felt so ashamed of my inexcusable omission that I even offered to make up his losses, but he refused with true Japanese dignity.

I was in complete charge of the "statistical" department at N.H.&L., which now bears the more respectable title of "research" or "investment research." My assistant was a former college mate, Leo Stern, about two years my junior. When I left, Leo took over most of my functions; in due course he became junior partner, full partner, and finally one of two senior partners—the other being Lester Newburger, the youngest of the four brothers I had worked under. Leo and I handled all inquiries, whether in person or by mail, about security lists or individual issues. From time to time we issued circulars which analyzed one or more securities in considerable detail. These generally included recommendations to buy a favored issue or to switch from a less to a more attractive security. For example, we recommended in 1921 that holders of U.S. Victory 4¾s, due in two years and selling at 97¾, should exchange them for the longer-term U.S. 4¼s which could be had for a lower price, around 87½. It was our view—correct, as it turned out—that the then high interest rates would subside and that the long-term governments would advance to par or better, while the short-term ones had very limited possibilities of gain. Our circular was advertised in the newspapers under the title "Memorandum to Holders of Victory Bonds." Promptly after it appeared, the New York Stock Exchange asked to see a copy. There had been an unwritten but stringent rule prohibiting stock exchange mem-

bers from recommending switches out of government bonds
into other securities. But they had no criticism to make of our
proposal, which was not only unobjectionable from the patriotic angle but proved quite profitable to those who adopted it.

Another circular, not so smart, was of a routine variety, carrying a detailed comparison of all the listed tire and rubber
stocks. On the basis of the statistical record, we observed that
the shares of Ajax Tire appeared most attractive. A few days
later a tall, handsome gentleman strode into our office, identified himself as Horace de Lisser, president of Ajax Tire, and
demanded to see the author of the circular. He was the more
noticeable figure because he was wearing a straw hat in the
midst of winter—one of his several idiosyncracies. As my
cousin Miriam, then my secretary, delights to tell the story,
Horace de Lisser was directed towards our department, found
me doing something just outside my office, and in an imperious
voice commanded: "Boy, take me in to see Mr. Graham." His
error in taking me for an office boy may have been due in good
part to myopia but also to the fact that I was young for my
advanced position and looked quite a bit younger. (This impression persisted for years and gave rise to a variety of incidents.) I don't know which of us was the more nonplussed—he
to see a young kid analyzing his industry, or I to be confronted
by the strange man with a straw hat. The interview was
rather strained. A number of years later I came to regret that
circular and to wish I had visited Mr. de Lisser before I had
published it. Ajax Tire flourished only a little while and then
declined into bankruptcy.

One of the most important and rewarding friendships of my
life grew out of one of my analytical circulars and in quite
unexpected fashion. In 1919, I was working on a detailed comparison of two railroads—the Chicago, Milwaukee, & St. Paul
Railroad and the St. Louis & Southwestern Railroad. Let me
digress for a moment about nomenclature. Railroads were
referred to in our business by special names. When I was just
starting at the firm, I heard Murphy, our senior order clerk,

refer to something as "shortstop." I thought he was saying "short stock," and I kept wondering how anyone could buy a hundred shares of "short stock," but I didn't dare to ask Murph for an explanation. He was actually referring to St. Louis & Southwestern Railroad, whose ticker-tape abbreviation was "SS." As for the Chicago, Milwaukee, & St. Paul, the railway was generally known as the "Milwaukee," but not on the stock exchange, where the nickname was based on the ticker abbreviations. The most amusing example was the Atchison, Topeka, & Santa Fe. No railroadman or customer would ever dream of calling it anything but the Santa Fe. But for countless years its ticker symbol was ATCH, and so it was always called "Atchison" or "Atch" in Wall Street. For some mysterious reason, the Dutch stock exchange dubbed it "Topeka." So this mighty railroad was known in three different markets by each of the three cities in its title.

Before I entered Wall Street, there had been both a preferred and common stock of the Northern Pacific Railroad, and they had been known to all the financial world, respectively, as "Big Nipper" and "Little Nipper." The preferred had been retired, as an aftermath of the famous Northern Pacific corner and panic of 1901, but thirteen years later I often heard people referring to the common stock as "Little Nipper." A much more harmful instance of this penchant for special nomenclature concerned the Great Northern Railway, the neighbor, rival, and one-time partner of Northern Pacific. As a result of its financial maneuvers, its own common stock had been retired, and its original preferred took the place of the common, being in every way equivalent to any other common stock. Yet for countless years it bore both the official and unofficial title of "Great Northern Preferred"; it was listed by Wall Street houses among the railroad preferred issues for investment; and it was naturally thought by most Wall Street amateurs to have the special protection of a preferred stock. It took some years before this inexcusable misbranding was corrected by the New York Stock Exchange.

Then there was the metamorphosis of the term "Big Steel." When U.S. Steel started its fluctuating career on the stock exchange in 1901, the higher-priced preferred was immediately dubbed "Big Steel," and the extremely speculative junior issue became known as "Little Steel"—as in the case of Big and Little Nipper. Eventually the price of Steel common passed that of the preferred, something that few Wall Streeters of 1901 would have predicted, and the old nicknames fell into disfavor. One day I was startled to hear an analyst use the term "Big Steel," but to find out that he was referring to U.S. Steel *common*. It had become "Big Steel" because its company was the largest. No doubt a long essay could be written about the vicissitudes of Wall Street nicknames.

To get back to the story: my comparative analysis of the Milwaukee and SS showed quite convincingly that SS common and preferred were more attractive buys than the correspondingly priced issues of the Milwaukee. Indeed, the Milwaukee appeared in a highly unfavorable light, so I felt it would be both fair and prudent to submit my findings to an officer of the company before publishing the circular. I went to see the financial vice-president of Milwaukee, Mr. Robert J. Marony, who had his office at 42 Broadway. He was surprisingly young for a railroad vice-president, only about forty or so, a little Irishman with a lively intelligent glance. With some embarrassment I told him why I had come. He looked over my material rather rapidly, then handed it back to me, saying: "I don't find anything to quarrel with in either your facts or your conclusions. I wish our showing was a better one, but it isn't, and that's that." Then he asked me some questions about my work in general. Soon we were talking about arbitrage, which was becoming one of my specialties, and in which he too was quite knowledgeable. I mentioned an interesting situation which was new to him. He listened intently to my explanation and then gave me an order to do a thousand shares for him. This was the least likely outcome that could have been predicted for my visit to the Chicago, Milwaukee, & St. Paul office.

That strange episode was the beginning of a business and personal association which has lasted until the present day (June 1960). Bob Marony became an investor in the Benjamin Graham Joint Account, then a substantial stockholder and director of Graham-Newman Corporation from its inception to its dissolution, a member of various protective committees which we organized, and finally a director with me of the fabulously successful Government Employee Insurance Group (GEICO). We have been good friends through prosperous and tough times. Once he gave me part of a profit on a successful deal because he thought I needed the money to help me out of personal financial difficulties. Some years before that he, his wife, Beatrice, and his daughter Marjorie, were my guests on Dr. Herman Baruch's yacht, the *Reposo*, which the amiable physician-turned-stockholder had lent me. Not so long after that happy trip, Bob and Bea were to lose their only child under especially tragic circumstances. The perennially youthful Marony suffered a stroke some years ago while in our office, and he has never recovered full control over his speech.

In these thirty-eight years of close association, Bob and I have never had a disagreement over anything. This is a remarkable record, considering the financial vicissitudes we went through together, the numerous important matters on which difficult decisions had to be made, the necessity for reaching agreement on such ticklish matters as division of profits and other forms of compensation, and, finally, the not unnatural tendency of Marony to get his Irish up from time to time—but always against someone other than me. Yet I must confess, in honesty and with regret, that even Bob, whom I have liked as much as any man on earth, was never a pal or crony. Perhaps I can sum it up in a single phrase: we never hung out together. What a simple, easy thing that seems to be for some people—and how elusive I have always found it!

I made a literary effort on behalf of N.H.&L., a series of three little pamphlets, bearing the title "Lessons for Investors." At the cocky age of twenty-five, I didn't realize the pretentiousness of that title nor my arrogance in presuming to instruct an investment public that averaged at least twice my age. Yet I believe that what I said made good sense. I am particularly proud of my strong argument for the purchase of sound common stocks at reasonable prices. Its crux was the then revolutionary statement that "if a common stock is a good investment, it is also an attractive speculation." For, said I, if it gives the investor full value for his money, if its market value is substantially less than its intrinsic value, it should also have excellent prospects for an advance in price. This was indeed a sound conclusion so long as the huge general public didn't act upon it. When that happened, several years later in the great bull market of the 1920s, investors forgot all about the safeguard of a responsible price and thus turned what formerly were sound investments into the most exaggerated and dangerous speculations.

My work as security analyst was by no means the major part of my job as junior partner. In addition, I handled all the operations of the firm for its own account (these being limited to arbitrage and hedging); I was the tax expert; I did the over-the-counter trading (including the Japanese bond operation); I was in charge of insuring the efficiency of the office systems; and, of course, I had a growing number of customers of various kinds who paid substantial commissions to the firm.

After World War I, U.S. tax laws and regulations—blessedly simple before—became increasingly complicated as well as onerous. I studied the subject quite thoroughly because of its bearing on the earnings of the corporations I was analyzing. The fact that I knew a little more than other people soon made me an expert, and I earned modest fees by making out tax returns for several of our customers. Towards the end of 1920 many of these suffered substantial paper losses on securities, while at the same time finding themselves subject to large taxes on their regular income. Like human beings everywhere, they were reluctant to sell those securities, believing that they would come back. I pointed out, citing chapter and verse from the income tax law, that such stocks could be sold, to establish the loss, and immediately bought back to reinstate the position. The cost of the operation would be limited to commissions and transfer tax. When the word got out, we received a large number of these lucrative "sell and buy" orders. I flatter myself that we were the first firm to execute such orders on the New York Stock Exchange, but before the end of the year everyone was doing it. (The next year, I think, Congress ended that picnic by requiring a thirty-day interval between sale and repurchase.)

My most ambitious research into the tax law and its consequences had to do with a calculation of the then jealously guarded goodwill or "water" component in corporate balance sheets. The excess-profits tax of 1917 allowed a credit of certain percentages on tangible invested capital, plus minor allowance for the intangible items in the balance sheet—goodwill, patents, and so on. (Patents were almost always lumped together with the tangibles in the published "property account.") By a series of formulas I was able to work back from the three known items—taxes reserved or paid, income before tax, and property account—to estimate how much of the property account was in the goodwill category. I incorporated my findings in an article published in *The Magazine of Wall Street*. Barnard Powers, the editor, told me: "Ben, neither I nor anyone else around here can make head or tail of your formulas. It looks as if you've done the whole thing with mirrors. But I've enough confidence in you to publish the article anyway." Given the many possibilities of error arising from misleading published figures, my computation proved later to have been quite accurate. It was only many years later that companies first revealed and then wrote off the water in their capital structures. By that time, however, the asset values had become so unimportant as against the earnings and growth of earnings that these disclosures had no effect upon the financial community.

I might add that my computations reveal that all the 500

million par value of U.S. Steel's common stock, and even a good part of its 360 million of preferred stock, had originally been nothing but water. In a subsequent article, I showed, by similar calculation, that U.S. Steel must have overestimated and overpayed its taxes for the year 1918. This deduction proved to be correct, and U.S. Steel secured a considerable refund from the government.

Although I never made a special effort to secure stock or bond customers for the firm, it was inevitable that a number of connections should develop through the years. Some of these were accounts that I actually managed; they were pretty well restricted to my special field of arbitrage and hedging. The Tassin account continued as one of these. In others, I recall, I assumed no share of losses but received 25 percent of the cumulative net profit. One of these was opened by my old public school chum, Sydney Rogow. My standard procedure was to buy convertible bonds around par and to sell calls against them on the related common stock; or else—in a more elaborate variant—sell the common stock short and sell puts against our short position. The amount received in these puts and calls was substantial and in effect guaranteed us a satisfactory profit on the whole deal, regardless of whether the stock advanced, declined, or stood still. I spare the reader a technical explanation of the complicated business, but it was as successful as it was ingenious.

We had one such elaborate operation going in Pierce Oil bonds in 1919, selling puts against our short position. The market went down; the puts were exercised in part; but a two-hundred share put, worth about $400, was not presented when it expired. It did come in a day late. "Doc" Dougherty from the back office came to me and said the other firm had overlooked the matter and was asking whether the customer would accept it now. I asked Doc what was generally done in cases like that. "Oh," he said, "anyone would be a damn fool who took in a put or call when he didn't have to." Not wishing to be thought a d.f., I said no on behalf of my customer. When I reported this minor windfall to Syd, he suggested that we spend the money by going to Atlantic City together that weekend (with our wives, of course). This we did, staying at the best hotel, spending money with most unaccustomed lavishness, and having a wonderful time. I tell the story to point up an anomaly that has impressed me many times during my life. Businessmen usually have one set of values for their business operations and a much reduced set for their private expenditures. A hundred dollars is a minor matter in a day's business; but at home, it may assume major proportions and cause much dispute between husband and wife. This divergence is natural enough psychologically and is probably necessary to avoid an unsound family budget, but it does give businessmen a sort of dual personality in money matters. In the Atlantic City incident, the special quality and richness of the experience lay precisely in our being able, for this once, to transfer a given sum of money—modest enough—directly from our financial to our private lives.

Uncle Maurice Gerard opened a personal account with me in 1918 which was destined to be crucial for me. It started with a few thousand dollars and proceeded quite satisfactorily. Then, in 1920, he came to me with a startling proposal. He had just finished a job as efficiency expert for General Motors, for which he had received a fee of $20,000. He wanted to add all this money to his account, to retire from his profession, and to live on the profits that I—or perhaps he said "he and I"— would make from his capital. He warned me that since I would now be handling a large fund, I must work on a grander scale than heretofore. I'm sure I did not encourage my uncle in what appeared to me to be a dangerous move, but I accepted the trust. From then on he came regularly to our boardroom and watched the market. He never did any trading himself, nor can I remember his interfering in any way with my conduct of the account. This is extraordinary (if my memory is accurate), for he was by nature a most interfering man.

For the next ten years his decision appeared entirely justi-

fied. Despite monthly withdrawals for living expenses his capital increased to a handsome total. The story after 1929 was
different and most depressing. He died in the thirties, when
the recovery of all our fortunes was just underway. Nonetheless he left an estate sufficient to cause major disputes and
hard feelings between his widow and the children of his first
marriage. As arbitrator, I was able to settle the dispute, but
not the hard feelings.

Another client was a schoolmate of mine, Douglas Newman. His account was speculative, and I assumed no advisory
responsibility. It seemed he received his market tips from a
big operator. In due course this operator started to trade with
us, and I witnessed some real speculation. Two stocks he
favored were Mexican Petroleum and Pan American
Petroleum, among the most active and volatile performers on
'Change. He traded in good sized blocks, on both sides of the
market. He was always making or losing what seemed huge
sums without turning a hair. He was a born gambler, with all
the attractive features of a gambler's temperament. He went
broke in the decline of 1920 to 1921, and I never saw him
again.

In 1919 we enjoyed a quite typical bull market, marked by
callous manipulation on the part of insiders, and the usual combination of greed, ignorance, and childish enthusiasm on the
part of the public. Some fifteen years later, during my play-
writing period, I decided to write a drama about Wall Street.
The spectacular and tragic events of 1929 to 1932 were then
fresh in mind, but I rejected that period as too extreme to
meet the standards of art. Instead, I went back to my recollections of 1919 to 1921. I included a number of characters I had
observed in our own boardroom, for example, the monomania-
cal chemist, Riddle, whose only interest was the stock of
American Coal Products, which was going to make him a millionaire, and the Brothers Friedman, shoe store owners, who
had come into our office first to buy the most conservative
bonds available, then to invest cautiously in odd lots of the

"best stocks," and who ended by losing their business and everything else in wild speculations.

Of course, I put myself into the play as hero, the bright young man who profits from someone else's flagrant manipulation without running any financial risks. I conveyed this theme through a plot concerning the transformation of a few small Pittsburgh concerns into a hugely inflated transcontinental oil company. I called the play "Angry Flood"—after the lines from *Julius Caesar:*

> Dar'st thou, Cassius, now
> Leap in with me into this angry flood?

It was never produced, and I do not know where the script is now. It doubtless deserves its oblivion.

Actually, I came through the dangerous period of 1919 to 1921 extremely well. Having learned much from my shattering experience with the Tassin account in 1917, I did not let the angry flood engulf me. My operations were nearly all arbitrage and hedging, affording limited but satisfactory profits, and protecting me against serious loss. A typical operation: one of the speculative favorites of the time was Consolidated Textile, a recent conglomeration of rather second-rate cotton mills. I had bought some of their convertible 7 percent bonds, considering them sufficiently safe, and later, as the common stock advanced, I sold the corresponding amount of shares at prices which assured me a good gain, whatever happened thereafter. Dan Loeb was an enthusiastic bull on the stock and carried many thousands of shares in his customers' accounts. I remember suggesting to him that he replace the stock with the 7 percent bonds, pointing out that he would have virtually the same chance of profit, would run much smaller risks of loss, and would have a better income return into the bargain. To this Dan replied that his customers didn't want to bother with convertible bonds, that they liked to see their stock appearing constantly "on the tape" and that it wasn't necessary to pay the extra point or so for the added safety of the bonds because a big further rise in the stock was absolutely certain. In a year's time the stock had fallen from 70 to 20, while the 7 percent bonds were actually refinanced and paid off at a premium above par.

It's not undue modesty to say that I had become something of a smart cookie in my particular field. Still, I was capable of doing some foolish things in other areas of Wall Street. One day, when I was chatting with Barnard Powers about an article for *The Magazine of Wall Street*, he told me he was thinking of retiring soon, as he had just made a killing in a stock called Ertel Oil. A close friend had invited him in on the ground floor. He had been part of the original group which had bought the shares at $3. A few days later trading had begun on the Curb Market at $10. The syndicate manager had sold out all the participants' stock at this figure, and Powers had just received a large check as his share of the profit. I was unduly impressed by this story and may have uttered some words of envy. Powers good-naturedly offered to let me in on the next deal of this sort, if there was room for my money.

Sure enough, another and apparently promising deal did come along soon afterwards, and a limited participation was available. A new company had been formed, called Savold Tire, which had a patented process for retreading automobile tires. Retreading was then a new idea, and was especially attractive because of the relatively high price of tires. The subscription price of the shares was to be $10, and they were expected to open on the New York Curb at a much higher figure. I think I put up $5,000. As by clockwork or magic, a few days later trading began in the shares at 35, amid considerable excitement. Before the week was out, I had received a check for some $15,000 in return for my $5,000.

In spite of my innate conservatism and commonsense understanding that operations of this kind were essentially phoney, cupidity ruled me. I eagerly sought other deals of this kind, and so did a few friends to whom I had communicated the glad tidings. The price of Savold Tire kept advancing. A large electric sign quickly appeared on Columbus Circle, which first flashed "SAVE," then flashed "OLD," and then deftly combined the two words into "SAVOLD." Soon I heard some exhilarating news. The parent company had decided to license its process to affiliated companies in the various states, and these companies, too, would have shares on the market. Barnard Powers promised to put my money in along with his own.

Action came fast. Four weeks after the original Savold made its appearance, the second company—New York Savold Tire—was organized, and we invested something like $20,000 in the syndicate. Our subscription price was $15 or $20 a share. The stock opened on the Curb at 50, and on sales of 96,000 shares advanced immediately to a high of 60. This was the week of May 10, 1919; I celebrated my twenty-fifth birthday in a blaze of excitement. Promptly I received a fat check for our contribution plus some 150 percent in profits. (No accounting came with the check, and we wouldn't have dreamed of asking for one.) When I announced their share to each of my friends, they all told me to keep their money for them and be sure to put it all in the next deal. After all, there were forty-eight states in the union, weren't there?

Disappointment was in store for us. A third company—Ohio Savold—was duly floated in June, but it was a relatively small affair; we were told that there was no room for our money in that one. It came out on the Curb at 28, advanced the next month to 34, but did not imitate the pyrotechnics of the two previous companies. Nevertheless, we were worried. Was our wonderful party at an end? Powers reassured us. A very large deal was cooking, and we would positively be taken into it. But this company—Pennsylvania Savold—was to be the last of the series. It would have production rights for the whole country except New York and Ohio. Management had decided that more than four Savold companies would be cumbersome and confusing. We neither understood nor approved of this restraint, but we prepared to profit to the hilt from our last gorgeous opportunity. When funds were called for, I sent over some $60,000, half of which was contributed by three wealthy young brothers named Hyman. Maxwell Hyman had been an old schoolmate, friend, and customer. (Once, when we were still bachelors, we had teamed up to win a tennis-doubles tournament at a weekend party at the large summer home of four sisters named Jacobs.)

In August 1919, the world was harassed by a host of problems growing out of the collapse of Germany. But in Wall Street the market continued a headlong advance, especially in stocks of the poorest quality and the rankest speculative flavor. The original Savold was active and strong. In fact, at the beginning of the month it soared to 77¾, but fell back immediately to 53 in the same week. We waited impatiently for Pennsylvania Savold to make its spectacular debut, smacking our lips over our impending killing.

The promised day arrived, but trading didn't begin. There was a "slight delay" for reasons explained neither then nor later. Suddenly all the Savold issues were acting very badly; we wondered what was wrong. Came September and still no trading in our stock. Suddenly a complete debacle occurred in the Savold markets. The parent issue fell to 12½! A few more trades, and then the coup de grâce was announced: "No bid for any of the Savold issues." After October 4 all three companies disappeared completely from the records—as if they had never existed.

I had many conferences with Barnard Powers, who had invested most of his own money, and that of his friends, in Savold. He told me that the arch-promoter who had managed all these flotations had diverted our money to other uses. We could put him in jail, but that wouldn't do us any good. Powers and I formed a committee to represent his victims, and we visited him in his office close to the Curb. I still remember the beautiful blue shirt and expensive cuff links he wore at our meeting. Powers did all the talking, except once. That was when the promoter asked me if I would like to have a very low number for my automobile license. He could get one for me, since he was a close friend of New York Secretary of State Hugo. I declined with cold thanks.

The upshot was that the promoter turned over about 10 percent of our contributions in cash and certificates for shares of companies he had been promoting. In one way or another we managed to sell some of these, and finally returned about 33 cents on the dollar to our respective groups.

What happened to the Savold companies themselves? I never really knew. Presumably they went into bankruptcy—if they ever really existed. There is no trace of any of them in the financial manuals of the following year. All that we—as so-called insiders—ever knew about those enterprises was the (supposed) nature of their business and the number of shares alleged to be outstanding. This information appeared in a flimsy "descriptive circular" of unknown origin. Yet, gullible as we were, we had felt highly privileged to put our money in this manipulative scheme, relying on a speculative public even greedier and more foolish to pay us a huge profit. In the six months between April and September 1919, thousands of shares of the three companies changed hands on the Curb, in trades involving millions of real people's real dollars. But as far as I know, the only thing real about Savold Tire itself was the electric sign at Columbus Square which bore its name. Also, as far as I know, nobody complained to the district attorney's office about the promoter's bare-faced theft of the public's money.

Clearly, Wall Street was quite a different place in 1919 than now. In those days, it reflected the widest imaginable spectrum of ethics. Among themselves, the stock exchange members and the stock exchange houses behaved impeccably. They were highly reliable, also, in the execution of their customers' orders and in their handling of cash and property on deposit. But most of them condoned, and many of them participated in, rank manipulation; they encouraged customers to speculate, knowing full well that nearly all of them would lose heavily in the end. They did virtually nothing to protect the public against gross abuses like the Savold swindle.

Not only many Wall Street brokerage houses but the New York Stock Exchange itself was guilty of these devious practices. It permitted the bucket shops to flourish in their midst with resulting enormous losses to the portion of the public least able to afford it. The bucket shops took a short position which offset their customers' purchases and in one way or another simply pocketed all the margin their customers had put up. To stay within the letter of the law, actual transactions were necessary on both sides of the market, and these trades were made for the bucket shops by certain stock exchange firms allured by heavy commissions. It is impossible that these firms did not know the nature and result of the business they were putting on their books. Nor can I understand how the New York Stock Exchange could have been ignorant of the nature of the bucket shop rackets and the part necessarily played by certain of its members.

Our firm knew pretty well what the bucket shops were up to, and we virtuously refused—on several occasions—to accept lucrative business from them. But I admit that we felt no civic or professional duty beyond such refusal; like all our fellow brokers, we were businessmen, not reformers.

CHAPTER TEN

The Great Bull Market of the 1920s: I Become a Near Millionaire

While I was in school, I held a dozen different part-time jobs in as many fields. But my career in Wall Street included only two: the first was as employee and then junior partner at a brokerage; the second was as head of my own business. Before I went into business for myself, I was seriously tempted to leave the brokerage to become a financial writer for *The Magazine of Wall Street*. Writing had been my early love, and this was an opportunity to combine "literature" with finance. But when I announced my tentative decision to my "partners" at N.H.&L. they managed to dissuade me from it.

After the birth of my eldest daughter, Marjorie Evelyn, in 1920, we decided it was time to try suburban life. We moved to the upper half of a two-story house in Mt. Vernon. It was but a

half-block from the Mt. Vernon Country Club, which I soon
joined as a tennis member. There we made a number of new
friends, joining a rather exclusive clique of Jewish residents of
Mt. Vernon, with whom we soon found ourselves associating
almost day and night. One couple of this group were the
Horvitzes, Aaron and Gertrude. He had been a classmate of
Fred Greenman's at Harvard; he had studied law, but never
practiced. Instead he became the right-hand man of another
classmate, Lou Harris, who with his brothers was operating
the highly successful Harris Raincoat Company.

Horvitz got to know a lot about my financial ideas and special methods of operation. The Harrises made a momentous
proposition: I was to give up my connection with N.H.&L. to
operate a large account for them on a salary and profit-sharing
basis. They would put up a quarter of a million dollars and
promised that unlimited additional funds would be available if
the quality and results of my work should warrant it. I could
bring in my other accounts as part of the original capital. I was
to receive a salary of $10,000 per year; the capital would be
paid 6 percent and I would then be entitled to one-fifth of any
remaining profit—all on a cumulative basis. This proposition
was worked out between us in early 1923.

I anticipated some difficulty in getting my firm to let me go.
However, luck was on my side. The stock exchange had tight-
ened its rules regarding the amount of free capital required of
a member firm in relation to the money it owed as a result of
its customers' margin trading. This trading was expanding so
rapidly that N.H.&L. could not spare capital for the arbitrage
operations I had been conducting with such success. Thus they
had reluctantly been forced to say no to some of my good proposals. They could not but recognize that my special talent lay
in that field and that it was unfair to ask me to stay in a company where my best activities would be strictly limited. No
doubt they calculated also that they would get the benefit of a
juicy big account, plus most of the business of my numerous
customers, without having to pay the usual tribute to a cus-

tomers' man. So they released me from my obligations (entirely moral) rather more readily than I had expected. We agreed that I would do all or nearly all my business through them; they in turn would give me the use of an office rent free, plus a private stock ticker and various other services. (All these concessions were quite permissible then, though later severely limited by NYSE rules.)

The new business was incorporated under the name of Graham Corporation. In order to save part of our corporate income tax, we issued participating bonds to represent all the capital, except for some shares of common stock for voting and other purposes. The old order ended, and the new one began on July 1, 1923, just nine years after I started at N.H.&L. at $12 per week. I made the change without regret. For a long time I had felt that I did not belong in the brokerage business, which repelled me at bottom because I felt (then, at least) that it could prosper only at the expense of its clients' losses.

Not many years ago I read the first volume of the memoirs of Bernard M. Baruch (whom I was to meet in 1927). After recounting the great financial successes which were to make him a millionaire, Baruch recorded a bit of soul-searching. Now that he had achieved fame and a large fortune, what should he do with his life? After paragraphs of discussion, he announced a momentous decision: he would give up the brokerage business, have no contact with or responsibilities to the public, and operate solely for his own account in the stock market. I recall smiling somewhat disdainfully in reading what I considered a lame and egoistical conclusion. How discreditable, I thought, for a highly gifted and enormously wealthy young man to dedicate himself totally to making a lot more money, all for himself. And then, into the bargain, to write this down in his memoirs, without the slightest pang of regret or self-criticism.

But was my decision any more creditable than Baruch's? I too was leaving the brokerage business, where at least I was giving helpful counsel to the public, to limit myself exclusively to a money-making venture. But I was far from a rich man by Wall Street standards. And I had been making good profits for friends and relatives who needed the money. I persuaded the rather unwilling Harris group to allow me to continue to handle my old clients' accounts as part of my corporate capital.

The Graham Corporation operated for two and a half years, to the end of 1925, and was then dissolved. It was a successful venture and returned a high percentage on the capital. I limited investments to my standard arbitrage and hedging operations, plus securities I thought very cheap on value. The first thing I did was to buy some shares of Du Pont and to sell seven times as many shares of General Motors short against it. At that time, Du Pont common was selling for no more than the value of its holdings of GM, so that the market was really placing no value on its whole chemical business and assets. So Du Pont was greatly undervalued by comparison with the market price of General Motors; in due course a goodly spread appeared in our favor, and I undid the operation at the projected profit.

Another operation ended in a goodly loss with comical overtones. I had come to pride myself on being able to detect both greatly overvalued and significantly undervalued common stocks. I would operate on pairs of such securities, buying a cheap stock and selling a dear stock short against it. One of the stocks I considered overpriced was Shattuck Corporation, the owner of Schrafft's Restaurants. The company was doing well, but the speculators had inflated the price of the shares to what I thought was ridiculous heights. So I bought one of the numerous undervalued issues I was always digging up and shorted a few hundred Shattuck shares against it.

From the start I had arranged a regular weekly luncheon to discuss my exploits. As it happened, these meetings took place at a Schrafft's Restaurant which was a favorite with Lou Harris. When we went short on the stock, we all felt it was against our interest to support the enemy with our lunch checks, so we found another place to eat. Time went by and Shattuck stock continued to go up. (It is an inconvenient characteristic of these popular and therefore overvalued issues that they sometimes continue to be popular and grow more overvalued than ever before they drop to a normal and proper price.) When the price had advanced from our 70 to a most bothersome 100, we held a council of war and decided it was unwise to "fight City Hall" any longer. Anyway, we couldn't expect every operation to turn out well; our overall batting average was high enough; it was good discipline to accept a loss now and then; and so on. So we undid the operation, with a loss of some thousands of dollars. Lou Harris's comment was "Well, one good thing about taking this loss is that I can go back to eating lunch at Schrafft's." We needed the laugh.

But these lunches contributed to the termination of our business relationship. Lou Harris was full of ideas, recommendations, even tips of various kinds picked up at various brokerage houses—very few of which had any place in our carefully worked out scheme of operations. Those that didn't succeed he forgot all about and never mentioned again; those that would have shown a profit he remembered only too well and never failed to bring up at subsequent lunches. After a while I found myself getting fed up with all this second-guessing and Monday morning quarterbacking. It is difficult to work for a long time with a person who has the right to give advice of all kinds without taking any responsibility for what he says.

By 1925 the great bull market was well launched, and more and more people were coming into the market. It was a period in which most customers' men ran discretionary accounts for their clients, which gave them the right to buy and sell what they pleased without specific authorization or orders. Many of these accounts were operated on a fifty-fifty basis, with profits divided evenly between a customer and his customers' man. The customers' man did not have to pay any share of a net loss. I had many friends in Wall Street who told me I was foolish to work for a mere 20 percent of the profits; they could bring me all the money I could handle, with a 50 percent cut (some part of which would be turned over to them).

I began to feel that I was being taken advantage of by the Harrises. At thirty-one I was convinced that I knew it all—or at least that I knew all I needed to know about making money in stocks and bonds—that I had Wall Street by the tail, that my future was as unlimited as my ambitions, that I was destined to enjoy great wealth and all the material pleasures that wealth could buy. I thought of owning a large yacht, a villa at Newport, racehorses—perhaps even mistresses, though I think I was still too naive to include them in my list. I was too young, also, to realize that I had caught a bad case of hubris.

In mid-1925 I proposed a new arrangement to Lou Harris. I would give up my annual salary; instead, after the 6 percent allowed on the capital, I wanted 20 percent of the first 20 percent earned, 30 percent of the next 30 percent earned, and 50 percent of all earned above 50 percent. This seemed to me a neatly logical arrangement. But Lou Harris was horrified at the idea that I would want as much as half of any profit, even after 50 percent had been earned on the capital. We rather quickly agreed to terminate our arrangement and dissolve the corporation at the end of the year. Had the Harrises tried to work out some compromise, I'm sure I'd have agreed, for I have never been stubborn about particular demands. But later I learned that they were already willing to part company with me, even though I had done so well for them. The reason? After two years in intimate contact with my operation, listening to a full explication of the pros and cons of each purchase and sale, they felt that they were now equipped with the brains and expertise to go it alone. Why pay me 20 percent or more of the profits when they might do even better by themselves? So I made my arrangements for 1926, and they made theirs. Since we were both quite satisfied with the change, we parted good friends.

Before writing finis to the Graham Corporation episode, I

must mention an affiliated account bearing the title "Cohen & Graham." The Cohen of the partnership was a thin, myopic lawyer of about 35, also a Harvard classmate and close friend of Harris and Horvitz. He was a student rather than a practicing advocate. He had some capital—$100,000, I think—and Lou Harris was kind enough to make a special arrangement for him, similar to but separate from Graham Corporation. It, too, proved successful, but was terminated at the end of 1925. Why do I mention this unimportant detail? Because the Cohen of Cohen & Graham was none other than Benjamin V. Cohen, destined to join Tommy Corcoran in the famous team of Corcoran and Cohen, the devisers of much important New Deal legislation, and aides to President Roosevelt in pushing laws through a sometimes balky Congress.

Years later, in 1934, Ben Cohen sent me a draft of the proposed Securities Exchange Act—the second of the series of bills that set up the SEC and completely revolutionized many of the practices of the financial world. He asked me for comments. My only observation was about one provision that required that proxy statements sent to stockholders for annual meetings contain, among much other information, "a list of those to whom the statement is being sent." This harmless-sounding phrase meant that a company like AT&T would have to enclose its entire stockholders list of several hundred thousand names. Ben Cohen thanked me for discovering this gaffe and deleted it from the bill, which soon became law.

On January 1, 1926 I transferred my services and my own funds to the "Benjamin Graham Joint Account." Most of the capital was contributed by old friends including Fred Greenman, Bob Marony, and the Hymans. The financial arrangements were exactly what I had proposed to the Harris group —no salary, but a sliding scale of profit-sharing up to 50 percent. (Little did I think in my egregious self-confidence that six years later I should have to ask, as a favor, that a provision of the original Graham Corporation be revised—to pay me a modest salary in difficult times.) The participants were to receive quarterly payments at the annual rate of 5 percent chargeable against their capital or profits.

The Benjamin Graham Joint Account started with $400,000. Three years later our capital was around 2½ million, most of the addition from profits; a good deal of it belonged to me as the reinvestment of most of my ample compensation plus the earnings on my growing capital. Each year new friends were eager to place funds in the account, the fame of which was spreading by word of mouth. I made no effort to attract additional investments; in fact, I refused to accept money from people whom I did not know personally. But the number of my acquaintances kept growing.

The original group included Douglas Newman, a classmate from Boys High School and Columbia College and a successful lawyer. Some years before he had introduced me to his younger brother, Jerome, who had followed us by three years in the same high school, then had gone through Columbia College and Law School. He had married the daughter of a wealthy cotton converter and mill owner named Reiss. Instead of pursuing the law, he had entered his father-in-law's business and soon was second in command. I had handled some investments for Reiss and also, more modestly, for Jerry Newman.

Towards the end of 1926 Jerry came to see me; he said he wanted to leave the Reiss business and go into mine. Evidently Reiss was not the easiest man to work for. Jerry wanted to come to work for me without salary until he had proved himself of value. He would also make a fair-sized investment, representing the fruits of his work in the cotton business. The idea appealed to me, but I insisted that he accept a modest initial salary of $5,000 per year. This was the beginning of an association which lasted throughout my subsequent business life, ending only with my retirement to California and the dissolution of the two businesses—Graham-Newman Corporation, and Newman & Graham—which had succeeded the Benjamin Graham Joint Account.

Jerry Newman proved invaluable to me almost from the

start. He had a quick intelligence and an excellent head for business in all its practical aspects. He was much better than I at the details of a commercial operation. He was shrewd and effective at negotiating deals of all sorts and was completely honest and dependable—qualities essential for lasting success in Wall Street. However, he was not a theoretician nor especially inventive in the field of finance. I must claim credit for having devised virtually all our strategies and the greater part of our individual transactions.[1] He did have a few negative qualities as well, chief of which was a lack of amiability. He was a hard taskmaster, like the father-in-law whom he couldn't get along with, impatient to have his orders obeyed, critical of small errors, somewhat too tough at a bargain. Yet he was intelligent enough to recognize, in important cases, that the other man must be treated right.

On the whole, Jerry Newman was far from popular, even among his friends, of whom he had many. He had numerous quarrels with close associates, almost always over business affairs. He showed considerable rancor against these opponents, but he surprised me by ultimately making up with almost every one of them. Nearly all have asked me how I found it possible to get along with Jerry Newman for so many years. But in all that time we had virtually no disagreements or arguments. The only one I can remember occurred towards the very end of our partnership: Jerry got the idea that I was unfairly taking all the credit for the success of our business. He was mistaken about certain statements appearing in *Fortune Magazine*.

After two years Newman became an equal partner with me in the management of the business, and he remained so to the end. We had many revenues to divide: salaries, fees for services rendered, profit-sharing arrangements on deals, and so on. We made an agreement, embodied in a very short letter to each other, to divide up all such extraneous or additional earnings on an equal basis. After a number of years, however, Jerry's deals became considerably more important than my outside activities—which were chiefly testifying as an expert in valuation cases. It then appeared proper to both of us to reduce to 25 percent the participation of each in the external earnings of the other.

Again, that certain aloofness in my character—which is one of its chief defects—kept Jerry and me from ever becoming cronies or chums. We were always on the best of terms, but we actually saw little of each other outside business hours. His wife, Estelle, always treated me with affection. I spent a few days at their country house on the New York–Connecticut state line, but I don't remember their ever staying with us. Nor did we ever take a trip together. We spoke very little to each other about our personal lives—including love affairs, a subject which often leads to confidences between male friends far less closely associated than we were.

Jerry lived a far more uniformly successful life, outwardly, than I. He was also much shrewder in handling his personal finances, and he came through the bitter difficulties of the post-1929 years with no real embarrassments. When we started again on our upward path, he was in better financial condition by far; because of that advantage he was ultimately able to amass a much larger fortune than I. But that's not important; more to the point is that on various occasions he was very generous to me. Fortunately for him, unfortunately for me perhaps, I never had the opportunity to be of like assistance to him.

Estelle Newman, of course, had the same given name as my wife. The identical names caused us some amusement through the years, but less confusion than one would have expected, because our social relationship was never really close.

Estelle Reiss was three years older than Jerry Newman and not very attractive. Naturally people said he had married her because of her father's money; but Jerry's kind of ambition made him the last person in the world to want to benefit from anyone's success but his own. Like many women considered homely in their youth, Estelle showed continuous improvement in her appearance as the years passed. She never seemed to look any older, retaining her black hair and her lively glance. Naturally, she took advantage of all that the beautician's art could do to improve upon nature. She had a somewhat distant quality about her, which the well-disposed might have called aristocratic, but the critical—of whom there are always more than needed—described as snobbish or "stuck up." But she was a consummate hostess and always exceedingly gracious to those she liked. Estelle had inherited much of her father's business sense and powers of application. When I became president of the (then) New York Guild for the Jewish Blind, I succeeded in interesting her in our work. She founded the Woman's Division, which did a remarkable job of raising money through a variety of social events. She soon became one of the forces in this increasingly important philanthropy. She and Jerry jointly donated the large funds needed to construct a hospital building on the grounds of our Home for the Blind. It bears their name.

When I reflect on the way lives develop, I am always struck by the large part played by accidental events or circumstances and especially by geographical location. People become close friends because they live close to each other; most love affairs are born out of contiguity, usually aided by the fact that certain *other* parties are *not* on the ground to interfere. Perhaps the chief reason that the Ben Grahams never became social intimates of Jerry and Estelle was that we always lived in different sections of metropolitan New York. For perhaps 25 years the Newmans inhabited a large house in Lawrence, Long Island, an elaborate wedding present from the father of the bride. During all that time I continued to live on Manhattan Island, quite far away. When Jerry and Estelle finally bought an apartment on Fifth Avenue, we had moved up to Scarsdale and had our circle of friends there; then came our emigration to California.

But while distance was to prevent a really close association between the Newmans and the Grahams, propinquity was to establish one between them and my brother Victor. After his marriage in 1927 to the pretty and lively Sylvia Goodman, he bought a nice new house in Lawrence. This made them neighbors of the Newmans, fellow members of the Cedarhurst Golf Club, and soon close friends. Later Victor's reverses forced him to sell their home and leave Lawrence.

Our staff in 1927 consisted only of a stenographer and a bookkeeper. The latter was someone whom I had first met on the tennis courts at the Hunt's Point apartments in the Bronx more than ten years before. We established a close friendship, based entirely on tennis, because he shared none of my other interests. But year after year we played singles, always closely matched, dividing our victories almost equally.

When I played my first tennis match with him, I was an impecunious young man from Kelly Street; his father had a prosperous shoe business, and they lived in one of the best Hunt's Point apartments. A few years later his father died suddenly, and the family's prosperity melted as did ours after my father's passing. He had a modest job with Statler Hotels, and he was glad to come to work for us at a somewhat higher wage.

Each year—except during 1929 to 1933—we paid him a year-end bonus, and in most years we raised his salary. For these purposes he used to prepare elaborate historical exhibits, comparing his earnings with the profits of the business. At our later directors' meetings, the subject of his salary and bonus would come up for discussion every January. He eventually earned as high as $16,000 a year with us, which was really good pay for those days and for the rather mechanical work he did. However, he and his wife lived on a liberal scale (they had no children), and he did some investing of his own with indifferent success. During twenty-five years of association we found him faithful and reliable within the limits of his competence.

He died suddenly in his bed one night of a heart attack. We went over his accounts and discovered some minor peculations, totaling a few thousand dollars. Jerry and I never spoke of this to anyone. Years later I thought of this incident and my reaction to it in reading the *Journals* of the Frères Goncourt. In one entry, they describe the death of their maid, a woman who had served them with unselfish devotion from their childhood. In a second entry they tell their shock at what they had soon discovered about the secret life of this homely and self-effacing domestic, well along in years. She had been spending all her salary to buy the sexual services of various young men. The Goncourts philosophized over the difference between what is seen and what remains unseen in the lives of people quite close to us.

CHAPTER ELEVEN

The Northern Pipeline Contest

O f the many transactions carried out by the Account, two are especially memorable. The first involved the Standard Oil Pipeline Companies; the second the Unexcelled Manufacturing Company, the largest maker of fireworks and firecrackers in America. The first represented a great success; the second a lot of trouble, for no ultimate profit.

When the Standard Oil monopoly was broken up in 1911 by order of the U.S. Supreme Court, eight of the thirty-one companies emerging from the giant combine were rather small operators of pipelines, carrying crude oil from various fields to refineries. Little was known about the finances of these concerns. They published only a one-line "income account," which stated the net profits of the year, and a balance sheet in the most abbreviated form possible. Only two Wall Street houses specialized in the markets for all the Standard Oil subsidiaries. They published a monthly bulletin containing news items and figures regarding each subsidiary, but these bulletins gave no data about the pipeline companies' finances except to reproduce their highly inadequate income and balance sheets.

One day I was looking through an annual report of the Interstate Commerce Commission to obtain certain detailed data regarding railroad companies. At the end of the volume I came across some statistics of the pipeline companies, which the tables said were "taken from their annual report to the Commission." It occurred to me that such reports might contain information not sent to the stockholders and that such information might be interesting and valuable. I wrote the ICC to send me, if possible, a blank copy of the reports filed by the pipelines. A bulky envelope came back, containing a report form of some fifty pages, replete with tables covering every detail of their operations and financial condition. I was especially interested in a table which required the companies to set forth a list of their investments at cost and market value. All the pipeline companies had listed a large number of investments in their annual statements, but since no details were given, it was impossible to know what they consisted of.

The next day I took the train to Washington, hied me to the ICC building, entered the record room, and asked to see the annual report of all eight pipeline companies for 1925. They were duly brought me, and I soon found I had treasure in my hands. To my amazement I discovered that all of the companies owned huge amounts of the finest railroad bonds; in some cases the value of these bonds alone exceeded the entire price at which the pipeline shares were selling in the market! I found, besides, that the pipeline companies were doing a comparatively small gross business, with a large profit margin, that they carried no inventory and therefore had no need whatever for these bond investments. Here was Northern Pipeline, selling at only $65 a share, paying a $6 dividend— while holding some $95 in cash assets for each share, nearly all of which it could distribute to its stockholders without the slightest inconvenience to its operations. Talk about a bargain security!

Here was I, a stout Cortez-Balboa, discovering a new Pacific with my eagle eye. Imagine! Carl Pforzheimer & Company and other brokerage firms had given years to the study of these Standard Oil companies, and apparently they didn't know what I knew now, for they surely would not have left the shares to sell at such low levels had they seen such bond portfolios. (After all these years, I'm still amazed that no one in the brokerage business thought of looking at the ICC data.) Not even counting its hoard of cash and bond assets, how could Northern Pipeline be selling at 65 if it paid a $6 dividend, and continued to turn a profit? The answer is that the pipeline stocks were completely out of favor. They had formerly earned much greater profits and paid larger dividends, but the new tankers had taken away much of their former business. Wall Street, with its usual disregard of details and concentration on the "trend," seemed convinced that these companies had only a dismal future. Investors actually took the high dividend yield—over 9 percent for Northern Pipeline—as a warning of trouble ahead rather than as a reason for buying.

I had copies made of ICC reports for several years back and returned to New York in high excitement. I concentrated on acquiring Northern Pipeline shares since this company possessed the largest amount of bond investment in relation to its own market price. By careful but persistent buying, I acquired 2,000 shares out of the total small capitalization of 40,000 shares. This made me the largest stockholder of record after the Rockefeller Foundation, which owned about 23 percent of all these companies. It seemed time now to persuade Northern Pipeline management to do the right and obvious thing: to return a good part of the unneeded capital to the owners, the stockholders. Naively, I thought this should be rather easy to accomplish.

I made an appointment to see D. S. Bushnell, president of the company, at his office in the Standard Oil Company's impressive building at 26 Broadway. That was the first time I had ever entered those legendary quarters. Two old men were waiting to see me, looking suspiciously alike. One was President Bushnell, and the other his brother, general counsel to the company. (It is the custom in all areas of high finance to have more than one company official present at such interviews, in case testimony might later be needed as to what was said.)

I spoke my piece and made my case. I pointed out that the company was doing only about $300,000 in gross business; hence it was absurd for it to be carrying $3,600,000 in bond investments that had no relationship to its financial needs. I showed that this $90 per share in surplus cash assets could not be properly reflected in the stock market, which had long been valuing Northern Pipeline as a declining business, not as a repository of railroad bonds, whose existence it did not even suspect. Clearly the stockholders' interest required that this property be distributed to them where it could have full value in their direct possession, instead of having less than half its value as it was presently confounded with the other pipeline assets.

"That's impossible," said the Bushnells promptly. "Why?" "Because we haven't any surplus to speak of, so we can't pay out any more than our earnings; actually our distributions are very liberal." "Oh," said I, confidently, "That's easy to arrange. All you have to do is to reduce the par value of the stock from 100 to, say 50 or 25 per share, and then you can pay out the difference or pay out 50 to 75 as a return of capital." A new tack by the Bushnells (they proved much more resourceful in finding reasons to hang on to the stockholders' pile of gold than ways to increase the profits): "The company can't afford to do that. It needs all its capital." "But why? It can't need millions of dollars of capital, practically all in cash assets, to do $300,000 of business."

"The bonds represent our depreciation reserve. They must be retained for the ultimate replacement of our pipeline."

"When would that be needed—approximately?"

"We can't tell exactly." (The Bushnells wouldn't even try to guess at any possible year. The fact is that those underground pipelines last practically forever.) "But you don't mean to tell me that you would actually use the $3,600,000 of the stockholders' money to replace a pipeline that was doing only $300,000 of gross business. That would be crazy." (The Bushnells winced whenever I mentioned their volume of business, which they had so carefully kept from the stockholders' knowledge.)

Still another tack by my hosts, reminding me of the fable of The Wolf and the Lamb. They couldn't eat me, but they were determined to send me away empty-handed: "We might decide to build an addition to our lines. There are a number of possibilities, and we must be prepared for any of them."

"But, Mr. Bushnell, you have only a little trunk-line segment, running from the Indiana border across the corner of Pennsylvania to the New York border. You are a small part of the old Standard Oil main line. How could you possibly extend your plant in any logical way?"

It was time for the coup de grâce and my *congé*. The Bushnells were running out of arguments. So:

"Look, Mr. Graham, we have been very patient with you and given you more of our time than we could spare. Running a pipeline is a complex and specialized business, about which you can know very little, but which we have done for a lifetime. You must give us credit for knowing better than you what is best for the company and its stockholders. If you don't approve of our policies, may we suggest that you do what sound investors do under such circumstances, and sell your shares?"

There it was, the complete story. I was to hear it again, with only minor variations, countless times in my business career. There was a special reason why this happened to me so often. My operations consisted largely of buying common stocks that were selling well below their true value as determined by dependable analysis. The most reliable indication of a substantial undervaluation occurs precisely in the Northern Pipeline kind of situation—where there were large realizable assets employed at small profit and withheld from the stockholders. It was my policy first to acquire a substantial interest in such

companies and then to endeavor by one means or another to
bring about the appropriate change in the company's capitalization or operating policies. Almost invariably management
resisted my endeavors, utilizing the same arguments as did
the Bushnells. The favorite weapon in their arsenal was the
claim that the business was a very special one, that I knew
very little about it, and they were much better qualified than I
to judge what policies were required.

When, in all innocence, I made my first effort as a stockholder in 1926 to persuade a management to do something
other than what it was doing, old Wall Street hands regarded
me as a crackbrained Don Quixote tilting at a giant windmill.
No experienced person would waste his time trying to change
any corporate policy from the outside, especially not in the
stronghold of Standard Oil. "If you don't like the management
or what it's doing, sell your stock"—that had long been the
beginning and end of Wall Street's wisdom in this domain, and
it is still the predominant doctrine. More than that, an outsider
who tried to change anything was deemed either crazy or suspect. Many years before, a crafty character named Clarence
Venner had made a lot of money and an unenviable reputation
by bringing many suits against management for alleged financial misdeeds of various kinds, some entirely technical. So now,
if you just asked politely for something to be done, you were
rebuffed, more or less courteously. If you then persisted and
indicated an intention to institute a legal action or to ask for
stockholders' proxies, your motives were immediately im-
pugned, with broad intimations that the company was being
victimized by a "holdup artist, another Venner." In most of
these cases the stockholder pressing for relief had not owned
his shares for a long term. The reason for that is simple. If he
had bought them in the old days when the price was high, he
would be neither knowledgeable nor vigorous enough to see
what needed to be done and to work for it. The only people
who were likely to carry the ball for themselves and the other
stockholders were knowledgeable professionals who had

bought at low prices—i.e., fairly recently—and aimed at what they considered a legitimate profit in return for their efforts.

Managements rarely failed to emphasize this fact of recent acquisition, suggesting that the troublemaker was a Johnny-come-lately, and therefore a mere self-seeker. I have never had any question or qualms about the ethics of my endeavors. What I accomplished benefited not only my own people but all the other stockholders, old and new, who were thereby getting only what they were entitled to as owners of the business.

In the early days, the business of Wall Street was largely a gentlemen's game, played by an elaborate set of rules. One of the basic rules was: "No poaching on the other man's preserves." This meant that no one who was "in"—a member of what we would now call "the Establishment"—would think of making any move contrary to any other similarly situated person's vested interests. Banks and brokers always turned their annual meeting proxies automatically over to management. (That is still largely true.) A corporation or a banking group would never think of making a merger or a purchase offer to the stockholders or some concern without first having worked out the deal with management and having made ample provision to "take care" of same. Since investment bankers wanted to stay in the good graces of corporate managements generally, none could afford to get the reputation of not playing the game. In parallel fashion, corporate officials never supported any move that would threaten the jobs or perquisites of the officers of another company, for they expected the same courtesies to be extended to them by all the other club members. It was like the preferred treatment always accorded to officers taken prisoners of war. Their officer-captors made them quite comfortable because they expected the same amenities for any of their own officers who might be taken prisoner by the other side.

Times have changed somewhat. Buyers of corporations no longer hesitate to make purchase offers to stockholders over the heads of, or without prior consultation with, management.

The same is true of investment bankers acting for themselves or clients. For instance, a purchase offer was made and accepted in 1964 for majority control of Franco-Wyoming Oil Company. The situation was similar to that in Northern Pipeline: corporate managers held a large amount of marketable securities having no relationship to business operations.

Before I left Bushnell's office, disappointed and exasperated, I told the brothers that I would like to come to the next annual meeting to express my views in an oral memorandum to the other stockholders and for the record. They seemed surprised at this suggestion but soon answered that, of course, I would be welcome to come to the meeting. With that I said good-day and left.

The annual meeting was held early in January 1927 in Oil City, Pennsylvania, a town truly in the sticks. One had to take the train to Pittsburgh, and then make a rather poor connection for Oil City. I made the journey alone, overnight in a pullman berth and then in a rickety local train on a bitter cold and snowy day. The company's offices in Oil City were meager but large enough to hold the assembly—consisting of five employees and myself. I looked in vain for outside stockholders. In the meantime Mr. Bushnell's minions scrutinized me as if I were some curiosity from another planet, which I practically was. After some formalities, an employee read a prewritten slip which moved the adoption and approval of the annual report for 1926. Another employee immediately seconded the motion. I rose and was recognized.

"Please, Mr. Chairman, where is the annual report?" A moment of embarrassed silence.

"We are sorry, Mr. Graham, but the report won't be ready for several weeks."

"But Mr. Bushnell," I asked in bewilderment, "how is it possible to approve a report that isn't ready and available?" A whispered confidence with the other Bushnell.

"We have always handled the matter this way. Those in favor say 'aye.'"

All the proxies except mine were voted for the motion. After a few more formalities the chairman said that a motion of adjournment was in order. I rose again, hurriedly. "As we agreed in New York, I should like to read a memorandum for the record relating to the company's financial position." Another brief conference.

"Mr. Graham, will you please put your request in the form of a motion?" I did so.

"Is there any second to this motion?" A pause of a few moments. Silence. I had not thought of this and had failed to bring any one with me from New York to back me up.

"I'm sorry, Mr. Graham, I hear no second. The motion must fail."

"But, as you are well aware, I made the long trip here just to put this memorandum in the record. You encouraged me, Mr. Bushnell. I think you owe me the courtesy of seeing that my motion is seconded and carried." Another brief conference, and then:

"I'm very sorry, but no one seems willing to second your motion. Do I hear a motion to adjourn?" In a moment the meeting was over. With ill-concealed snickers, the Bushnells' minions filed out.

I felt humiliated at being made a fool of, ashamed of my own incompetence, angry at the treatment given me. I was able to control my feelings just enough to say quietly to the president that I felt he had made a great mistake in not permitting me to have my say. For I would come back the next year, and then I would have a second with me, and more.

I amply justified and fulfilled my threat. Actually, what I took to be a dismal personal failure in January 1927 turned out to be a great piece of financial luck. For now I had a whole year to prepare a plan of campaign and to enlarge my financial stake. With increased capital available, I bought more shares of Northern Pipeline. I committed as much of the partnership's funds as I could risk. As counsel, I engaged Fred Greenman's highly regarded corporate law firm, Cook, Nathan, &

Lehman. The senior partner was Alfred A. Cook, a man of
great ability and prominence, but—I must add—of even
greater pompousness and vanity.

In my financial reading, I had come across a fact that was
little known at that time. I discovered that a number of states
had passed laws requiring corporations to elect directors by
cumulative voting. By casting all proxy votes for one director,
a shareholder with only minority support could insure his own
election. Pennsylvania was one of these states, and Northern
Pipeline Company was incorporated in Pennsylvania. Given
its small board of five directors, it took only the proxies of one-
sixth of the shares to elect one director, and only one-third to
elect two. I circulated the stockholders, asked for their proxies
in favor of a resolution to reduce the capital, and for the election of two of the directors to represent the rank and file of the
owners. We did not propose to elect a majority of the board,
for that would have given us responsibility for operating the
company, and we knew we had no right to assume that.

Alfred Cook asked for a list of stockholders, and we were
allowed to make our own copy from the company's records.
Evidently the Bushnells thought we had no chance of accom-
plishing anything; otherwise they might have made us fight a
costly legal battle to obtain the list. We prepared a letter setting forth our case. Cook, Greenman, and I worked hard over
it, and I must say it was pretty good. The company replied in
its usual lordly way, dodging all the real issues, asserting its
superior competence to decide what was best for the company,
and ergo its stockholders, and impugning the motives of us
interlopers by not so subtle innuendo.

There were not many large shareholders, and we arranged
to visit personally all who owned more than a hundred shares.
The company made similar efforts through its employees and
the Bushnells. (This was before the days of the large organiza-
tions which are used nowadays by many companies to solicit
proxies even when there is no contest!) Our most important
objective was the proxy of the Rockefeller Foundation, owner

of 9,200 shares, or 23 percent of the total. I was able to arrange an interview with Bertram Cutler, financial adviser to the foundation. He listened courteously, but said rather decisively that the foundation never interfered in the operations of any of the companies in which it had investments. (This statement, too, I was to hear too often in my later career from investment managers who should have taken their true responsibilities more seriously.) I tried to establish that the question at issue had really nothing to do with the *operations* of Northern Pipeline; this was simply a decision to be made by stockholders relating to the use of their surplus capital. But I returned empty-handed.

This was the second time I found myself in close proximity to John D. Rockefeller, Jr. The first was when I received an invitation, over his signature, to lunch at the Recess Club as one of a group to help him finance the establishment of the Phi Beta Kappa Foundation. I suspected that this lunch might prove expensive, but the distinction of meeting the billionaire philanthropist appealed to my vanity and overcame my prudence. So I went. He asked the rather small group gathered at his table to join with him in this enterprise by contributing what we could afford. Swallowing hard, I came through with $500. I felt it was a rather unique experience to be helping out John D. Rockefeller. The Phi Beta Kappa Foundation was soon established, and ever since has been publishing a fine journal called *The American Scholar*.

But back to 1927 and the Northern Pipeline proxy battle: Greenman and I met Cook at the Recess Club to discuss strategy, particularly in relation to the Rockefeller Foundation's proxy. By chance, we espied John D., Jr., sitting at the very next table to us, having lunch with a youngish man in a sport coat, who turned out to be Andrew Mellon, Jr., son of the multimillionaire financial magnate, art collector, and then U.S. Secretary of the Treasury. We were so struck by this happenstance that for a minute Alfred Cook seriously considered approaching Rockefeller and asking him to discuss our proxy fight and to solicit his Foundation's support. But soon we dismissed the idea as ill-advised.

Nonetheless, we did surprisingly well in garnering our other proxies. In retrospect now I am amazed at our success, for further experience was to teach me that a strong, logical case does not go very far when one is appealing to the mass of feckless stockholders over the heads of and in opposition to the company's entrenched management.

The annual meeting day arrived in January 1928. I went again to Oil City, but this time not alone. I had with me three lawyers from Cook's outfit, including the redoubtable Alfred himself, and also Henry Schnader, partner in a prominent Philadelphia firm, our Pennsylvania counsel. (Schnader was soon to be elected attorney general of his state.) We also had a goodly store of proxies, enough to give us what we wanted. To be sure that nothing misfired, we arrived in Oil City a day in advance and installed ourselves in the best (or perhaps only) hotel. A pourparler with the Bushnells resulted in an agreement to go over the proxies that evening, to save time at the meeting. The management group was surprised and discomfited to see how many of their own proxies had been superseded by later-dated ones given to us. After all this time I still remember old Bushnell's involuntary exclamation of pain when we established our right to one proxy for three hundred shares. "He's an old friend," he gasped, "and I bought him lunch when he gave me his proxy."

Before the meeting started the next morning, the management asked for a conference. We had proxies for more than 15,000 shares, enough to entitle us to two directors. (Thus we had obtained about half of the votes other than those belonging to the Rockefeller Foundation, which we hoped might at least be withheld from the management.) President Bushnell was now very suave. He saw no reason for an open contest at the meeting, with its accompanying embarrassments to everyone. He would be very happy to accept the nomination of two directors by our side and put them on the company's slate, thus making the elections unanimous. Alfred Cook proposed Schnader and myself as directors. Bushnell made some effort to have Cook himself—or almost anybody—substituted for me, for whom he evidently didn't care much. Without consulting me, Cook answered with a flat no. This had been my battle, he said, and I was entitled to the victory. The Bushnells gave in; the single slate was duly nominated and elected, and the whole meeting went off quite smoothly.

I was now the first person not directly affiliated with the Standard Oil system to be elected a director of one of its affiliates. Even though Northern Pipeline was tiny compared to most of the others, I was mighty proud of my exploit.

During that truce conference in Oil City, President Bushnell offered the conciliatory remark that it ought to be possible, at an appropriate time, for us all to reach an accord on the company's financial setup. We thought then that this was a little soft soap, with no real significance. However, a few weeks later he invited me to his office for a discussion. In dulcet tones the old hypocrite said, "You know, Mr. Graham, we were never really opposed to your ideas on returning capital to the stockholders; we merely felt that the time was not appropriate. As matters now stand, we are ready to present a plan which we think will meet with your complete approval."

The plan was to reduce the par value from 100 to 10; to give $50 in cash and three new shares in exchange for each old share, and to carry the balance of $20 per old share to capital surplus. Bushnell added that some additional distribution might be made later out of that capital surplus. But first some proper provision must be made for pensions for the faithful employees. In fact, the full $70 per share was eventually distributed, and the aggregate value of the new Northern Pipeline stock plus the cash returned ultimately reached an aggregate of more than $110 per old share.

We wondered what had brought about this sudden change of heart in our formerly obstinate opponents. Alfred Cook later learned that the Rockefeller Foundation, through their proxies made out to management, had indicated that they would favor distribution of as much capital as the business could spare. (They could find good philanthropic uses for the money.) This explanation is most likely true because virtually all the pipelines later followed Northern's example and made corresponding distributions to their stockholders.

The third time I met Rockefeller came many years later and represented an independent act on my part of which I am quite proud. It was 1945, and I had become a member of the rather stuffy New York State Chamber of Commerce—partly as a civic matter, but chiefly, I think, to take advantage of their luncheon club facilities. The Democrats in Congress were backing the rather revolutionary proposal now known as the "Full Employment Act of 1946," which committed the government to take all proper measures to maintain high-level employment. Businessmen generally mistrusted and disliked the Democrats, and this measure revolted their conservative instincts. A committee of the New York Chamber of Commerce brought in a report roundly condemning the bill, and the report was unanimously approved by the members present (I was not there that day). But in the fall of 1945 the measure passed the U.S. House of Representatives. This was viewed with such dismay by our good chamber members that the committee thought it proper to bring in a second report, again condemning what was soon to be the law of the land, to show the public that its business leaders would have no truck with these new-fangled ideas.

When I read the proposed second report in the monthly circular, I felt it was up to someone in the New York State Chamber of Commerce to tell his fellow members that the political and economic climate had changed significantly since, say, 1929. I wrote the secretary asking for permission to address the next meeting—when the report would come up for adoption—for not more than three minutes. My request was granted, as a matter of course.

As it happened, the meeting was to hear a principal speech

by Winthrop Aldrich, president of Chase Bank and Rockefeller's son-in-law. On this occasion, Mr. Rockefeller attended the gathering, and I found myself seated in the chair next to him. When the resolution on the employment act had been presented, my name was called as the only one who wished to speak on the report. With some understandable nervousness, I read my three-minute harangue, ending with a rather impertinent admonition to my fellow members not to show themselves "as Bourbons who learned nothing and forgot nothing." My words were received in complete silence by the entire assemblage, including Mr. Rockefeller, whom I brushed by in returning to my seat. When the vote was taken the "ayes" supporting the committee's condemnatory report were overwhelming, and I heard but one "no" added to my own.

Another battle that I had with the Rockefellers was not a proxy contest but a legal maneuver relating to National Transit Company, a Standard Oil subsidiary which operated both pipelines and a pump-manufacturing subsidiary of its own. Management had applied to the state authorities for the right to take some action, which we resisted on behalf of the stockholders. They wanted to use most of our large cash assets for some unattractive purpose. Anyway, they withdrew their application and later—probably under Rockefeller Foundation prodding—made a substantial distribution of cash to the shareholders, of which we had become one of the largest.

I mention the National Transit matter for two reasons. Many years later, we acquired control of that fairly important enterprise, in partnership with Wertheim & Company, a leading New York Stock Exchange firm. Some interesting details of that transaction I'll reserve for later. The other reason has to do with a consequence of my early investment success and involves the magic name of Baruch. As our business expanded, we had given up our little office at N.H.&L. and taken quarters in the Cotton Exchange Building at 60 Beaver Street. Here the old NYSE firm of H. Hentz & Co. had its main offices. Its two senior partners were Jerome Lewine and Dr.

Herman Baruch, both of whom I came to know well. A younger partner was Arthur Neumark, whose family were friends of ours in the ancient days in England. (I had tutored Arthur in geometry, when I needed the money badly, and years later I had helped him start in Wall Street in the research department of *The Magazine of Wall Street*. He then moved on to Hentz as statistician, proved good at developing business, and rose to a partnership.) For a number of reasons—chief of which was to widen our means of borrowing stocks in connection with our arbitrage and hedging operations—we found it advisable to have two brokerage accounts in addition to the original one at N.H.&L. Through Neumark we were persuaded to become clients of Hentz; and in some other way we added Goodbody & Company to our list.

Dr. Herman Baruch was one of three brothers of Bernie Baruch, all four over six feet tall. He had followed in his illustrious father's path and had practiced medicine for a brief time in the Long Branch area. Then—at the request of the surviving residents, the unkind tradition went—he had made the unusual change to Wall Street brokerdom. (Actually, all three of Bernie Baruch's brothers became brokers, a fact easy to understand.) When I first met Herman, he was in his early fifties, very imposing with his tall figure, his debonair manner, his copious white hair, and flowing white beard. He had acquired an estate called Bagatelle, rather far out on Long Island, which one of the Vanderbilts had first presented to the ravishing Lina Cavalieri. There he had begun to grow Christmas trees as a hobby; it eventually developed into a large and profitable business, with substantial tax advantages, it seems. He was also the proprietor of a large and luxurious craft, ninety-three feet long, half-yacht, half-houseboat, named *Reposo.*

In the spring of 1929 he told me that he had followed my example and bought a lot of National Transit shares, on which he had made a highly satisfactory profit. He felt he owed me some reward since I had worked hard for all the stockholders without any pay from them. So he offered me the use of the *Reposo* for a week. It would cost me nothing except some suitable gratuity to the captain and crew. The yacht slept six, and I could invite whomever I wished.

So my work and success in the National Transit matter led to eight glorious days as honorary skipper of Dr. Herman Baruch's luxurious *Reposo*.

Another operation and would-be coup was destined to bring me much bother, little profit, and some odd experience. The chief beneficiaries of this episode were my children, for— much to everyone's surprise—I became vice-president of the largest fireworks manufacturer in the country. Here's how that happened.

Our successes with undervalued securities had made us well known in the large over-the-counter houses—those dealing in issues not listed on any stock exchange. Perhaps the most important was J.K. Rice & Company, whose chief trader and salesman was a man named Bill Currie. (He invariably introduced himself over the phone as "Currie of Rice.") He came into our office one day in late 1928 with an elaborate proposition concerning the fireworks manufacturer, Unexcelled Manufacturing Company. This concern was rich in cash (I thought) and quite prosperous. A large block was for sale at only $9 per share, which was less than the working capital alone, and only six times the current or recent earning of $1.50 per share. The most important part was that the purchase of this block would ensure the transfer of control from the old president, B. V. Bingle—described as a heavy drinker—to a new group, centering around the steady and capable vice-president, Tom Jardine. Currie had suggested to this group that I would make an excellent financial adviser in the new set-up; if I bought the block, they were ready to make me vice-president, at a suitable salary for part-time work relating to the company's money matters.

The whole thing appealed to me greatly, not the least attraction being election as officer in a fair-sized corporation.

Jerry and I decided to buy 10,000 shares for the Benjamin Graham Joint Account and to place the balance in good hands. The hands in question belonged to none other than Bernard Baruch, who had heard of me and was becoming increasingly interested in my type of operation.

The Unexcelled annual stockholders' meeting took place in January 1929. This was the first time I saw E. V. Bingle: he was old, stout, and quite jovial in appearance. A strange thing happened. When it came time to read the annual report—not previously published, but in the president's hands—he saw me in a front seat and said: "You look like a clean-cut young man. Come up and read the report to the meeting." This I did, even as it dawned on me that I was a leading player in a conspiracy that would end the career of a man who had never done me any harm. Did I have a presentiment that I would live to regret this action? If I didn't, I should have.

The meeting went off as planned. We won by a rather narrow majority of the votes. Bingle was amazed and discomfited. He said angrily that he had made Tom Jardine, and now his minion had betrayed him. In any event, he added, Jardine hadn't an ounce of ability in his body and would be a complete failure at running the great company that he, Bingle, had built up over twenty-five years. With which he stalked out of the meeting. I was told that he returned later to the office he was about to give up, quite drunk, and caused a big commotion. In the meantime we had had our meeting and elected the new directors, with Jardine as president and Graham as financial vice-president—salary $6,000 per annum.

CHAPTER TWELVE

Family and Other Affairs

My beloved son, Isaac Newton, was born in May 1918. Two years later our first daughter arrived. We named her Marjorie Evelyn, for no special reasons and after the usual long discussions. By coincidence, 1920 was also the year of the song "Margie," a quite ordinary composition that somehow lasted for many years. Our Marjorie immediately became Margie (later, Marj) for all of us (also "pie-face," because of her full-moon visage as an infant). I often tried to soothe her by singing "Margie, I'm always thinking of you, Margie," and so on in my off-key voice, but without much success.

Exactly five and a half years after Marjorie, our second daughter was born, a blue-eyed, golden haired baby, whom we called Elaine Dorothy. The name Elaine was a romantic recollection of Tennyson's *Idylls of the King:*

> Elaine the fair, Elaine the lovable, Elaine the lily
> maid of Astolat...

Dorothy was my mother's name.

Newton was a wonderful boy, from his earliest infancy to his heart-breaking death just short of his ninth birthday. No doubt the passing years have led me to exaggerate his virtues; for indeed it is hardly possible for a child to have been as perfect as I remember him. He was very handsome, full of charm, highly intelligent, considerate, and accommodating.

I remember taking him at three to the New York Hippodrome, a palace of fabulous spectacles no longer in existence. It was famed for its large water tank, which always occupied an important place in the entertainment. The moment would come for the tank to be uncovered, numerous mermaids to take their places, and then to dive gracefully into the water. The audience would watch in intent silence. Suddenly a very young, but very clear voice piped up, "Mommy, why are they taking a bath? Are they dirty?" That voice, of course, was our Newton's.

When Grandmother Mazur came to the house, she slept in his room. The next morning we asked him how everything went. "Fine," said he, cheerfully. "But do you know, we snored so that the castle shook." The phrase, which he had heard many times, describes the ogre sleeping in *Jack and the Beanstalk.* By saying "we snored," the boy delicately sought to spare his grandmother's feelings, but his report made us all laugh.

In his last weeks at Mt. Sinai Hospital, we brought him the news that his sister had been awarded the blue ribbon for the best work in her class. Newton's face lit up, and then he said seriously: "You don't appreciate Margie properly. She is really very smart."

Even when they were very young, Newton and Marjorie understood each other in ways that we couldn't. Though Marjorie started to speak at the usual age, her enunciation was very indistinct, or rather she had a pronunciation all her own. We had great difficulty in making out what she said. But Newton, because he was with her so constantly, could understand her without trouble. So quite regularly, when Marj was trying without success to communicate something to us, we would turn to her four-year-old brother and ask him what she was saying. He always told us without hesitation.

As a baby Marjorie's "pie-face" seemed quite homely, but she was destined to grow soon into an attractive child and a beautiful young lady. (I still consider her one of the loveliest *looking* women I know, as well as the loveliest in character.) Her early disposition was very different from Newton's. Whereas he was invariably sweet and docile, she could be rebellious and troublesome. When we returned to New York City from Mt. Vernon, and Margie was about three, we engaged a governess for the two children. Louisa Gohl, always called Fräulein, came from Stuttgart and was very Germanic in her ways. She quickly showed that Newton was her favorite and tried her Teutonic best to make Marj behave properly. Evidently she was the wrong person for our daughter, but we didn't realize it at the time. For a while we viewed Marj pretty much as a brat, which she probably was. Fortunately for her and us, she grew into a model daughter as a young teenager, an outstanding student and a fine athlete. Since the age of thirteen or so she has given me nothing but joy and feelings of pride.

Marjorie was not only very bright, but she had a great desire to excel and to do an outstanding job in everything she attempted. Early in life she learned to stand on her head, and she would keep that pose until we begged her to stop. I recall one of those occasions, when she was perhaps six years old; from her little mouth close to the floor came the serious question: "Daddy, what's the world record for standing on one's head?"

But she did use the stunt to advantage later when she was a member of the swimming team at Lincoln School and regularly took first place in the back-dive from the headstand position. She showed considerable aptitude for music, especially for original composition. Marjorie and two other gifted Lincoln Schoolers wrote and produced a play called "Seventeen

Million Dead," which recalled the slaughter of World War I and made an eloquent plea for peace. Marjorie also composed the music for a movie her class made called "The Brothers of Altamira," about cavemen. Her young English teacher would show the film at various meetings of educators. Since Marj never wrote down the score of her accompaniment, she would be taken to these projections to play the music accompanying the film on the piano.

I remember her composing an exciting piece called "Civil War Rhapsody"; I suggested to her that she finish it by combining an imitation of Tchaikovsky's *1812 Overture* with "Dixie" and "Yankee Doodle." This she accomplished very adroitly, I thought. She also set to music my versification of those famous lines in *History of the World* which Sir Walter Raleigh composed in prison: "O eloquent, just, and mighty Death." My version began as follows:

> Eloquent Death, mighty and just,
> Thou dost persuade whom none could advise;
> What none hath dared that thing thou dost;
> Whom the world flatters thou dost despise.

To combine music and head-standing is not easy, but Margie managed it. For a while she took piano lessons at home with a young teacher. Regularly at the half hour she would take a minute off to stand on her head, and then return, refreshed, to the keyboard.

Margie made a remark at the age of eleven that I have always treasured as most perceptive. One of her schoolmates was Fifi Garbat, daughter of a stomach surgeon famous for his skill and enormous fees. Mrs. Garbat was something of a lion huntress in the jungles of musical celebrities. Marj was invited to Fifi's birthday party, and Hazel and I were allowed to bring her and stay. This was indeed a privilege, because the youthful guests included Yehudi Menuhin, his talented sister Yalta, and another boy wonder, Ruggiero Ricci. These celebrities in short pants maintained a grave and decorous mien throughout the party. That same evening a giant of a Russian tenor, perhaps thirty years old, named Maxim Karolik, came to our home for a visit. As was his custom, he behaved like a cutup, saying a lot of outlandish things accompanied by ridiculous gestures. The next day, when we were commenting on the visits of the previous day, Margie observed sagely: "Aren't artists funny, Dad? When they're children they act like grownups and when they're grown up they act like children."

We had met this Karolik through musical friends in 1923. He was a Russian Jew and a tenor; he also looked a lot like Abraham Lincoln. When we met him, he was close to starving. We were living on the ground floor of 160 Riverside Drive, and at dinner time it was not an uncommon experience for us to hear a familiar knock at our window. "That's Maxim," we would say, and we would invite him in for a bite with us.

Not so many years later Karolik was engaged to sing at someone's house in Newport, Rhode Island. (Though a professional, his voice was neither very bad nor very good.) There he won the hearts of two immensely wealthy maiden sisters of patrician lineage, the Misses Codman, who were thirty or more years older than he. In what seemed like a trice he married one of them. I never heard how it was decided which of the two would become Mrs. Karolik. Like a male Cinderella, Maxim now entered the dazzling world of Newport, Washington, and Boston society, with the Fahnestocks and the like for close neighbors and every luxury within his reach. He was even able to give two recitals at Carnegie Hall, which we duly attended, and the notices of which were ambiguously respectful. Rather rarely he was allowed to make brief visits to New York. At such times he would come up to us for a meal, to enjoy our cooking, he would say, instead of to still his hunger as in the old days. He would regale us with reports of his success with the bluebloods of Newport society, who must have considered him a Heaven-sent rescuer from their ennui. At one time he described with gusto how he had started a new

craze in the colony—breeding pigeons, now carried on in Newport mansions almost exactly as it had been done in his tiny
native village in Bessarabia. In due course his wife made a
sumptuous gift to the Boston Museum of a large part of her
collection of American furniture. Instead of perpetuating the
ancestral name of Codman, as might have been expected, the
estimable lady made the gift in the joint names of Mr. and Mrs.
Maxim Karolik, and the rooms set aside in the great museum
to hold these treasures bear this inscription.

Of all the many transformations of fortune and of destiny I
have witnessed in my long life, that of our dizzy young friend
Max Karolik was undoubtedly the strangest. Was the game
worth the price he paid to take part in it? I don't know, but I
am inclined to answer "Yes."

My second daughter was to become Elaine Graham Bell,
Ph.D. and later the wife of Cyril Sofer. Elaine started out life
in 1925 in a little blaze of glory, a compound of blue eyes,
golden hair, lovely features, and a winsome disposition. She
was universally beloved, as much by her brother and sister as
by the rest of us. (Since they were seven and five years older
than Elaine, they showed none of that sibling jealousy that we
hear so much about from psychologists.) Fräulein Gohl quickly
transferred her fiercely concentrated affection to the new little treasure, showing herself even more intolerant of Margie's
little misdemeanors. Hazel remarked often enough that Elaine
was the best behaved of her three babies. Fräulein quickly
took to calling her "Besty," and this rather invidious title was
accepted without complaint by the other children, remaining
her sobriquet for quite some years.

I composed a poem for Elaine's first birthday, and Newton
recited it at her little party. (He was not to live to see her second.) I can still hear his clear, childish voice reciting:

Gaily we greet the little traveler
On this first milestone of her life's long way;
May every day be happy as this day,

And goodness, health and love watch over her.
Sweet was she when she came and sweeter still
Day after day and month by month she grows;
While loving hands hold our dear Besty close
And watchful eyes guard her from every ill.

This Besty was to develop a character all her own, containing some unexpected traits. She thought and acted for herself, sometimes erecting an unmistakable wall between herself and everyone else. (This trait I'm afraid she inherited from her father, with some variations of her own.) Her basic independence was manifested at quite an early age, to the point where she had encounters with the police while only a child. At the age of six she decided to get up early in the morning to hear the birds begin singing in Central Park. She arose, dressed herself, and slipped out of our apartment one Sunday morning at about six o'clock, taking along her little brother, the second Newton, who was then only three years old. We learned about this when we were awakened by a policeman who found the two infants wandering in the park—never a safe place to be at odd hours. Did we punish the charming child for this strange escapade? I don't remember.

A second adventure was both stranger and more serious. At the age of twelve Elaine and a chum from Lincoln School took into their heads to go off somewhere. They boarded a bus which carried them 150 miles to Lancaster, in the heart of the Amish country of Pennsylvania. (They explained this choice by saying they wanted to see some "real country sights.") Trudging along a road outside of Lancaster, they stopped at a farmhouse and asked for milk. The woman there was the mother of a state trooper, who happened to pass by. He took the two girls to the county jail and held them as vagrants for further disposition. Late that night we anxious parents in New York were told by telephone where our missing daughters were. The girls were put on the bus for New York the next morning. We met them at the terminal; they were evidently happy to be home again but reticent about the details of their experience. Later we learned they had spent the night in jail with drunken women and prostitutes—our innocent little Besty!

Both Marj and Elaine were fortunate to attend Lincoln School, a fabulous institution financed by the Rockefellers and operated by Teachers College of Columbia University. Its purpose was to experiment with a number of promising ideas in primary and secondary education. It attracted a teaching staff of the highest quality, and the student body was carefully chosen, with preference given to the children of the Columbia faculty, which I had joined. My children benefited greatly from the liberal and challenging atmosphere of Lincoln School. When Elaine entered it at an early age, she was warned that she would have difficulty living up to the great reputation already established by her older sister—who was to be valedictorian of her graduating class. But Elaine did not fall far behind. Actually her teachers felt that she had a keener natural intelligence than Marj, but lacked the latter's indefatigable drive. Like her father, Elaine did not spend too much time over her schoolbooks and got through her work in half the time her sister took.

At an early age Elaine gave us several occasions to be proud of her. Before she was nine she had appeared on the stage of both Town Hall and Carnegie Hall. The children attended the Diller-Quaile School of Music, which taught music in new ways. Each year the pupils gave a performance at Town Hall. The first graders, all aged about seven, generally appeared as a little percussion band, with drums, triangles, cymbals, and whatnot. After a tryout Elaine was selected to lead the orchestra. There she was, our little treasure, giving each instrument its cue in a highly nuanced version of "The Campbells Are Coming," in perfect command of herself and her group. A lump arose in my throat as I watched her, and I cast furtive glances to see if others were as entranced as I by this extraordinary performance. A year or two later Elaine took ballet lessons at the Neighborhood Playhouse School of Dancing, under the aegis of the Lewisohn sisters. The school put on an ambitious performance of La Boutique Fantasque, engaging, as sole professional, the redoubtable Alexis Kosloff. In one of the dances Kosloff was accompanied by a little poodle dog on either side of him, who rolled over and did somersaults and other tricks. Guess what! One of those poodles was Elaine, and Carnegie Hall rang with applause when she and Alexis Kosloff finished their number.

When we moved back to New York from Mt. Vernon, we lived first on the ground floor of 160 Riverside Drive, at 88th Street, next to the imposing Schinasi mansion and two blocks from the Soldiers and Sailors Monument. Our apartment seemed large and luxurious to me at the time, and I was proud of our Riverside Drive address, which spoke of financial success. We signaled the latter also by choosing for our summer residences the exclusive—or at least snooty—town of Deal on the Atlantic Coast of New Jersey. We spent our first summer there in 1925 at the Hathaway Inn. In 1926 we rented a nice house near the Casino, which of course we joined as members.

In New York I had also joined the City Athletic Club, which at that time had as its first rule "There shall be no cardplaying anywhere within the club building." (As the original members grew older and less athletic, the rule was abrogated; visiting the club many years after I had resigned, I was surprised to find cardplaying on almost every floor.) At the C.A.C. I took lessons in two new sports—squash and golf. My squash teacher was a young man who was then the world's champion professional. (An enthusiastic C.A.C. member whom I spoke to recently declared flatly that he was the greatest player of *any sport* who ever lived.) He made a handsome living by giving most of his pupils a handicap of 19 points per game for a $5 bet, and then proceeding to win 21 points easily before any of us could take the bare 2 points we needed. But at an early age this young man had a nervous breakdown and committed suicide. I never heard the full story—I suppose there must be one. As far as I could see, he hadn't a nerve in his body nor a care in the world. How little we know of what goes on in other people's minds.

My golf career was entirely without glory. Like everyone else, I often thought I had found the right track, only to slip back into the morass of slices, hooks, and general ineffectuality. It did not take me long to develop a strong prejudice against the game, on the ground that it gave full rein to the player's egotism. The endless discussion of one's own good and bad shots, the boasting and the beating of breasts, the arguments over how many strokes somebody took on a hole, the invariable wagers—all this revolted anyone who had grown up under the strict and gentlemanly rules governing tennis behavior. After seven years of wandering in the wilderness of golf, I gave up the game for good and went back to tennis, where I belonged. I was to continue to enjoy that exhilarating sport into my sixties. I had to quit it at last for health reasons: I could never play an easy-going game.

I also enjoyed skiing, a sport which I began at the Dean House at Lake Mahopac in Winter 1924. There was lots of snow, and skis were available for guests who wanted to risk the sport. The skis had the most elementary bindings, consisting only of a single strap over the toes. There was a little slope leading down from the inn towards the lake. I took quite naturally to skis, as did our little Newton. We had an early amateur motion-picture camera, given to us, along with projector and screen, as a Christmas present by my old firm of N.H.&L. (They had gotten a lot of business from me in the previous year without having to pay for it.) The family archives still contain the first reel made with that camera; it shows us enjoying ourselves hugely that first time on skis.

Hazel's introduction to the Bell & Howell movie camera had more significance for her than she expected. Photography was later to be her career. For many years she was the official photographer of the huge Hadassah organization, as well as being a longtime member of its national board as well. Her films of life and landscapes in Israel have been shown to appreciative audiences everywhere.

In my nearly forty years of skiing, I have seen its development from the smallest beginnings to a sport of the masses, involving huge facilities on innumerable slopes. But in 1924 even towropes were largely unknown. The first time we went up to Stowe, Vermont, Mount Mansfield had neither lifts nor ropes. We spent four hours climbing the mountain by the carriage road (using skins under our skis to keep from slipping back) and then coasting down the same way we came up in twenty minutes. We had heard of such things as christiana and telemark turns, but they were for Scandinavians who were born with a pair of skis on their feet. We relied on the good old toes-turned-in snowplow both to brake and to turn. Many years later I mastered the christy pretty well, and I've never forgotten the thrills I got from showing off my technique to whoever was willing to watch.

Some of the happiest and most exuberant periods of my life occurred on skiing vacations. We often went up to Lake Placid on the night train for the Christmas holidays. Much of the skiing there was done on the quite simple Stevens Hill, near the hotels, which had a single towrope. At first, the hill was thronged by beginners who seemed to be scared out of their wits; someone fell every moment in front of me. The towrope had to stop constantly to permit sprawling neophytes to crawl or be dragged out of the path. Five days later, I was amazed at the difference. The frightened and awkward beginners seemed to have turned into comparative experts; the rope ran smoothly, and nobody seemed to fall. (I suppose the hopeless cases had given up Stevens Hill and gone to an even easier place, but in any event the improvement seemed miraculous.)

A later Christmas vacation at Lake Placid we spent with our good friends the Charles Goodmans and their children. The oldest of them was a charming college boy, Robert. I recall our staying up a good part of the night, sitting in one of our lower berths and talking philosophy, reciting poetry, and having a wonderful time. As I write this, three decades later, I know that Robert Goodman and his wife are somewhere in Mississippi, hoping against all hope that their dear son Andy will somehow be found alive. For Andy is one of the three devoted workers for civil rights for negroes who disappeared twenty days ago, leaving no trace except their charred automobile.[1] My heart goes out to the bereaved father, Robert, whom I knew as a serious-minded, idealistic student so long ago, who communicated his ideals to his son and now must somehow learn to accept Andy's martyrdom. My own sympathy is the more poignant because my own son—Benjamin Jr. (Buz)—is now (July 1964) in Mississippi with hundreds of others risking their lives to do the humanitarian work which their conscience tells them must be accomplished by people like themselves.

But back to Lake Placid, and an occurrence which sheds some light on the clashing temperaments of Hazel and myself. Since we were to be at the hotel for New Year's Eve, I decided to take my formal clothes with me. For some reason Hazel was against participating in formal affairs—possibly her hairdo wasn't right—and tried to dissuade me as well. I said that I knew the Goodmans were taking their outfits, and I wanted to do the same—and I did. Of course there was a gala New Year's party at our hotel; the Goodmans went up to dress for it, and so did I. In our room Hazel begged me not to wear my evening clothes; she would be greatly embarrassed if I were dressed and she was not. I was adamant. I said the whole thing was one of her caprices; she had no reason to leave her evening dress behind; I was tired of always obeying her orders; it would be silly for me not to wear my outfit after taking all the trouble to bring it.

As the argument waxed hotter, Hazel took the dress shirt I had laid out on the bed and threw it out the window into the snow below. I calmly took my other dress shirt out of the drawer and prepared to put the studs in it. Hazel seized that shirt out of my hands and threw it after the first. I had no recourse but to surrender—with bad grace, I am sure—and to go down to dinner dressed sheepishly in an ordinary suit. Hazel retrieved the snow-covered shirts, and we gave some awkward explanation of the incident to our friends. When we finally returned to our room, we found that some wag (it was Bobby Goodman) had carefully laid my evening clothes out on the floor, as if they were being worn by some horizontal manikin. This closed the incident on a humorous note.

No doubt a psychologist or a Simenon could have deduced a good many things about the state of our marriage from that incident. In my view, Hazel and I were good people whose virtues greatly outweighed our faults. We had a fairly wide community of interests—primarily our children, but also theater, opera, concerts, vacation travel, sports, and charitable activities. It was Hazel who, before our marriage, had interested me in work for the blind. She had taught dancing to the children at the Dyker Heights Home for the Blind, and later taught at the newly founded New York Guild for the Jewish Blind. (In the year that I write these lines, the guild, under a slightly changed name, is celebrating its fiftieth anniversary.) Through Hazel's interest I began as a "big brother" to one of the very handicapped blind boys. Later I was to become a director, chairman of the budget committee, and finally president of the guild, whose annual budget grew from $30,000 to a recent $1,300,000, a percentage increase matching that of the U.S. gross national product.

We had more reason to expect a happy and successful marriage than do many couples. Why did we fail? The less important reason, probably, was a certain lack of physical compatibility. We were too young and inexperienced to recognize this at the time of our marriage. But the chief difficulty, I am convinced, grew out of a defect in my character which prevented me from dealing, as I should have, with a defect in Hazel's. My wife's outstanding qualities were her energy and her many practical abilities. But, more than most people, she had the faults of her virtues. She was sure she could handle anything better than anyone else; she naturally took the lead in all prac-

tical arrangements; this led her in turn into the habit of boss-
ing those around her, including her husband. I was not the man
to tolerate that treatment. Though I liked to oblige and hated
to quarrel about anything, I was strongly independent and
inwardly resented all forms of domination.

If I had known at twenty-three what I know now, our marriage would have gone quite differently. From the very beginning I would have refused to be told what to do, would have
insisted that my wishes in all matters carry equal weight with
Hazel's, and would even have invented wishes different from
hers to make sure that she would not always have things her
way. I would have studied more carefully the countless wiles
and devices she used to put herself in the right and me in the
wrong. I would have devised effective countermeasures. Instead, I made the great mistake of assuming that each issue
that came up was trivial and therefore not worth fighting
about. What really counted, I thought, was my great financial
success—to the surprise of many, especially my mother, who
had known me as a dreamy youth—and my steady climb
towards affluence and social position.

Our marriage was doomed to failure—nay, was already a
fundamental failure—before either Hazel or I suspected that
there was anything radically wrong. In the summer of 1926,
living at a comfortable vacation house in Deal, I was playing
golf on Wednesdays at the swanky Deal Country Club with
Bert Parker, manager of the local office of McDonnell and
Company, with whom I had placed purchase and selling
orders. Life seemed comfortable, luxurious, interesting, rewarding in many areas. My brother Victor visited us one
weekend, and he commented on how wonderfully well things
were going for us. I agreed, and then added: "Perhaps things
are going too well, and there is some great unhappiness in
store for us." That this proved to be a prophetic remark is not
surprising. I was married and had three children; in Bacon's
phrase I had "given hostages to Fortune," and I was more vulnerable than I dreamed.

In early March of the next year we returned from a vacation in Florida to find that Newton was suffering from ear trouble. We called in Dr. Friesner, the great ear specialist of Mt. Sinai Hospital. He diagnosed our child with mastoiditis which required an operation. After the operation, spinal meningitis set in, and Newton died on April 20, 1927. He would have been nine years old the following May 12.

Many painful incidents connected with Newton's illness and death are engraved on my memory, but I don't have the courage to recount them—for which the reader may indeed be grateful. If I tried, mine would resemble that abortive and pathetic account that Daedalus tried to cut in stone about the flight and fall of his beloved son Icarus. Virgil's lines are dear to me.[2] Years later I was to weep when I was reminded of our loss by the account of a child's death in Aldous Huxley's *Point Counterpoint*.[3] Alas! so many parents have suffered what we did. But what a consolation it is to reflect that penicillin has conquered meningitis, along with diphtheria and the many other ills that took such a toll of children's lives and parents' hearts.

Newton was buried in our plot in Westchester Hills Cemetery. As members of the Free Synagogue, we had acquired it not long before, little thinking that we would soon use it. The little footstone bears the words: "SWEETEST, BRAVEST, MOST BELOVED CHILD." He was all that, and more. My mother was then in Europe, visiting her numerous family. (Hazel had taken happy films of her departure, the last that show Newton alive.) We had tried to keep all news of Newton's illness from her. At the last she suspected some disaster and beseeched us to tell her. It was I who took that sad duty on my shoulders, hiding my own grief as best I could and invoking what philosophy I could command to soften the heavy blow that was to bow her head. She answered in a letter of poignant consolation to me, and across the wide ocean I knew that her tears were flowing with mine.

Hazel and I felt closely united in our grief, but this sense of union indicated to us more clearly than we had realized how we had been drifting apart. Shortly after the funeral we lunched together in a Chinese restaurant. We talked about starting a new and better life together. Hazel felt that she should tell me things about her life she had kept hidden from me. I had been a cold, relatively unresponsive husband, too immersed in my career to give much of myself to her. She had needed more warmth and understanding and had obtained it in a friendship with our family doctor. She said it was a close friendship, nothing more. I did not question her, accepted her avowal, and promised to be a better husband from then on. Hazel, too, promised to be less dominating.

We were both eager to have another child—dreaming of another Newton to reincarnate the boy we had lost. In due course Hazel was pregnant, and everything should have gone smoothly between us. But that was not the case. A great grief and the best of intentions are not enough, alas! to correct deep-seated conflicts between a husband and wife. We soon drifted back towards our old patterns. In the fall, despite her pregnancy, Hazel announced her intention of making a trip through Russia with one of her closest friends, Pauline H. Naturally, I was too busy making money to go along.

Thus I was left alone for two full months, and thus the first liaison came into my life, at the age of thirty-three, after ten years of marital fidelity. It is not my intention here to write of my sexual adventures, à la Frank Harris, nor even to emulate the candor of Rousseau's *Confessions*. But neither shall I imitate the disingenuous reticence of that great lover, Chateaubriand, who in some three thousand pages of *Souvenirs d'Outre Tombe* refused to disclose any of his famous affairs. Without the aid of editorial notes, the reader of those extraordinary memoirs might innocently wonder how it happened that Chateaubriand, in over fifty years of married life, spent so little time with his wife. I propose to be more frank, if only in hopes of shedding some light on human character.

In an important sense my sexual life has been lived in reverse. In Victorian novels it was taken for granted that young men would drink and gamble and wench, sowing many bushels of wild oats before they settled down in marriage to become pillars of respectability. But in my own youth I sowed not even a half-wild oat. I didn't drink, smoke, chew tobacco, gamble, swear, or use obscene language. Never once did I go to a burlesque show, even though Minsky's sultry and buxom beauties beckoned me from countless hoardings. The idea of visiting a brothel never entered my head, although in my adolescence, friends often talked of such matters. For some reason, which I never examined, I considered myself different from other young men—and no doubt superior in both ability and character. (What a prig I was!) At bottom I knew I had the same sexual instincts and impulses as everyone else, but it seemed my clear duty to suppress and deny them. My success was far from complete; I had a long struggle with masturbation, and from time to time I succumbed to such books as Pierre Louy's *Aphrodite* or Petronius's *The Golden Ass*. But I did relatively little erotic reading, and always with a guilty feeling. It took several decades for me to free myself from this sense of guilt.

Some years ago a teenage daughter of mine was staying in my house, and entering her room I found a copy of *Fanny Hill* by her lamp. The only thing I knew about the book was from a footnote to an entry in Boswell's *Diary*, in which he mentioned spending some time with John Cleland. The footnote remarked soberly that Cleland was the author of *Fanny Hill*, "considered the most pornographic book ever published." Even though I was then in my late fifties, the discovery of the book in my house shocked me. I read a few pages at random, shuddered to think of my own daughter wallowing in such filth, and threw the obscene work from me. As I am writing these pages here in Alassio, Italy, fifteen years later, I refresh myself with daily reading of such volumes as Graves's *The White Goddess*, *The Letters to Milena* of Kafka (what a hopeless neurasthenic!), *The War Letters* of Rilke (much less neurotic), two of Simenon's casual masterpieces, *Tropic of Cancer* by Henry Miller—and *Fanny Hill*. The latter unspeakable tome I find indeed to be as pornographic as anyone could want or fear, but at least it is written with verve and sparkle and a proper eighteenth-century regard for the decencies of language. *Tropic of Cancer* is quite another matter. In the introduction, Karl Shapiro hails Miller as an, or the, authentic prophet and genius of our time. Miller does have many original observations that strike home, but much of the book appears to me like the graffiti in men's lavatories in public buildings. Perhaps if I live long enough, I'll learn to appreciate and enjoy Miller's enthusiastic use of four-letter words. I'm not anxious to reach that stage of enfranchised taste; but my present enjoyment of *Fanny Hill* costs me no qualms of conscience, and I deem that a sufficient advance.

Before my marriage at twenty-three, my chapter on "Sleeping with Women" would have read like Holinshed's account of "Snakes in Ireland." There is still a considerable body of opinion that favors virginity for both bridegroom and bride. Theoretically, I think differently about that matter now than I did then, but my practice is not so different. I believe that people should live their sexual lives in accordance with their overall character and temperament, rather than by some norms imposed from the outside. But if I had had that view in my earliest manhood, would I have behaved much differently than I did? Very likely not; my innate disposition, I think, would in any case be to move from asceticism to sexual hedonism rather than the other way around.

Let me describe my first extramarital affair in the soberest fashion. The girl—let us call her Jenny—was about my own age, by no means beautiful, noted for plain-speaking and a rather sharp tongue, a close friend of ours for fifteen years. She was unmarried and never seemed much interested in men. I had kissed her in friendly fashion over the years, and in quite a bit more than friendly fashion during the summer before we started our affair. One evening, while Hazel was far off in Russia, I took her home from a concert. Everything was propitious for a love affair to begin, and it began. To my mind the prescription for a liaison consists of one part attraction and four parts opportunity. Two lines of our dialogue should be reported because they reflect our respective temperaments:

> I, meditatively: 'If we should consummate our love, I wonder if it would bring you more happiness or sorrow.'
>
> She, without hesitation: 'There's only one way to find out, and that's to try.'

What was a man to do next? Perhaps I should characterize the entire liaison from Jenny's viewpoint in the jocose terms I once used to describe an old maid's idea of rape: "It's a fate worse than death, but better than nothing." I was far from an ideal lover. I was hardly a lover at all in the romantic sense of the term; at bottom I always considered Jenny a very good friend who appealed to me physically, and whom I liked to be with. Because of unfortunate experiences in my marriage, turning about the twin scourges of possessiveness and jealousy, I had come to be wary of romantic love. It seemed to me that the ideal relationship, for my temperament at least and perhaps for people generally, would be a combination of sincere friendship with sex. This combination appeared to offer most of the advantages of love without any of its serious disadvantages. Comparatively few women have shown enthusiasm for this practical formula. It appealed to Jenny more than to most women because of her intensely practical spirit, but I am sure even she was hardly satisfied with my rather carefully measured-out devotion.

Our love affair operated under numerous handicaps, chief of which was the fact that I was intensely busy. We could see each other only seldom and briefly. I remained faithful to Jenny in my fashion for nearly seven years. During all this time she behaved in exemplary manner towards me, rarely finding fault or asking for more than I offered her. But in 1933 or 1934 she told me that the affair was too unsatisfying and too wearing on her and that she had decided to terminate it by spending an extended time in Mexico. We parted very good friends; in fact I have a sentimental memory of the last hour we spent together in the cabin of her Ward Line steamer. (Little did I think then that my firm was later to control that old-established steamship company.) Jenny is still a very good friend of mine. All in all, our relationship has been a rewarding one for both of us, despite the shortcomings of its erotic phase.

It seems callous or frivolous to pass from describing a liaison to hailing the birth of a child, but human nature permits us to do many contrary things and to experience many inconsistent emotions within a short space of time. Was it not Goethe who speaks of the brief instant that it takes the mind of man to pass from good to evil thoughts? And vice versa.

Our second Newton was born on April 10, 1928, ten days before the anniversary of the loss of our first. His birth brought great happiness to Hazel and me: it seemed an especial kindness of Providence to send us a boy. I recall waiting anxiously in Doctors' Hospital in the early morning for the fateful news. When it came, some force from outside my mind seemed to dictate a triumphant poem, which I jotted down in a few minutes. Here it is:

RESTORATION

He has returned
From the dark, vacant night
Where no star burned.
He has returned
Our child, our hearts' delight
He did not vanish *quite*
He has returned.
He has returned
Tho' the grave claimed him then
In stillness urned.

He has returned:
As the year blooms again
Back to our wilful ken
He has returned.
He has returned
As he went forth, in Spring.
Dull Death he spurned;
He has returned
For Love's new treasuring
Our hearts in rapture sing
He has returned!

The second Newton was a beautiful boy, with large brown eyes, and a halo of black, curly hair. Never was a child received with more enthusiasm and surrounded with more loving care. But our family doctor of many years, May Wilson (who devoted much of her life to seeking a cure for cardiac rheumatism in children) had some disquieting news. It seemed that all was not well with the baby's thymus gland, and there was some possibility of serious trouble in the future. This apprehension caused us to take special care to protect him against illness. (We had already moved from our Riverside Drive apartment because we felt the raw winter winds that blew there might have caused our first Newton's ear trouble.)

With heavy heart I write now that, after the first few years, our second boy was to bring us little happiness and much concern and sorrow. He did not seem really at home with us; he was extremely difficult to get along with; it was soon evident that he was highly neurotic, and in all probability schizophrenic. At times we have blamed ourselves because we gave this child our first Newton's name and endeavored from the start to consider him our first-born returned to us. Did this give him a confused sense of his own identity? Did he resent having to stand comparison with the matchless vanished paragon of our family? Did the special physical care lavished on him weaken his char-

acter? I am quite convinced that there is no substance in these
speculations and that it was simply Newton's misfortune and
our own that he was born to be what he was.

I had sought an additional occupation for my mental ener-
gies, as well as a distraction from my grief. For some time previously I had been thinking of writing a textbook on security
analysis. I felt that the texts then available were outmoded
and generally inadequate, especially because they paid little
attention to the new importance of common stocks or to the
quirks and pitfalls of corporate accounting. I decided to work
up a college course in the subject before I put my ideas in
printed form. I approached Professor James Egbert, head of
the Extension Division of Columbia. He liked my idea and set
the course—called "Security Analysis"—for the fall of 1927.
Everyone was surprised at the response. The course was completely swamped by more than 150 registrants. In retrospect,
that phenomenon is easy to understand. The bull market of the
1920s was now in full swing; the public was eager for information, instruction, and—most of all—good tips; there were no
similar courses being given elsewhere by a practicing Wall
Street man. The registration was closed at some high figure,
and it was necessary to station people at the door to make sure
that no one crashed the gate. Although I warned my students
that any stocks mentioned were for illustration only and under
no circumstances were to be taken as recommendations to
buy, it did happen that some of the issues I discussed as undervalued subsequently enjoyed substantial advances—though
very likely no more than made by the soaring market as a
whole. The few such incidents were enough to give my course
the reputation of being a sure moneymaker for those who took
it. In the fall of 1928 the registration was even greater than
the year before; many people insisted on being allowed to take
the course over again in expectation of being introduced to a
new crop of profitable current examples.

Thus began my academic career, which was to last over
forty years and to include professorships with various titles at

Columbia and UCLA, as well as lecture courses at other institutions. One of the students in the fall of 1927 was David L. Dodd, then an assistant professor in the School of Business at Columbia. He was to become my coadjutor in teaching, the co-author of our "Bible of Wall Street," *Security Analysis*, an associate in important financial ventures, and an unfailingly loyal friend. From the questions that arose in my mind as I prepared my first year's lectures it was evident to me that I was far from ready to write a satisfactory textbook. Indeed, it was seven years before *Security Analysis* made its appearance; it would have proved a great mistake to have published it earlier, for by 1934 I was able to pour into it wisdom acquired at the cost of much suffering.

In the summer of 1928 I made my first trip to Europe since my visit to England as a seven-year-old at the turn of the century. Hazel was nursing Newton and had to stay behind. (We had taken a cottage for the summer at Galen Hall, a large hotel complex in the hills near Reading, Pennsylvania.) I arranged to meet Mother in Europe, and to travel with her to England, France, Germany, Switzerland, and Austria. My main objectives were to hear a Wagner series in Bayreuth, the Mecca of us Wagnerites, and also the summer festival at Salzburg, Mozart's home.

At Bayreuth we put up at the best hotel, called The Golden Anchor, which had been constructed about 1750 but appeared a good deal older. It lacked every modern convenience. We forgot about these discomforts the first evening, when we walked up the hill to the Festspielhaus. There, by a common accord as it were, the audience stood in their places and looked curiously around at each other. It was a dazzling sight, what with the women's gowns, jewels, and coiffures, the men in full evening dress, and the sprinkling of Indian turbans and officers' uniforms. The series of six operas consisted of *Der Meistersinger*, the four operas of the *Ring*, and *Tristan*. The performances were indescribably thrilling to me. That they were well done is unquestionable; but it was the atmosphere, redolent with tradition and deep musical significance that gave everything the cachet almost of the supernatural.

The Wagner family was very much in evidence. Siegfried Wagner—he of the *Idyll*—conducted three of the performances. Siegfried's wife Winifred sat, blond and queenly, in the box in the rear. Her identification with Hitler lay unsuspected ahead. Everyone went to visit "Wahnfried," where the family lived, including Cosima, Richard's legendary widow, who was 90 years old and said to be on her deathbed. (Actually she lived several years longer.) The tourists were allowed to go upstairs and peek in through the door of her room. Mother and I thought this was unseemly, and we stayed below. Instead we went over to the children's rooms. In one of them the boys—Wolfgang and Wieland—had arranged an exhibition of Dürer's etchings (in reproductions) and asked some small admission charge. The two fair-haired boys, scarcely in their teens, seemed very businesslike and cute. The next time I saw them they were rather portly men in their forties, in full charge of the Bayreuth Festivals and having to answer to their grandfather's ghost and to a number of living citizens for the radical changes they had introduced into the sacred procedures that governed the festivals for so many years. I did not see their sister then—she must have been very young—but I was to meet her years later in the United States, as a rebel against Hitler and her mother.

Naturally I was impressed by the typically Wagnerian lines that the great (and impossible) composer placed on the facade of his home:

Hier wo mein Waehnen Frieden fand,
Wahnfried sei dieses Haus genannt.

(Here where my imaginings found peace
Let this house be named "Wahnfried")

Returning to America, I suggested to a German dentist I

knew that he call his chair "Zahnfried" ("tooth-peace") and kindly offered him a suitable motto to go with it:

> Hier wo mein' Zähne Frieden fand,
> Zahnfried sei dieser Stuhl gennannt.

For some incomprehensible reason he rejected my suggestion.

Wagner performances at Bayreuth are different from those everywhere else for many reasons; not the least important are the eating arrangements. The first thing you must do is to reserve a table in the restaurant near the Festspielhaus; this requires a surprisingly large tip to the head waiter. Then, before the opera starts—or maybe the night before—you order *two* meals in advance. I well recall the strange time schedule for *Götterämmerung*, which began at 4:00 p.m. At about 3:45 we all walked towards the Festspielhaus in our full evening costumes. The first act took exactly two hours, and was followed by the "Kleine Pause" of one hour, at which one ate fairly copiously. Then promptly at seven o'clock the second act commenced; this took only an hour and a half, and was followed by the "Grosse Pause" of a like duration. Here the eating and drinking was something to behold. It brought us to ten o'clock and the third act, which ran for two full hours and eventually let us all depart, tired but happy, for a midnight snack. It was an eight-hour day for sure, an unforgettable combination of heavy music and heavy eating.

From Bayreuth we went on to Salzburg. The chief thing we wanted was a good bath in a good bathroom. Fortunately, we had reservations for a nice suite at the Hotel Europa, of recent construction. When we got there after our exhausting journey by rail, we found a mob of people milling around in the lobby. I forced my way to the reception desk and asked smugly for the Graham reservation. After a long wait the clerk told us that he was sorry but he had no reservation for us and that no rooms were available. "Just look again please," said I, loftily. "Here is your signed cablegram confirming our reservations for today."

Now he was *very* sorry; somebody had made a regrettable mistake; but the fact was that there were no rooms available, and he could not do the impossible. Translated that meant that some other tourist had given them a large bribe and had been awarded our rooms. Angry and frustrated, we reported this enormity to the official Tourist's Office of Salzburg. Much shrugging of the shoulders, but no redress. What was worse, they said, was that because of the enormous influx of travelers from America, there were no rooms of any kind to be had in the town. At last they did find one room for us in the Gasthausstrasse, a street that lived up completely to its smelly name. How were we to manage with one room? The landlady rigged up a wash line down the middle and hung a sheet from it. For a bath there was the laundry basin, with a small amount of hot water— reminding me of the two baths I took at the Barman's farmhouse in the summer of 1910. So this was what our elegant suite at the Hotel de l'Europe had changed into.

Nonetheless, Salzburg was a great experience. I was privileged to see a performance of *Jedermann* in the Cathedral Square, with the famous Moissi in the title part, Helen Thimig (wife of Rheinhardt) as Die Glaube (Faith), and her sister in another role. I had taken the precaution to buy the text in advance, which I was able to follow in the late daylight of summer. Thus, I understood every word, and I found myself deeply moved by Helen Thimig's rendering of the great speech given to Faith. Moissi, of course, was matchless. I think it was at Salzburg too that I heard him as Orest in Goethe's *Iphigenie*, with Helen Thimig again. Fifteen years before I had written an elaborate study comparing the *Iphigenia in Taurus* of Euripides with that of Goethe. I felt almost as if that classic drama belonged to me, and to see it presented by two of the greatest stage figures of the time was a priceless experience. (Another time I saw Moissi in a memorable performance of Ibsen's *Ghosts*, given in German in the old Irving Place Theatre in New York.)

We spent some days in Munich, where I was amazed at the

enormous number of impressive public buildings, by the plentitude of Rubens' paintings in the Alte Pinacothek and by the incomparable Deutsches Museum of the technical arts. We went to the Ausstellungspark, a place of outdoor amusement, where we saw two pleasant entertainments. The first was a performance of marionettes entitled "The Woman with Two Husbands." The heroine was married to both an office worker, who was busy all day, and a footpad who did his business by night. As I recall it, most of the scenes took place in bed, with plenty of erotic movements effected by the expert string-pullers. I was amazed that a performance like that was permitted in a public park in 1928!

After the performance we went to a large outdoor restaurant. Mother, who always ate lightly, asked for "zwei weichgekochte Eier" (two soft-boiled eggs). The waiter was sorry. He could bring us scrambled eggs, poached eggs, and fried eggs, but not boiled eggs, because the latter were not on the bill-of-fare. My mother was incredulous—"If you can fry eggs you can certainly boil two for me." The waiter remained sorry, and that was that. Later reflection suggested that their eggs might have been too far gone to boil. When the pretty waitress in the old story asked the traveling salesman what he wanted, he answered "I want a plate of ham and eggs and some kind words." The plate was served in silence, whereupon the man asks "Where are the kind words?" "Don't eat the eggs" was the reply.

We were due to go on to Zurich to visit a niece of Mother's. The trip by train over the mountains would take a dreary eight hours. Mother had heard that one of the first air services had been established between those two cities, and the flying time was only two hours. Was I game to fly? Neither of us had been in the air before, except for a three-minute sightseeing flight I had made in a barnstormer's plane over Atlantic City. If Mother wasn't afraid, obviously I couldn't be. I remember us few passengers filing out to enter the plane, with curious visitors lined up on both sides, as if we were going to our execution. Nothing untoward happened. We flew over the Bodensee (Lake Constance) not far from Friedrichshafen, where the first huge zeppelins were being built and tested. The little lake steamers below us seemed like beetles crawling on the water. As we passed from German to Swiss territory, I noticed a single change in the landscape. The German fields had trees at their corners, but the Swiss fields had one tree in the center, where the farmer could more readily seek its shade.

Of our stay in Zurich I recall only a curious scene in natural history. The cousins and we went to Lake Zurich for some kind of picnic. Sitting near a large rock, I noticed two armies of ants in furious combat. One set had wings and the others were wingless. It was a war to the death; I watched for a long time, to the displeasure of the others who showed no interest in the sight. But I was thinking of the line from "Dover Beach"— "where ignorant armies clash by night"—of the strange passions or even stranger calculations that drive both ants and men to conflict and wholesale destruction.

In the fall of 1928 the Ben Grahams were ready to make another move, this time to something really sumptuous. Enormous office buildings and scarcely less impressive apartment houses were going up in all the finer districts in New York. We heard that the old hotel Beresford at 81st and Central Park West—where our close friends the Greenmans had lived for some years after their marriage—was to be replaced by a thirty-story apartment building of ultimate luxury. That was what the high-flying Grahams wanted. From the plans we selected a duplex apartment, with terrace, on the 18th and 19th floors. It had ten rooms and Lord knows how many baths; there were also maids' rooms available near the roof. The rent was to be $11,000 per year, and the lease was to run ten years.

We were not at all apprehensive at taking on an obligation of such magnitude. These were small figures compared with those I was getting used to. For the year just closing, we were to show about 60 percent earned on our starting capital of

$1,500,000. My own gains exceeded $600,000 before taxes. I had done this by following what I thought to be highly conservative methods, keeping my risks of loss to a minimum compared with the crazy speculation in overvalued securities whirling all about me. What a *Wunderkind* I was—before the catastrophe! The last thing I did that year was to sign the ten-year lease for our Beresford apartment—to take effect on its completion in the fall of 1929. We signed the lease in our drawing-room on a train taking us to Palm Beach for a Christmas vacation.

CHAPTER THIRTEEN

The Midpoint of Life's Way: The Deluge Begins

Nel medio del camin de mia vita
Mi ritrova nel una selva oscura.

(In the midpoint of the road of my life
I found myself in a dark forest.)

Thus Dante began his great poem, writing in the year 1300 at the age of thirty-five. His life's journey was in fact far more than half over, for he died in his early fifties—as had his idol Virgil; so did great Caesar, Shakespeare, Molière, Beethoven, Napoleon, and many others. In 1929 I turned thirty-five, the age at which my father died. But I am writing these words in the summer of 1964, so that this chapter does, in a very real sense, represent a middle point for me. It would be an exaggeration to suggest that, like Dante, I too was about to get a full taste of Hell. Yet, there were times when I thought I was descending into ever lower circles of trouble and discouragement, the gloomier because they contrasted so sharply with my days of glorious success. In his exile Dante must have known that feeling well, and he put its most famous expression in the mouth of Francesca da Rimini:

> Nessun maggior' dolore
> Che ricordarsi del tempo felice
> Nella miseria...[1]

(But why did he add "and that your teacher knows"? Virgil suffered no misery except from his own dissatisfaction with his immortal work.)

Actually, the first half of 1929 ushered in exciting and flattering events for me; and even the terrific shocks that came later in the year left me comparatively unharmed. My big troubles were to come in the following three years. Yet, in its implications, 1929 was as fateful for me as for the rest.

The January vacation included one adventure of which I was anything but the hero. Jerome Lewine, who at a young age was really *the* senior partner of the old brokerage house of Hentz and Company, invited me and two others to go sailfishing with him. The other guests were a famously successful financial lawyer, named Isidor Kresel, and another lawyer named Oscar Lewis. We set out in a boat that seemed mighty small to me at the start, and seemed to grow smaller as we got farther from land. In a half hour or so I wasn't feeling so well, and neither was Oscar. To console us, perhaps, our host unwrapped some pretty sandwiches and offered us our choice. Our hands had just about strength enough to wave them away. When the pint-sized Kresel and Jerry Lewine began eating with great gusto, the sight quite overpowered Lewis and me, and we crawled below, where we lay in the saddest state for what seemed like hours. Just when we were passing from the second fear (that we were going to die) to the third (that we were *not* going to die), we saw a figure in the hatchway: "Come up, Oscar, Ben," it shouted, "I've caught a sailfish." But we just moaned "Take us home" and turned our faces to the wall. Jerry reversed the prow towards port, and two hours later Oscar and I thanked him wanly as we tottered ashore.

I did not meet Kresel again, but I read later with a certain sympathy of his prosecution by Max Steuer relating to a somewhat technical infraction of the law in the Bank of United States collapse. Steuer was to submit me to three days of hammer-and-tongs cross-examination in the Kaufmann Department Stores valuation case in 1939. Oscar Lewis I was to meet again when he was special master in another valuation case and I was appearing as expert witness for a bondholder's committee. I didn't recognize him at first, but he called me to the bench in an intermission and asked me how I could possibly have forgotten our sailfishing expedition together.

And the sailfish that Jerry Lewine hauled in? There's a little story about that too. A month or so after the event I was invited to lunch in the Hentz Company's private dining room, where the proud host bade me admire a new ornament on the wall. It was that accursed sailfish, beautifully stuffed and expensively mounted, with a silver marker telling where, when, how heavy, and by whom. "Turn that damned thing around," I begged. "Just to look at it makes me seasick all over again." But the others just laughed. Despite this sad experience in Palm Beach waters, I came back to New York beautifully tanned—so much so that my large class of palefaces at Columbia greeted my swaggering return to the podium with a long and loud stamping of their feet.

During this period, various kinds of investment trusts were forming. The first ones had been fixed trusts, innocent enough in character, in which a bank held a specified portfolio of common stocks as trustee (hence the name), and stockholders each held a pro-rata share in this unchanging portfolio. Next came the management trusts—companies whose officers could vary the portfolio, just as we were doing in the Graham Joint Account. There was nothing inherently unsound in such an arrangement; indeed, it had proven itself successful for many

decades in England, although like any financial institution it
needed honest direction and sound policy. However, the speculative atmosphere of the late 1920s had seduced or corrupted
nearly everyone of importance in finance and led to unbeliev-
ably shaky practices by firms of heretofore unquestioned probity.

Not a few of the larger stock exchange firms formed their
own investment companies, selling shares to their clients.
They were lured into this practice by a threefold profit: a
markup or load on the sale of the shares, a management fee for
running the company, and the straight brokerage commissions
on portfolio purchases and sales. The Hentz partners decided
they were as fit as anyone to have their own fund—nay more
so, because they thought they could persuade Ben Graham to
head it up. I was by no means sure that I wanted the job, because I could not expect to have a compensation arrangement
approaching the 20 percent-50 percent cut I received from the
Joint Account (though, of course, I was dividing part of it now
with Jerry Newman). But the Hentz partners were rather
insistent. They spoke of a fund of 25 millions, of the prestige I
would enjoy as top man in so large a venture, of the guaran-
tees I could have under a long-term contract. Jerry Lewine
was enthusiastic about the possibilities of combining his well-
known talent for picking good market situations with my now
widely acknowledged supremacy in finding special or bargain
situations, and in security analysis generally. I was tempted
by the big numbers being thrown around, and we had several
conferences to see if we could put the thing together.

In the meantime Bernard Baruch came into my picture in
an unexpected way. A year or so before I had been privileged
to meet the great man and to suggest to him a number of Gra-
ham-type investments—all of which appealed to his keen
sense of security values. These included such issues as Plymouth Cordage, which sold at about 70, earned and paid a
handsome dividend, and had over $100 per share in working
capital alone. Others of the same type were Pepperell Manu-

facturing Company, long a household name in sheets and pil-
lowcases, and Heywood & Wakefield, a leading maker of baby
carriages. All were selling well below their minimal value as
judged by the ordinary standards of a private business, and at
ridiculously low levels in comparison with the prices of most
popular stocks at the time. These discrepancies illustrated the
peculiarly unreasonable character of the stock market of the
late 1920s, where all the emphasis was laid on an industry's
promise (favorites were electric utilities and chemicals), dom-
inant size (companies in the Dow Jones Industrial Average), or
else a record of recent growth, accompanied by speculative
and manipulative ballyhoo. Many substantial companies with
excellent long-term records which fell outside the favored categories, like Plymouth Cordage and Pepperell, were neglected
and sold for years on end at bargain-counter prices.

Mr. Baruch deigned to listen to my analyses, to approve of
my choices, and to buy substantial amounts of each. From his
point of view, no doubt, his concurrence alone was sufficient
reward for my pains. To some degree he was right, of course,
because the mere knowledge that his judgment backed my
own, and that we now had similar financial interests, was of
substantial value to me. On two occasions, Baruch was to
make an effort to secure my election to boards of companies in
which we both held stock; in one he succeeded. But these
moves he made not to help me but to improve his own investments. In the fairly numerous contacts I have had in my
career with this eminent personage, he never did anything
helpful or generous for me as a person, nor did I ever hear of
his doing so for anyone else. He had the vanity that attenuates
the greatness of some men, and it may have been this vanity,
rather than true generosity, that led him to give large sums to
charities and causes, sums for which he received the wide
recognition and acclaim he always coveted.

We had several general conversations in his office far up in
the forty-nine-story Equitable Building at 120 Broadway (our
fund was destined to be part of a group that controlled that

enormous structure). We both agreed that the stock market had advanced to inordinate heights, that the speculators had gone crazy, that respected investment bankers were indulging in inexcusable highjinks, and that the whole thing would have to end one day in a major crash. I recall Baruch's commenting on the ridiculous anomaly that combined an 8 percent rate for time-loans on stocks with dividend yields of only 2 percent. To which I replied, "That's true, and by the law of compensation we should expect someday to see the reverse—2 percent time-money combined with an 8 percent dividend on good stocks." My prophecy was not far wrong as a picture of 1932—and it was borne out precisely, under a different set of market circumstances, some twenty years later. What seems really strange now is that I could make a prediction of that kind in all seriousness, yet not have the sense to realize the dangers to which I continued to subject the Account's capital.

Once when I was waiting in Baruch's office, he emerged into the antechamber with a stoutish, round-faced man of about the same age at his side. After a moment's hesitation, he said: "Winston, allow me to present my young friend, Ben Graham, a very clever fellow." We shook hands. I knew of Churchill's record in World War I and of his present displacement from the British government. It was a moment I should have savored more than I did.

I owed another introduction to Baruch. Just after World War II, I was invited to hear a private lecture at Columbia by General Eisenhower on our military strength for the future. Baruch was there, and after the lecture he presented me, with a few flattering words, to the fabulous commander-in-chief. When I left the building, it had started to rain hard, and I opened the umbrella I had wisely brought. Just then General Eisenhower came out and stood for a moment next to me. "May I share my umbrella with you, General?" I asked. "Oh no, thanks very much," he replied and strode off into the rain. Military men in uniform are not supposed to use umbrellas, I guess. These two introductions I owe to Baruch, and I am grateful for them. But I can't help thinking, ungraciously perhaps, that the old man, now ninety-two (in 1964), owes me more than I owe him.

Back to 1929. A message came from Baruch that he would like to see me in his office. When I arrived, his famous secretary, Miss Boyle, told me he was occupied and asked me to wait. After about a half-hour the financier came out, apologetic for once. He had been taking his afternoon nap, but Miss Boyle should have told him I was there. When we went into his huge office, lined with plaques of all sorts attesting to his achievements (and, indeed they had been great in peace and war), he told me that he was going to make a proposal to me that he had never before offered to anyone. He would like me to become his financial partner. "I am now fifty-seven years old," he said, "and it's time I slowed up a bit, and let a younger man like you share my burden and my profits." He added that I should have to give up my present business and devote myself entirely to our new partnership. I replied that I was highly flattered—flabbergasted, in fact—by his proposal, but I felt I could not end so abruptly the close and highly satisfactory relations I had with my friends and clients. And for that reason—and another that will be explained—the matter was dropped. How different, how much better, the next seven years would have been for me had I accepted his terms without thinking of other people!

The negotiations with the Hentz partners for the establishment of a jointly run investment fund dragged on through subsequent months; I cannot recall what made them take so long. Then came the market's first serious sinking spell in August, and we decided to put the project on the shelf for a while. It was never taken down. Beginning in September, the terrific Crash cut stock averages in half in a matter of days, culminating in a hecatomb in which millions of shares changed hands, the ticker ran hours late, and the DJIA dropped nearly out of sight. The prospect of a Graham-Hentz Investment Fund dissolved into thin air. Newman and I turned our thoughts back to the Benjamin Graham Joint Account; there was plenty to think about.

Here was its position in the middle of 1929: our capital was 2½ million; we had shown only a slight gain for the first half of 1929 (a fact that should have augured trouble ahead). We had a large number of hedging and arbitrage operations going, involving a long position of about 2½ million, offset by about an equal dollar volume of short sales. In our calculations these did not involve any net risk of consequence and so needed only a nominal part of our capital. We had in addition as much as 4½ million in true long positions, or investments of various types, against which we owed some 2 million. As margins were then figured, we calculated ours at about 125 percent; this was six times the brokers' minimum requirement and about three times what was generally considered a conservative margin. We were also convinced that all our long securities were intrinsically worth their market price. Although many of our issues were but little known to active Wall Street hands, similar ones had previously shown a praiseworthy tendency to come to life at a decent interval after we bought them and to give us the chance to sell them out at a nice profit, replacing them by other bargain issues which we were constantly digging up.

In a typical hedge operation we would purchase a convertible preferred stock and sell the related common stock at just about the equivalent price. In weak markets the common would decline a good deal more than the preferred, and we could undo the operation at a good profit, despite the fourfold commissions that made our otherwise sluggish account a pleasure to our brokers. Originally, we had completed such operations by selling out the preferred when we bought back the common. But having found that we would often need to reinstate the position later, thus having to buy the preferred again at a higher price, we adopted a policy of only partially undoing the operations. We would buy the common, but hold on to the preferred, as an appreciably sound investment, until we could again sell the common at an equivalent price against it. In addition, we went in for partial hedges: we would sell only half the common shares called for by our preferred holdings, hoping to get a better price for the remainder when and if the price advanced further. Our idea was to make money whichever way the price of the common went. If down, we would cover our half-short position on good terms; if up, we would benefit from the increased value of the half-interest we hadn't sold.

In the tremendous declines after September 1929, we covered a large number of our short positions, making a nice profit. But in most cases we did not sell out the preferreds (or convertible bonds) since their prices seemed too low. We closed the year with a loss of exactly 20 percent compared to a much larger loss for the DJIA. Many of our participants had their own margin accounts whose losses had been much higher because of the pyramiding effect of the borrowed money. Practically everyone was pleased with the account's result for the year; in fact, I heard myself referred to more than once as a "financial genius" for not having lost more. The year 1929 ended in a period of some price recovery and of relative calm; most of us believed that the worst was over.

There was some delay in finishing the new Beresford Apartments, so we could not move into our regal duplex until October 1929, just when the holocaust in Wall Street was at its height. I was never really happy in that palace. I regretted the $11,000 rent and the ten-year contract as soon as they became realities. But, in addition, the whole place seemed too large. There were endless decisions to make about the decorations and furnishings, and these in turn put me in a dilemma. On the one hand, I have never had a real interest in such matters—indeed, in any sort of material possessions—so it was an annoying chore even to shop for furnishings. On the other hand, if I left all the decisions to Hazel, that would confirm more completely than ever her conviction that she was the boss of the family by right of superior knowledge on every subject. (I note, as I type this, an unused little ashtray in my room in Alassio, bearing the inscription: "Il padrone sono io; chi comanda e mia moglie.")[2] How frequent it is nowadays for the wife to command. I don't remember now how I resolved the dilemma. I do recall that we spent a not so small fortune on the furnishings.

We started off with a troupe of servants, including a combined butler and personal valet for me. It was about that time that I visited the new quarters of our friends Dave and Lisette Sarnoff on Fifth Avenue and found that the man who had risen from Russian immigrant to head of the huge RCA company had a room with a built-in barber chair where a barber would shave him every day. It was one of my valet's duties to give me a daily massage, which I soon came to regard as a nuisance and a waste of time. I insisted that he be let go. That was the first and last time that I had a full-time manservant.

On several occasions, Chateaubriand writes in his memoirs about his simple tastes, formed in part by his exile in England in poverty and hunger. When he returned to England in a special warship as French ambassador to St. James, he took with him his personal chef.[3] It is ironical that to nine Americans out of ten "Chateaubriand" means only the most expensive steak on the menu; in that sense it was his chef, inventor of the luxurious dish, who made the great writer's name a household word. (So much for Chateaubriand's simple tastes!)

Our Beresford apartment had a large terrace on the eighteenth floor, where a setback began, with a view both east, to Central Park, and south, to downtown. The three children played there with large toys and a pet rabbit. Our neighbors were Nathan Strauss, Jr., and family; Strauss was son of the philanthropist who had sold milk at a penny a glass to the city's poor, and nephew of Oscar Strauss, who had been our first Jewish ambassador (to Turkey), and whom I had heard speak as Bull Moose candidate for governor of New York in 1912.

To our chagrin we discovered one day, soon after they moved in, that the Strausses had erected a cast-iron wall between our terraces, which shut off our view to the south and was very unattractive as well. The Strauss wall became a cause célèbre for a while. We took it as a personal insult and an encroachment on our inviolable privileges. (I laugh now to think about the things that were important to me then.) We retained a lawyer, Mr. E. F. Greenman, of the eminent firm of C.N. Lehman & Greenman, to represent us, and heavy negotiations were carried on. Mr. Strauss claimed that we were keeping guinea pigs on our terrace, and he didn't want them to invade his domain. We retorted that the guinea pigs consisted of one small rabbit; he insisted on his right to privacy; and so on. Finally, a compromise of the great dispute was reached. The cast-iron wall was replaced by plants.

Years later I found myself sitting at the same table, at a charitable dinner, with the entire Strauss family. We recalled our "Berlin Wall" episode not only without rancor but even with a certain nostalgia. Then Mrs. Strauss was kind enough to remark: "We used to hear a lot about your daughter Marjorie, when our Nathan III was in her class at Lincoln School. He told us that she got A's in every subject, and he was too bashful to ask her to the dances."

For the winter months of 1930 Hazel engaged an apartment in St. Petersburg, Florida, where she would stay with the children, and where I would come for the longer holidays. Driving through that sunshine city for the first time I saw what I believed to be a large number of people with crutches, all gathered in a park. It turned out that these were the shuffle-board addicts. My January stay in Florida was marked by an incident which made little impression on me at the time, but which I was to recall often.

Hazel had met a man named John Dix, who was ninety-three years old. His father had founded the John Dix Uniform Company of Long Branch, New Jersey, and I had often passed their large factory on the way to Deal. I visited this Mr. Dix at his home in St. Petersburg and found him surprisingly alert for one so close to the century mark. He asked me all about my business, how many clients I had, how much money I owed to banks and brokers, and innumerable other questions. I answered them politely but with smug self-confidence. Suddenly John Dix said, with the greatest earnestness: "Mr. Graham, I want you to do something of the greatest importance to yourself. Get on the train to New York tomorrow; go to your office, sell out your securities; pay off your debts, and return their capital to your partners. I wouldn't be able to sleep one moment at night if I were in your position in these times, and you shouldn't be able to sleep either. I'm much older than you, with lots more experience, and you'd better take my advice."

I thanked the old man, a bit condescendingly no doubt, and said I would think over his suggestion. Then I hastened to put it out of my mind. Dix was not far from his dotage, he couldn't possibly understand my system of operations, his ideas were preposterous. As it happened he was 100 percent right and I 100 percent wrong. I have often wondered what my life would have been like if I had followed his advice. That it would have spared me much worry and regret I am sure; but whether my character and later career would have formed as they did after my ordeal by fire is another question.

The stock market in early 1930 had a nice recovery from the previous year's collapse. By April, the DJIA had reached 279, marking a gain of some 41 percent from the low point of 198 on November 13, 1929. But soon the entire economic picture clouded over because of the Credit Anstalt failure, and a second major decline set in which was to continue, with relatively short interruptions, until the DJIA reached the abysmally low level of 42 in June 1932.

Despite its encouraging beginning, the year 1930 was to prove by far the worst in the thirty-three-year history of my fund management. We were handicapped by the fact that we had already had to cover all our short positions. Owing a substantial sum increased the impact of market declines and put us at the mercy of our creditors. For about three years our great aim was to cut our debt service without sacrificing too much of the values we were sure were inherent in our portfo-

lio, despite the bad earnings picture that nearly every enterprise was showing.

Our loss for 1930 was a staggering 50½ percent; that for 1931
was 16 percent; but that for 1932 was only 3 percent—a comparative triumph. The cumulative losses for 1929 through
1932—before the tide turned—were thus 70 percent of our
proud 2½ million capital of January 1929. But we had stub-
bornly continued to make quarterly distributions of 1¼ percent—charged to Jerry and my capital—and these cut the
amount remaining at the end of 1932 to only 22 percent of the
original figure. A number of the participants withdrew all or
part of their capital. One of these was Bob Marony, who
explained most apologetically that he had to have his funds to
meet obligations elsewhere. (Fred Greenman told me then that
Bob—the imperturbable, fighting Irishman—had burst into
tears after disclosing the near-total loss of his fortune of far
more than a million dollars.) We gave Marony his pro-rata
share of the issues in our portfolio, against assumption of what
was then a quite small debt.

I think only one person made a new investment in our fund
during those difficult years. That was Elias Reiss, Jerry Newman's father-in-law, who put in $50,000 at what turned out to
be practically the low point of our fortunes. That meant that,
with his characteristic shrewdness, he was to reap a very high
return for his show of confidence in us. I have always been
grateful to Reiss for a very helpful gesture. Having heard of
our preoccupation with our debit balances, and the possible
selling that might grow out of them, he additionally offered to
put some of his large supply of U.S. government bonds at our
disposal, to fortify our position if required. As it happened, we
never had to take advantage of his generous offer.

We worked hard in those years to retrieve what values we
could and managed to make various beneficial arrangements
affecting our holdings. In one case we actually brought a suit
against some brokerage firms to recover losses on bonds of a
zinc mine. The prospectus had indicated very substantial earn-

ings in the past, but it had failed to state that they had been made by extracting all the good ore, so that what was left was bound to be relatively unprofitable. Our lawyers told us we had a meritorious—though unusual—case. Alfred Cook said the only way we could possibly lose before a jury would be if the other side got the almost invariably successful Max Steuer to defend them. What to do? Fred Greenman suggested that we retain Max Steuer ourselves as a consultant; in that way our opponents couldn't get him. We sent the redoubtable Steuer a check for his fee, $5,000, together with our summary of the facts. He said our case was a good one and well briefed, and pocketed the money. The upshot was that the defendants settled by buying back our bonds at two-thirds our cost— quite a substantial recovery for us.

One of our substantial holdings was the 8 percent cumulative preferred stock of Universal Pictures. This was a small issue which had been earning its dividend many times over before the Depression, but soon fell on evil days and passed the dividend. The price declined to 30 cents on the dollar, and this was a real blow to us. The president and founder, Max Laemmle, was continuing to pay himself a salary of three thousand a week plus a thousand a week to Carl Laemmle. These salaries exceeded the entire dividend owed on the preferred stock, and we felt they were excessive under the circumstances. I made an appointment to see Mr. Laemmle. After a wait outside his office I heard a cordial voice shouting "Hi, Graham, come in!" As I entered, a bit mystified, I saw a little man at his desk with a crestfallen face. "Oh," said he disgustedly, "I thought you were Graham McNamee" (Universal's celebrated news commentator). I wasn't able to persuade Laemmle to cut his salary, but we eventually unloaded our stock at a fairly respectable price.

Clearly, my family needed to cut down on its tremendous living expenses, especially since under the compensation contract the account paid me no salary but only a percentage of earnings for running the business. The chief problem was to get rid of that old man-of-the-mountain lease at the Beresford. By a stroke of luck we were able to sublet the apartment for most of a year (at nearly the rent we paid for it unfurnished) to Mrs. Marcus of Neiman-Marcus, the Dallas department store. Later we wiggled out of the balance of the lease by paying some indemnity, and we took another, much cheaper, but still quite impressive, place in the El Dorado on 91st Street and Central Park West.

The El Dorado had been constructed by our friend Charles Goodman, father of Bob and grandfather of Andrew. Charles was a self-made man, an engineer turned successful builder of subways. Like many similar ventures, his luxurious and enormous apartment house was finished just before the Crash. Apparently Goodman was never able to get the permanent financing needed to pay off the construction loans, and the building was taken away from him—with a loss of more than a million dollars. I don't know how much he had left, but it was enough to continue living in a large penthouse in what was once his prideful project, to have a lively summer place on Tupper Lake—where I learned to ride an aquaboard behind his Cris-Craft (was it cold when we fell off into the lake!)—and in general to live in ample luxury with his large family. But the loss of his El Dorado had turned him into a revolutionary. The only subject he would talk about to all and sundry was the iniquities of "the system"—which a pronounced lisp made him call "the thithtem." According to him, American capitalism was doomed and would have to be replaced by another "thithtem" in which the banks couldn't take over a beautiful building from a man who had put a large fortune and his heart's blood into erecting it.

Everyone has read about the ruined speculators said to have jumped out of brokers' windows in droves during the 1929 market panic. Those stories were greatly exaggerated, of course, as are all that appeal to the public's macabre sense or Galgen-humor ["gallows-humor"]. But it is true that many people did desperate things in those awful days, often because they considered themselves ruined, even though they weren't. An example was the uncle of Jenny, my first mistress; he had made a fortune in shoes and then gone into real estate. But worried over losses of various kinds, he locked himself into his garage with a bottle of whiskey and the car engine running, and thus put an end to his troubles. But the fact was that he was quite solvent and left his family in a comfortable position. Indeed, through their investment in our funds their wealth later turned into millions.

I can sympathize with the desperation of my old friend, and almost with his tragic end, because to some degree I went through comparable dismay and apprehension for more than three years. It is true that I wasn't ruined and that at the lowest point I still had means which would have seemed quite large to me only ten years before. But wealth and poverty are relative terms—a poor man in New York would be a rich man in Calcutta, and practically everyone who has lost four-fifths of his wealth considers he has suffered a disaster no matter how much he has left. The chief burden on my mind was not so much the actual shrinkage of my fortune as the lengthy attrition, the repeated disappointments after the tide had seemed to turn, the ultimate uncertainty about whether the Depression and the losses would *ever* come to an end. Add to this the realization that I was responsible for the fortunes of many relatives and friends, that they were as apprehensive and distraught as I myself, and one may understand better the feeling of defeat and near-despair that almost overmastered me towards the end. I expressed those feelings in a little poem I composed in the bleak winter of early 1932:

> Silent and soft as the gossamer snow:
> Mantles of Death drift over the lorn;
> Cold is his touch, but warmer than woe:
> Black is his night, but brighter than morn.
> Where shall he sleep whose soul knows no rest:
> Poor hunted stag in wild woods of care?

Earth has a pillow for his harassed head:
Dust has a drug to ease his despair.

The Crash reaffirmed parsimonious viewpoints and habits that had been ingrained in me by the tight financial situation of my early youth but which I had overcome almost completely in the years of success. I blamed myself not so much for my failure to protect myself against the disaster I had been predicting as for having slipped into an extravagant way of life which I hadn't the temperament or capacity to enjoy. I quickly convinced myself that the true key to material happiness lay in a modest standard of living which could be achieved with little difficulty under almost all economic conditions. I applied this new principle in two ways—one logical and creditable enough, the other quite small-minded.

It became my firm resolve never again to be maneuvered into ostentation, unnecessary luxury, or expenditures that I could not easily afford. The Beresford lease was a bitter but salutary lesson, and in the ensuing thirty-five years, I have avoided any and all real estate white elephants. But on another plane, that of purely personal spending, I must own that I carried economy much too far, and began once more to worry about dimes and quarters when tens of thousands of dollars were actually at stake. I would take the subway instead of a taxi, alleging to myself that this was quicker—and I was always in a hurry—but knowing well that I wanted to save the dollar or so involved. Similarly, I got in the habit of ordering the less expensive entrees on the menu, and even—I hate to confess it—of taking my mother to Chinese restaurants for our weekly dinner. In the days of my affluence I had provided Mother with a car and chauffeur (although I have never had a chauffeur for myself); now I felt that Mother, understanding my need for strict economy, could do without. Fortunately, I almost always made a sharp distinction between spending habits that involved others and those which affected me alone. I am reasonably sure that I was never considered miserly, though I might have been if the world knew how I was treating myself.

During the trying period of 1930 to 1932, I kept busy with many activities. I wrote three articles for *Forbes Magazine*, pointing out the extraordinary discrepancies between the low prices of important common stocks and the much larger current assets (even cash assets) that were behind each share. The title of one of those articles was "Is American Business Worth More Dead Than Alive?" a question that was to take an important place in financial phraseology. (Actually the phenomenon continued to affect the stock of many companies long after the end of the Great Depression.) I participated in many economic discussions with groups of various sorts. I continued to give my course at Columbia, though to much smaller classes, and in 1932 I set definitely to work on the textbook that I had first projected in the lush times of 1927.

I asked Dave Dodd to collaborate with me on the book. We agreed that I would be the senior author and write the entire text in my style. He would aid with suggestions and criticisms, would check the numerous facts and references, and work up the tables. We prepared a table of contents and a sample first chapter, and submitted them to McGraw-Hill & Company through Hugh Kelly, a bright young employee who had been one of our students. (He later became McGraw's vice-president.) McGraw submitted our material to their reader, a Harvard professor of finance. As an exception to the rule, we were shown his report, which was very favorable—his only doubt being whether we would have the stamina to carry the ambitious work to a conclusion. McGraw-Hill was so impressed with his recommendation that they offered us a straight 15 percent royalty, instead of the sliding scale that usually started at 10 percent. Dodd and I agreed to divide the royalties three-fifths to me and two-fifths to him. The contract was signed at the end of 1932, but it was to take a year and a half before the first edition of *Security Analysis* made its appearance.

Before the Crash ended, in December 1932, I had begun two

entirely new activities which were to play an important part in my subsequent life. One was as expert witness in valuation cases. The other was my invention of the commodity reserve currency plan, which was to give me a place in many textbooks in economics. I will defer discussion of these until I describe the next period of my life, which began with the inauguration of Franklin D. Roosevelt in March 1933.

CHAPTER FOURTEEN

The Road Back, 1933–1940

The DJIA touched bottom at 42 in 1932, ended that year at 59, declined again to 53 with the closing of the banks by President-elect Roosevelt, and then began its upward climb. It ended 1933 at 99, showed no net change in 1934, advanced to 144 at the end of 1935, and to a bull market top of 197 in March 1937. Our own operations again became successful; in fact, we did quite a bit better than the market. We started 1933 with $375,000 of capital, quite a fall from our $2,500,000 figure of four years earlier. But in 1933 alone our profit was better than 50 percent. With this encouragement I felt a new, if somewhat chastened, confidence in my abilities, a confidence shared by our participants, most of whom were old personal friends and comrades in misfortune.

One of them, Guy Levy, suggested that the financial arrangements made in 1926 be changed to give Jerry and me a chance to participate in current profits. The old agreement required that any losses be made up in full before we could receive any compensation. This meant that our profits would have to more than triple the Account's 1933 capital to restore the January 1929 balance before either of us could begin to be paid for our work. After brief discussions with the more important partners, the following new agreement was reached: they would give up their right to have the past losses made good; we, in turn, would limit our compensation to a straight 20 percent of the profits, rather than the one-third to one-half that we previously received. These arrangements would begin as of January 1934. The other participants were asked to accept the new contract, in a letter—very complimentary to Jerry and me—signed by the five with the largest interest. Happily, with one exception, every one of our partners signed up. The exception was a brother-in-law of mine. By December 1935 all past losses of the account had been made good, and it was with no small satisfaction that we were able to charge something to that brother-in-law's account for compensation to us under the old contractual terms.

However, a new complication arose. The Internal Revenue Service advanced the claim that our business was not really a "joint account" nor a true partnership, but rather "an association taxable as a corporation" under certain provisions of the law. Fred Greenman advised us to incorporate our business, saying that otherwise there would always be some doubt about our status under the tax law and that the Treasury would be likely to call us either a partnership or a quasi-corporation, depending on which would make for a larger total tax. This advice led to the termination of the Benjamin Graham Joint Account and its replacement by the Graham-Newman Corporation in January 1936.

I was also increasing my services as consultant. The U.S. Treasury Department had a lawsuit involving the estate taxes payable on the controlling shares of Whitney Manufacturing Company, maker of chains. Treasury wanted an expert witness to testify on the value of a stock not sold on any market. The Columbia School of Business people recommended me, I was engaged, and thus a new phase of my career began. The executors of the estate claimed that the value of the shares should be determined by the very low level of the stock market at the date of the owner's death in 1932, as well as by the fact that the company—like most others—was losing money in that year. It was my conviction that the shares should be valued like those of a private business since they represented the controlling interest and the owner could do anything he wished with the company and its assets. I concluded that the minimum value of the controlling shares should be based on the value of the business if liquidated. My assumption was that—in the absence of good evidence to the contrary—the reason a business would continue was that it had more value as an ongoing enterprise than as a liquidation. I estimated the liquidation value, and thus the shares, at an amount equal to the net working capital, without any allowance for the substantial plant investment. These views were consistent with the analyses and valuations I had made in many articles—particularly the 1932 series in *Forbes Magazine.*

The Tax Court found a value about equal to the one I had advocated and much higher than the estate had claimed. That was my first case and my first "victory" as an expert witness on valuation. It was to be followed by perhaps forty more, embracing a great variety of financial situations. I have described the Whitney case in some detail not only because it marked an important beginning for me but because it represents the philosophy of value I have espoused consistently throughout my financial life—in making investments, in writing and teaching, and in my reports and testifying.

My career as expert witness deserves its own chapter.[1] For its title I could borrow that used by my friend Lou Nizer for his best-selling autobiography, *My Life in Court.* Another consultation started in 1933 and was to take much time and thought. Six railroads operating in New Jersey were suing the state government to have their property assessments reduced, on the ground that such assessments (and the resulting taxes paid the state) were supposed, by law, to represent the true value of their property holdings in New Jersey. The tax

assessor, they claimed, had failed to recognize the great fall in
these values during the Depression. The amounts at stake ran
into many millions of dollars. The governor had selected one of
the state's leading lawyers to handle the case for the tax assessor, giving him the title Special Assistant Attorney General.
Deciding he needed expert testimony, the lawyer went first to
Professor James Bonbright of the Columbia School of Business, who had written the classic work (in two large volumes)
The Valuation of Property. Bonbright suggested that he en-
gage me, since an enormous number of figures were to be introduced and my talents were especially fitted to deal with
complicated calculations. The lawyer accepted the suggestion;
I was very happy to get this important job, as I needed the
money in those profitless times. Bonbright fixed the compensation for both of us at his standard rates for such work: $100
for each day of preparation and $250 for each full day of testi-
mony in court. These rates seemed to me quite generous, and
I adopted them as my standard fee in later cases.

Fortunately for Bonbright and me, it was not our task to
justify the valuations set by New Jersey on the railroad properties in the state. That we could not have done, and we would
not have attempted it. Under the law the burden was on the
carriers to propose a different method of valuing their property than that long in effect and to prove that their new
method would produce a "correct" valuation. Our job was simply to pick holes in the railroads' proposals by showing that
under various actual or supposititious conditions they would
produce contradictory or otherwise anomalous results. I can't
remember substantive details about the case, which went on
for a number of years, but peripheral bits of local color are
rather interesting. The most amazing aspect of the litigation
to me was the personal position of the lead attorney. His firm
was local counsel for the New York Central Railroad, one of
the petitioners for relief. When I asked him how it was possible for him to have his feet in both camps, he answered: "I had
no trouble in arranging that. What is more, I am also personal

counsel for Mr. Weaver." Weaver was the head of the Tax Equalization Board, before whom the hearings were proceeding, and the lawyer was representing him in a suit challenging his actions in another case. "And not only that," said he, "I have just agreed to handle the divorce case for the court stenographer." There he was, genial, popular, and unperturbable, representing in one way or another practically everyone having a part in the railroads' suit. The honorable Weaver, presiding in the case, looked like a Daumier caricature of a bloodless, wizened judge. I was the more surprised to read in the paper one day that this almost disembodied spirit had entered suit for divorce against his wife, alleging that the lady had been so unkind—in the midst of a marital quarrel—as to try to choke him to death with his own necktie!

A great day in our case occurred when Jim Bonbright offered testimony on the theory of valuation. Few subjects lend themselves so well to metaphysical reasoning, high-falutin' language, and general obfuscation. Since it was Bonbright's job to show how difficult it is to arrive at an airtight valuation of a railroad's property, I am afraid he didn't try too hard for clarity of expression and ease of understanding. He sprinkled his remarks liberally with foreign phrases—such as "faute de mieux"—and employed as esoteric a vocabulary as I have ever been privileged to hear. His testimony left everybody completely befuddled, a result not at all unsatisfactory to our sly counsel. It was unanimously agreed that the court stenographer that day had taken the biggest beating in his long career.

My own testimony was far more pedestrian, dealing largely with the mathematical implications of the numerous exhibits submitted by the railroads, and of those that I had prepared. My cross-examination, conducted by Mr. Stallman, chief counsel for the railroads, was most intensive and almost endless. Nobody seemed to be in any hurry to finish these cases—after all, in view of all the millions in taxes involved, legal fees and expenses would reach a tidy figure. I recall a day on the stand answering Stallman's questions and objections one after the other while watching our attorney sleep peacefully at the counsels' table. At the end of the session he told me he had no hesitation in taking a nap while I was on the stand, as he knew I could handle the questioning without his aid. I accepted that as a great compliment.

One summer's day in Trenton, I found it almost impossible to enter the courthouse where our hearings were held, so great was a mob of reporters and others gathered on the steps and in the square. It was a moment in the trial of Bruno Hauptmann, the accused in the Lindbergh kidnapping case, and some points had to be ruled on in the state's capital before the trial could start in nearby Leamington.

What happened to the railroads' cases? They brought them afresh for some successive years but were never able to win any of them, despite appeals of the Tax Court's decisions. They did get some relief, finally, through a voluntary agreement with the state. I have no reason to be proud of my role in this long litigation, for I am sure that equity was on the side of the overtaxed railroads. However, I am not ashamed of it either. I said nothing I did not believe to be true. Mine was basically a technical job, which the state was entitled to have done for it as competently as possible and which I discharged to my employer's satisfaction.

I continued to update *Security Analysis.* In the Second Edition of 1939, my views about investment remained conservative and monitory. This proved a wise position to take, I think, for the market's action in the next few years—while predominantly upward—offered many pitfalls for the average investor. The most recent revision, the Fourth Edition just published as I write [1962], proved the most difficult and took a great deal of time. But after wrestling with what seemed like insoluble problems of market analysis and evaluation, I found myself drawn irresistibly towards two almost ridiculously simple solutions. The first was a flat compromise on the question of how investors should divide their portfolios between stocks and bonds (or savings accounts). My answer was that they should always have a significant portion in each. This proportion should never be less than 25 percent in both bonds and stocks, and that the remaining 50 percent should be allocated in accordance with the investor's own conviction or sentiments about whether the market level for stocks was high, "normal," or low. If he has no strong opinion on this matter, it would be logical to maintain a fifty-fifty division between the two categories.

As to the selection of individual securities, my view is, first, that the bond component should be limited to high-grade issues, which might be U.S. Savings Bonds for comparatively small investments, corporate issues for larger sums if the interest were subject to a low tax rate, and tax-free bonds for higher-tax-bracket investors. In any case, the choice of the particular issues presents no problems and can easily be made for the investor by brokerage house analysts. My attitude about the common stock portfolio, for most investors, is quite similar. I have little confidence even in the ability of analysts, let alone untrained investors, to select common stocks that will give better than average results. (The reasons for this skepticism are too complicated to be given here, but they appear in *The Intelligent Investor.*) Consequently, I feel that the standard portfolio policy should be to duplicate, more or less, the Dow Jones Industrial Average. There are dependable ways to improve upon the results of Dow Jones, and I present these briefly in *The Intelligent Investor.* But for various reasons I doubt if they are likely to be followed by many investors.

In 1938 I was divorced from Hazel and married Carol Wade. Carol Wade was beautiful but impossible to live with, and we were divorced in 1940. Even though our relationship was stormy, I continued to socialize extensively. For instance, I was one of a group of security analysts who met once a month at the apartment of Helen Slade, to talk shop, to partake copiously of alcoholic refreshments—all except me, that is—and equally generously of the famous buffet presided over by Helen and her husband Henry Sanders. Helen Slade knew everybody who was anybody in the more intellectual areas of finance. There were a dozen prominent figures who found her indispensable, some speaking to her daily over the phone. For years—until her final illness—she was the moving spirit behind *The Financial Analysts Journal*. Her monthly meetings represented a kind of Wall Street salon, at which she presided, a twentieth century Madame Recamier—though a Recamier whose face would have stopped an oversensitive clock. No, a better comparison would be with Madame Verdurin in *A la Recherche du Temps Perdu:* Helen had most of the salient features of Proust's unforgettable character. Her endless vendetta against a one-time friend, A. Wilfred May of the *Financial Chronicle*, resembled Madame Verdurin's against the Baron de Charlus. My own relations with the Great Slade Goddess of Security Analysts remained most friendly until the end. Slade was the name of her (unmourned) first husband, and she retained it as a *nom de guerre*. Henry Sanders, her second husband, was as handsome as she was ugly; he had plenty of intelligence and industry, and rose from nothing to become vice-president of the Public Bank, and after its absorption by the Chemical National Bank to carry on as a vice-president of that august institution. His submissive devotion to his physically less favored wife reminded me of Disraeli's.

Helen was inordinately fond of cats, but her "incatuation" was carried to extremes that I have never dreamt of. She showered the following attentions (among others) on her favorite, Alexander: (1) she bought him a genuine pearl necklace which she draped around his neck in public; (2) she bought important shares of stock and registered them in his name; (3) after his greatly lamented death, she established an Alexander Prize, which she awarded annually for the best article published in *The Financial Analysts Journal*. The Alexander Prize was replaced, after her own demise not only by a properly named and administered Helen Slade Prize but also by an annual Graham & Dodd award. So in some indirect fashion I have succeeded to the honors originally bestowed on a dead cat.

Helen Slade was very choosy about whom she invited to her monthly get-togethers, and the invitations were highly valued by the financial analyst fraternity. She was a great and intensely loyal friend of mine, singling me out for high favor by allowing me to enter her bedroom—not for any purpose à la Guy Breton but, more agreeably, for a few minutes' conversation and a frolic with her three felines.

Carol and I were also extremely fond of cats. My own attraction to them has always verged on the irrational, and Carol's was not far behind. We bought a baby Siamese, whom we named Sheherazade—Sherry, for short. She grew up not only beautiful but affectionate and well behaved—uncommon virtues in a Siamese. Our love for her was one of the few feelings we shared. If it had not been for Sherry, the first year of our marriage might have proved an unmitigated disaster, instead of just a disaster.

In our Manhattan apartment Sherry spent all her time indoors, without seeming to suffer in health or spirits. When we moved out to Kew Gardens Inn, she had the run of the gardens around the hotel. This proved a tragic error because, in our ignorance of cat lore, we had not inoculated her against enteritis—a disease which alley cats readily survive but which often proves fatal to thoroughbreds. A few days after her first sortie into the garden, Sherry showed signs of illness. Two days later Carol called me at the office to break the news that our beloved animal was dead! The veterinarian's desperate efforts had been in vain. Carol was sobbing so loudly that I could scarcely make out what she was saying. I felt the loss keenly too, but it was my manly duty to comfort her; I promised her another Siamese from the same family who would be in all respects a second Sherry. But I felt much like Aeneas encouraging his men after their shipwreck:

Spem vultu simulat, premit alto corde doloram

(He simulates hope on his face, but deep in his heart
   he represses his grief)

Though less superstitious than many people, I could not help taking the loss of Sherry as a bad augury for my future with Carol. Our new Siamese was almost indistinguishable in appearance from the first. I wanted to call it O-Puss Two, and like all punsters I was inordinately proud of my wit. But better sense prevailed, and the new cat was given the name of her predecessor. We took anxious care of it in every respect, but it didn't give us the pleasure we had found in the first and unforgettable Sherry. Perhaps the second cat was not affectionate enough; perhaps we expected too much from it; perhaps it sensed our devotion to the memory of Sherry No. 1 and showed her resentment in her behavior. (I write these lines thinking not really of the two Sherries, but rather of my two Newtons, the first a marvelous boy who died a month before the age of nine, and the second who came to replace him just a year later, a son who in the end brought Hazel and me more sorrow than joy.)

After my divorce from Carol, I spent most of my spare time with my mother and my brothers. I was also busy putting the last touches on the 1940 Edition (First Revision) of *Security Analysis*, with David Dodd. Even though the modifications introduced were not nearly so drastic as those in the next revision, ten years later, it still required a lot of work to bring illustrations up to date and to incorporate the numerous changes wrought by the Securities and Exchange Commission.

My domestic difficulties were paralleled by the dangerous turn in foreign affairs. I was dismayed at the rise of Hitler and appalled by Chamberlain's surrender at Munich. These events were discussed at length at monthly meetings of a select group of financial analysts which I attended. When World War II started in September 1939, its effect on the stock market was quite the opposite of the shock caused by World War I. Prices immediately advanced strongly. Very little fighting occurred in the first months of the conflict, only a relatively few men were killed, and the American public became rather bored with what was often called the "phony war."

But in May–June 1940 came the gigantic and lightning-quick German offensive, followed in a sickeningly short time by the fall of France and the miraculous but still depressing escape of the British army at Dunkerque. It was then that I found myself really shaken by what was going on. I became nervous and depressed—a rare state for me—and less able than before to cope with my domestic problems. This mental dégringolade prompted unusual remedies. One of them will sound infantile. I went back to roller-skating, something I had rarely done since childhood. A strange sort of solace was provided by the continuous circling, the rhythmic movements of the body, the soothing music, and even the subdued roar of hundreds of turning wheels. I might begin the session with sad thoughts about the world situation and bitter hostility towards Carol, but eventually I'd find myself thinking of nothing but my skating maneuvers, and a most welcome peace would descend upon my soul.

The fall of France and the mortal danger to my native England continued to weigh on me after I became separated from Carol. To take my mind off these troubles, I added another recreation to roller-skating. I began to go to Ebbetts Field in Brooklyn to watch the Dodgers (then better known as the "Bums"). To plunge myself completely in the atmosphere, I sat far out in the bleachers, surrounded by coatless fans, who by turns gloried and lamented, cheered and booed, passed from hope to despair and back again to hope—as if their lives, their fortunes, and their sacred honor depended on every pitch. Instead of finding their enthusiasm absurd and their emotionalism distasteful, I steeped myself in this childish melodrama as in a revivifying bath. I can't say that I ever acted like a true Dodger fan, with all the trimmings; but those half-dozen afternoons in the bleacher section of Ebbetts Field made me an aficionado of the "Bums" for life. They changed their home, as if to rejoin me after I had moved out Los Angeles way. From "Bums" they became "Angels." I remained faithful to them after I had established myself in Europe; this year I rejoiced when Koufax won the pennant for them in the very last game of the 1966 season and mourned loyally their loss of four straight in the World Series.

CHAPTER FIFTEEN

My "Career" as a Playwright

During the period of my most intense professional activity, I somehow found the time and energy to write one one-act and three full-length plays. Of these, one saw the light of production on two different stages.

My first play had a curious origin. In 1930, while looking for some old papers, I found a cardboard box on a shelf in our apartment in the Beresford. I opened it casually enough and discovered it contained a number of letters written to my wife by a married artist whom we had known for many years. Some of these letters were fairly incriminating, even though excisions had been made—no doubt of the more lurid passages. At that time my relations with Hazel were already fairly strained. We were descending into a long period of diminishing love and eventual estrangement that had begun clearly with her trip to Europe without me in the fall of 1927 and was to end in a difficult divorce in 1938.

These letters could have been of great strategic value to me at the time if I were willing to make use of them. But I never did—except once in a very private way, between her lawyer and mine, at the end of our marriage. Why this reluctance? I had two reasons, I think. One was that I was then engaged in my own extramarital love affair, which had started during Hazel's absence in Europe, and my sense of fairness told me that she had an equal right to find happiness in someone else's arms. My second was undoubtedly my great dislike for anything approaching a public scandal which would affect our family.

I kept only two of these letters—out of a prudence which proved justified by later events. I did not tell Hazel that I had seen the letters. Strangely enough, I have never spoken to her about them, even to this day, despite contacts of all sorts that we have had in the ensuing thirty-five years. But the incident gave me an idea for a play, on which I soon found myself hard at work. (Would psychoanalysts call this a sublimation of a traumatic experience?)

The name I gave the play was *China Wedding*, referring to the twentieth wedding anniversary of the couple who are the chief protagonists. They are a very superior pair (another sublimation!). He is a highly successful lawyer; she a beautiful woman, active in many good works. There is a French artist on the scene, with whom my heroine has had a love affair some years before. It came about, says she, because her husband was too intellectual and logical, refusing to give himself fully to the wife of his bosom. (A little self-analysis here.) But later, the love between the wife and the artist ripened into friendship, and their romance ended.

The wife, however, has kept Raoul's ardent letters; they had been addressed to a private box at the post office but were inadvertently left in a folder on her husband's desk two days before the play opens. The big question is whether or not the husband has found these letters and read them. He never mentions them in the play, but the wife realizes that it would be in character for him to know her secrets and say nothing about them. The play ends with the question unresolved in her mind—it is for each member of the audience to decide whether the husband knows or doesn't know. There are subsidiary characters, of course—chiefly an eighteen-year-old daughter, and the daughter's fiancé, to whom the lawyer gives very unconventional advice about sex. In portraying the young fiancé, I tried to give a (quite idealized) portrait of the author as a young man. He makes a pun in Latin and recites two romantic poems he has written himself. The husband is, of course, myself ten years hence, while the wife has many of Hazel's traits as well as something of her history. I gave Hazel the script to read after it came back from the typist. She returned it saying that she liked the play very much. Not a word about the subject matter; not a sign of surprise or chagrin that I had discovered her own secret. O women!

At that time we were friends with Sylvia Golden, an editor of *Theatre Magazine* and sister of John Golden, the producer. She, too, liked the play and thought that the great David Belasco might produce it. I sent it to him and a little later had an interview in his office at the David Belasco Theatre. I wish I could remember more of that occasion. The author of *Madam Butterfly* wore his famous semiclerical costume; he spoke to me politely, I am sure. What is even more sure is that he turned the play down.

Later the play was accepted by a leading firm of theatrical agents, Young and Rubsaman, but that was the only acceptance it ever received. There was a near-miss, however. Johns Hopkins University asked annually for the submission of American dramas by new playwrights, of which one was chosen for production. I sent them my play, which they kept so long as to give me high hopes. But in the end they returned it to me, not without a very nice letter, saying that the final choice lay between *China Wedding* and another entry. Despite the fact that mine was "a strong play," they had given it second place in the contest. It was some consolation, but I could not help recalling the lines Goethe puts in the mouth of Thoas in *Iphigenie auf Tauris*: "Der Andre hört nur das Nein."[1]

But there were other ideas in my head and other plays to write. A plot for a one-act vaudeville sketch came to me, and I wrote the dialogue almost at one sitting. The play was called *The Day of Reckoning*. The scene takes place in a barbershop. Many years before, the barber's wife was seduced by a rascally friend, who also took off with the couple's savings. A heavily bearded customer enters and asks the barber to shave him clean. Soon the barber recognizes the man in the chair as the cause of their misfortunes. Tableau. The play ends with the villain dying of fright beneath the menacing razor.

I gave this somewhat-less-than masterpiece, along with *China Wedding*, to an old friend of Hazel's named Harry Delf, who, with his sister Juliette, had made a profitable career in vaudeville. His specialty was dancing, hers, imitations and monologues. But Harry had also been a playwright, with one solid success to his credit, entitled *The Family Upstairs*. When he returned the sketch, he told me that it was well written but that it had a plot almost identical with that of *The Emperor's Barber* (whose protagonist is Napoleon). Furthermore, he said, vaudeville had fallen so low that there was virtually no chance of anyone's producing a new sketch in that market. That was the end of *The Day of Reckoning*, which lies somewhere in my archives.

Shortly thereafter, Harry Delf sought me out with a proposal. He had a wonderful plot for a three-act comedy, had been impressed by my skill in writing dialogue, and thought that we could collaborate on a box-office "knockout." However, there was a small complication—which really would prove an advantage to me. He was suffering from Buerger's disease—medically known by the awe-inspiring name of thrombo-angiitis-obliterans—which so affected his legs that he had to give up his performing career. But he had had the foresight to protect himself by substantial insurance policies, from which he was now receiving a goodly sum each month under their "disability clause." Such payments would cease, however, if he once again became self-supporting, and the insurance companies were keeping close watch on his activities. Under the circumstances, he felt it would be dangerous for him to be known as the coauthor of a new play; thus our joint work would have to appear under my name alone. Still, we would share equally in the large profits to be reaped, to which movie rights might well make a large contribution.

All this sounded very good to me, and I accepted his offer without much reflection. Viewed in retrospect, this was a far from creditable action on my part. I was assisting a beneficiary in taking advantage of—"cheating" might be the better word—certain insurance companies. Since I had always had a somewhat holier-than-thou satisfaction in my own financial rectitude, I set down this transgression with as much wonderment as chagrin. Could I have thought, along with nearly everyone else, that it is no crime to outsmart an insurance company? This seems the more incredible to me now since for many years my chief financial gains have come from ownership of shares in insurance concerns. Alas, it matters so much whose ox is gored!

Harry Delf's idea, tentatively entitled *True to the Marines*, was about an enormously influential editorial writer, clearly patterned after Arthur Brisbane, then the grand pundit of the Hearst newspapers. Our man has a mistress, a beautiful, scatterbrained blonde. But this apparent ninny has the knack of making spontaneous remarks about current affairs which give the editor great inspiration for his columns. There are other characters, of course, among them an attractive youth with whom the blonde is really in love. Another is the editor's wife, who recognizes the importance of the young lady to her husband's happiness and career and who actually tries to repair the great damage done to him by the love affair of the two young people.

I started work on the play in the summer of 1933, for I recall traveling once a week to Harry Delf's place at the seashore for long conferences. We finished it at last to Harry's satisfaction, and he took over the job of getting it produced. He came up with a deal that was not very impressive but better than nothing. A stock company which performed in a certain Red

Barn Theatre in aristocratic Locust Valley, Long Island, agreed to try the play out for a week or two to open their season. We were to be paid a nominal amount for our permission. The first performance actually took place in June 1934, almost the moment that *Security Analysis* made its initial bow. I attended two performances in Locust Valley, which was quite far from my home. I can't remember what kind of a reception it received; my sense is that it was called "reasonably successful."

The almost simultaneous appearance of my first book and the production of my first play gave me a feeling of great satisfaction, verging on vanity. My euphoria was enhanced by the excellent profits being turned by the joint account, which promised a definite end to my own financial troubles and to my worries for my clients. In addition, I was increasingly in demand as an expert witness, a most remunerative sideline. I had now reached the age of forty—which a French writer has described as "the adolescence of old age." To my own surprise, I found myself gliding, as it were, into a period of romantic attachments of a quite different nature than I had known before. Perhaps my exposure to the atmosphere of the theater, as well as the variety of my other activities, exerted an unrealized influence on my erotic life.

Harry Delf actively sought a Broadway producer for my play *True to the Marines*, which we had agreed to rename *Baby Pompadour.* (We detected or imagined a certain resemblance between the situation of Madame Pompadour at the court of Louis XV and of our heroine in the sanctum of our eminent editor.) After some months of maneuvers our agent found a man ready, willing, and able to back our play on Broadway. Harry told me that the contract was not perfect, but he thought we should accept it. It included the standard $500 advance to be paid to us against future authors' royalties.

We could indeed have wished for a better deal. The producer-to-be was named Irving Steinman. As one of the principal owners of Palisades Amusement Park—an extensive playground situated across the Hudson—he was experienced and successful enough in one area of the entertainment business. But this was his first venture into legitimate theater, and it was one not totally prompted by business interest. *Cherchez la femme,* of course, the *femme* here being a young lady to whom he was engaged to be married. Shirley Miller came of a good Jewish family; her father was a Wall Street broker. Her interest since childhood had always been acting. She had taken a number of principal parts in dramatic-school productions, and she was convinced that she was now ready for a professional career. But instead of starting at the bottom, as everyone else did, she aspired to instant stardom.

Shirley had seen the play at Locust and had immediately decided that the part of our heroine had been made to order for her. She confided to me later that it had been no easy task to persuade her hard-headed fiancé to back the show, but she won her point in the end by simply threatening to break off the engagement unless he did. Hence, the major stipulation in the arrangement between Steinman and ourselves was that Shirley—an unknown neophyte—was to play the leading part.[2] It is easy to see, looking back, that this guaranteed the failure of the play. But such was our eagerness to have our work produced that even the experienced Harry Delf found reason to believe that we had a good chance of success.

I appeared at the office of our agent to sign the contract. Naturally Steinman asked me about myself, and I told him I was in finance. We soon found ourselves in an animated discussion of the prospects of the stock market and the virtues of certain of his investments. The astonished agent remarked that this was the first time in his experience that this kind of a conversation had taken place between playwright and play-backer. The result of my display of financial knowhow proved not very good for me. It seemed that Steinman was looking for $2,500 to complete the $15,000 he was putting up for the production. (What a minuscule sum compared with present-day costs!) I let him talk me into putting up the $2,500, on the same basis as his own $12,500. *He* had to risk his money in order to win his girl, but

why did I risk mine? I suppose that the play itself was my darling then, just as Shirley was Irving's; perhaps I had as much
justification for being unbusinesslike as he had.

In any case, the papers were signed, the money was put up,
and we were ready to go. Someone dug up a producing firm for
us. Its name was Kinnecott and Werner; they were two young
men just starting their careers as full-fledged producers. Kinnecott, a tall, handsome fellow, had put up the money;
Werner—small, bald, bespectacled—had contributed the experience, based on some years as assistant to various producers. It seemed they had already put on one play, which had
quickly folded, but—as always—there was a good explanation
for the failure.

Despite this unpromising beginning, our play enjoyed at
least one bit of class, namely, Clarence Derwent as director.
Derwent was an Englishman of considerable standing in the
theater, as witness the fact that a Clarence Derwent Prize is
now awarded annually for the best directing job on Broadway.
He must have been hard up for employment to have associated himself with our venture. But he did his work conscien-
tiously. The director and the producers together selected the
cast, except, of course, for Shirley Miller. As far as I can remember, they all had had ample experience and seemed competent enough to me. (But I must confess that my critical faculty about acting, as well as countless other things, has never
been well developed.)

Werner, the active man of the producing firm, announced
that he had engaged the Vanderbilt Theatre, on 44th Street,
for the play. He said that others were available at a somewhat
lower price, but the Vanderbilt had a fine name and a reputation for many successes.

The six weeks or so required to put on the show were a
period of intense interest and excitement for me. I attended
the rehearsals fairly regularly, after business hours, and I was
consulted at times about possible changes in the text. It was
fascinating to watch the actors gradually learning their lines,

the director Derwent prescribing changes in business and expression, the sets and costumes arriving (perhaps the best part of the whole business), and, finally, the dress rehearsals.

Not long before the opening date, we decided that the play needed a different ending—most of the last act had to be done over. After reaching agreement with Harry on the new material, I undertook to have it ready the following day. I spent most of the night at the typewriter, kept awake by copious quantities of coffee supplied by the ever-efficient Hazel. The new version was delivered as promised, and received with approval.

The night of the initial performance finally arrived. I recall two incidents of the few days before. Somebody—a stagehand or messenger boy—came over and congratulated me, saying that the word was all over Broadway that *Baby Pompadour* was a sure smash hit. (Did he say this out of kindness, or did he expect a tip?) The other incident was more meaningful. The young assistant producer took me aside and, almost in tears, said: "Mr. Graham, what is happening here is a crime." "Why?" I asked innocently. "But your play isn't ready. There's a lot to be done on it still. It should have at least two weeks of tryouts—in New Haven, Atlantic City, anywhere—before it comes to this theater." What could I answer? Only that I hoped that the producers and Mr. Steinman knew what they were doing—and anyway there was no money available for tryouts. The young man raised his hands despairingly and walked off. Of course, he was entirely right.

Someone from the Theatre Program Company had approached me at the Vanderbilt and asked for biographical material to be used in the program. I answered his questions frankly. Unfortunately, the program notes made it only too clear that I was an amateur playwright, that this was my first offering, and that my real career was in finance.

The theater was well attended the first night, and many of us donned evening clothes as befitted the occasion. The play seemed to go off all right, with a fair number of laughs, but the applause was far from exuberant. As the last curtain fell there were a few feeble cries of "Author, author!" (from friends or relatives, no doubt), but no one seemed to want to stay. As I walked out I heard two men in untidy costumes talking. Said one to the other, "Not even one good curtain call." My heart sank. I just knew they were newspaper critics.[3]

In accordance with custom, the cast, director, and crew gathered at my apartment in the El Dorado for a first-night party. There were coffee, cakes, champagne. Someone suggested that the party continue until early morning when the first editions of the papers could be bought, but everyone else seemed tired and wanted to go home. They knew what was coming. The criticisms were about as bad as could be. They referred to the dubious wisdom of mixing a Wall Street career with the Broadway theater. There was, however, one rather favorable review, and—strangely enough—it appeared in the very *New York Evening Journal* for which Arthur Brisbane was the chief editorialist.

In short, the production was a fiasco. The play ran for one week to very meager audiences. Steinman had various plans for papering the house and carrying the play along for some additional time, in hopes the tide would turn—as in some other cases he knew about. Also, he suggested that I change the text to introduce various kinds of vulgarities, which he thought would draw the crowd. He wanted me to put up half the money for the continuance. I had no stomach for his ideas and refused. At the end of the week the play was off the boards, the actors received their modest indemnities, the scenery was sold back to the designers for a pittance, the various bills were paid— and no money was left to be returned to the backers. *Baby Pompadour* had laid an egg.

Was the play so very bad? How am I to judge? I must have considered it pretty good at the time, and so did a number of other people associated with it. Undoubtedly, it had a few good ideas, some good scenes, and a number of witty lines. It's thirty years since I've read it, and I don't remember it well enough to venture a mature and considered verdict. The probabilities are that it wasn't good enough for Broadway and that it deserved to fail.

I recall Harry Delf shaking his head resignedly over the debacle and saying to me more sorrowfully than indignantly, "Ben, you should never have told them that stuff about your being in Wall Street. It was poison." For a year or so thereafter Harry made efforts to sell our play to Hollywood. I think he got a very small offer, which he turned down, and then nothing. I lost sight of him completely in the following years. On the whole, he was a nice enough fellow and a good sport about the affair. (At least he did get $250 out of it and was smart enough not to invest a nickel in the venture.)

The day after the notices appeared, I received a copy of the most virulent review with the word "Ha, ha!" scrawled over it. Nothing else. Evidently I was not without enemies. But I also received a few copies of the *Journal's* encouraging review, with congratulations from friends who evidently hadn't read the others. I told my dear friend Professor Tassin how downcast I was about its failure. He felt quite otherwise. "How can you talk like that, Ben, merely because the play didn't succeed? Look at me. I've spent a lifetime as actor, writer, and teacher. I've written a half-dozen plays, which have been published at my expense. My great ambition has been to get one of them produced somewhere other than by amateurs, and that's never happened. Now look at you. You write your first play (that wasn't quite true) and you get it produced twice, the second time on Broadway. I call that success, not failure." I'm sure dear Algernon meant what he said.

I wrote one other play, at the urging of Saul Levy, lawyer, expert accountant, and good friend, who felt I was the ideal man to write a play about Wall Street. I called it "The Raging Flood," the title taken from *Julius Caesar.* I thought first of placing it in the years just before and during the Great Crash—say, 1928 to 1932—but I decided that the events of those years were so extreme as to obscure the traits of any characters I might invent. So I went back to the speculation of 1918 to 1919 and the bear market of 1920 to 1921 for my framework. I used a number of characters I had observed rather closely in my early years with N.H.&L. The hero is, of course, myself as a young man, who comes through the Crash triumphantly by doing things entirely differently from everyone else. But nothing much happened with the play, and so ended my fruitless courtship of Thalia and Melpomene.

Thereafter, I continued my interest in the theater, but not as a participant. In 1936, the New School for Social Research, under my long-time friend Alvin Johnson, started its "University in Exile," to give teaching posts to eminent professors who had fled Hitler's Germany. A big fund-raising drive was launched, capped by an elaborate dinner attended by hundreds of people. The guests were assigned to tables according to their business or profession. To my surprise I found myself seated at the *theatrical* table. I was even more pleased than amused, for others at the table included George Gershwin, Edward G. Robinson, and Sam Jaffee. Needless to say, I did practically no talking but a lot of listening. First the conversation was about *Porgy and Bess*, then in rehearsal. Gershwin spoke about painting as a hobby, and Robinson about his art collection, which would ultimately become one of the most valuable in the country. I forget what Sam Jaffee talked about, but I remember congratulating him on his performance as King Lear, which I had seen in the theater of the New School.

Alas, George Gershwin was soon to die at the height of his powers. Many years later I was introduced to Robinson in the Imperial Hotel in Tokyo. I told him I was especially glad to meet him again because many people had mistaken me for him. (Once during World War II, when I was giving blood at the Red Cross headquarters on Fifth Avenue, the rumor went around that Edward G. Robinson was there under an assumed name, and lots of nurses ran in to look at me.) I'll always remember Eddie's response to my remark, for it flattered my vanity so. "Mr. Graham, if I looked like you, I'd play glamour parts." In after years we became friends in Beverly Hills. There I also got to know Sam Jaffee quite well since he was a cousin of my close friend and supporter Irving Kahn.

I had little later contact with my erstwhile theatrical associates except for Werner. He came to my office and told me that he had been living from hand to mouth but that now he had been offered a job as assistant to a film producer in Hollywood. Could I lend him the money to get to California? I made the loan, got a nice letter from Hollywood some weeks later telling me that things were going well, and then the usual complete silence thereafter.

How precarious are the careers and the earnings of nine-tenths of the people connected with the theater! By the nature of things there must always be far more employables than employed. When there is a good season and many plays are running in New York and elsewhere, there are always plenty of actors, managers, directors, and crew to meet the personnel requirements. But what happens to half of these, and more, when show business is poor? There are pitifully few permanent jobs in the theater; scarcely anyone knows if he will be receiving regular pay a year from now.

There is a brief stage description in *Waiting for Godot* whose implications are devastating. One of the characters is described as extremely tall and thin, to the point of emaciation. Beckett could specify such an unusual physical appearance with full confidence that a *good* actor could be found to fit the description closely—whenever and wherever the play was to be put on. But how many other roles would be available to such an ungainly player in his lifetime? There must be many actors and actresses ready to meet such outrageous specifications, but how can such extreme types expect to find regular employment in the theater? In Paris I saw a little actor magnificently carry off the part of Napoleon in *Madame Sans-Gêne*. He dominated the stage and magnetized the audience. But what parts could this undersized and overstomached follower of Thespis find when he wasn't playing Napoleon?

CHAPTER SIXTEEN

The Commodity Reserve Currency Plan

If my name has any chance of being remembered by future generations—assuming that there will be future generations—it will be as inventor of the Commodity Reserve Currency Plan. To describe this plan, I must start with a disclaimer. My formal study of economics was confined to four weeks under Dr. Muzzey at Columbia College in 1912. I quit the course, along with all my others that fall, to take on my daytime job for the U.S. Express Company. When I returned the next February, I could not fit economics into my schedule, and I gave it up with scarcely a second thought. This scanty training in the "dismal science" did not prevent me from setting up later as an authority in the theory and practice of security investment, in corporate finance, and, indeed, in economics, in the professional sense of the term. I have learned whatever I know about economics in the same way I learned about finance—by reading, meditation, and practical experience.

An economic invention of mine has found its way into most of the standard works on monetary theory, and—even as I write this in mid-July 1965—it seems to be in the minds of some economists.[1] The great Lord Keynes wrote an (admittedly ambiguous) article about my idea, and a letter from him to me on the subject will be part of his collected works, when published.

The notion of a commodity-based reserve currency—or CRC, as I shall call it—first came to me in the Depression of 1921 to 1922, when the world had perhaps its first real exposure to poverty in the midst of plenty. There was an excess of production of raw materials generally, as against the effective or cash demand. Commodity prices fell disastrously, producing all kinds of financial embarrassments, which in turn led to increasing unemployment and the vicious cycle of economic depression. From the outset of my study of that depression, with its attendant widespread suffering, I felt that it was all basically unnecessary, and a recurrence should be preventable. If a nation lacks the means of production—in fertile land, manufacturing capacity, technical knowledge—then its standard of living must necessarily be low. But it seems logically absurd for a country like ours, blessed with so many resources, to find itself unable to buy its own products, suffering at once from an excess of goods in the warehouses and too few on the shelves of its families.

Seeking a solution for this anomalous problem, I considered, first, the position of the gold producers. They were exempt from the difficulties that bedeviled the rest of us. No matter how large their output, they could sell it immediately at an assured price—then $20 an ounce. They even gained substantially from the Depression itself since lower wage scales and lower prices for what they needed reduced their production costs and increased their profits. Many economists had suggested plans for stabilizing the general level of prices, but none had won widespread acceptance. The best known at this time was Irving Fisher's proposal for a compensated dollar, under which the amount of gold equivalent to a paper dollar would be increased or decreased to offset a rise or decline in the price level. My own meditation on the problem led me to a quite different solution. A better standard, I felt, was to give a designated bundle or "market basket" of basic raw materials a monetary status equivalent to that which had always been accorded to gold. This meant that owners (producers) of the whole group of commodities in their proper relative proportions could always turn them over to the Treasury for a fixed amount of paper dollars, while holders of paper dollars could always cash them in for the corresponding number of commodity baskets.

For why, I asked, should economic advantages be confined to the gold producers? Were not the ordinary necessities of life as important and as valuable as gold, and were not those who produced them entitled to similar advantages?

In my view, the commodity-reserve proposal had both an active and a passive merit. On the active side, it dealt as directly as possible with the problem of stabilizing the price level by *defining* the dollar in terms of commodities and by establishing a two-way convertibility between the paper dollar and its defined commodity equivalent. In a broad sense this would create a bridge between the world of commodities and the world of money—permitting commodity units to pass over into and be treated as money when they were not needed for consumption, and, conversely, for money to pass back into the world of commodities and consumption whenever necessary. The idea is reminiscent of the famous Biblical story of the seven fat and the seven lean years, and of Joseph's wisdom in storing the surplus against later need.

On the passive side, it did not attempt to stabilize the price of any *single* commodity, as had been tried in the past—quite unsuccessfully—by so-called valorization schemes. My plan permitted each separate commodity to fluctuate in price according to changes in its own supply-demand situation, while maintaining stability (at least within narrow limits) against the bundle of commodities as a whole.

The difficulties of putting this theoretically appealing idea into practice were evidently great. Should dress manufacturers, and countless similar businessmen, be enabled to sell everything they turn out to the U.S. Treasury at a fixed price? Obviously not—there are too many questions about quality, variety, fair prices, perishability, obsolescence, and so on. Most of all, assuming that the government found money to pay for all these things, what would it do with them?

If we pass from the universe of *all* products to the restricted field of basic raw materials, however, many of these problems vanish. A key role in booms and depressions is played by fluctuations in the prices of basic raw materials. As an example, the index of such prices in the United States advanced considerably from 1913 to 1920—as the result of World War I inflation and the postwar boom—but fell precipitously in 1922.

Suppose we limited ourselves to providing an unfailing demand for the most important raw materials? Since these form the basis of the goods economy in general, we could assume that securing their economic position in a way analogous to the assured position of gold would protect both the price level and the effective demand for most commodities against the eroding effects of recurrent depressions. The prices of basic commodities decline far more than do goods generally, and stabilizing the former might well stabilize the prices of consumer products. A comparatively few major raw materials—not more than thirty, say—account for a large part of the value and importance of all primary products. If the price level of these thirty could be stabilized, the economy as a whole might be protected against severe destabilization.

But how to best stabilize the price level of basic commodities? Could we set an unchanging price for a bushel of wheat, another for a pound of copper, another for a pound of coffee, and so on down the line of our thirty products? There are serious objections to doing this. The relative prices of these commodities—each against the others—had always been subject to wide fluctuations, resulting from changes in individual supply-and-demand factors. Are such changes merely temporary? If so, it would be a good thing to suppress them. But they are secular or quasi-permanent, in response chiefly to long-term changes in relative costs of production. A number of efforts had been made in the past to stabilize the price of individual commodities. In 1921 the historical example was sugar, but efforts proved rather unsuccessful. Economists were almost unanimously opposed to the so-called valorization of commodities or services. They liked to refer to the valiant but ultimately unsuccessful attempt to valorize commodities made by the Emperor Diocletian as far back as A.D. 301 as proof that valorization was impractical.

I was conscious of the inherent weakness of any plan to set the individual prices of a number of different commodities. The solution to the problem of stabilization, I felt, lay in fixing, within narrow limits, the price of a bundle or market basket of important commodities *taken as a whole*, while permitting the prices of the several components to vary in accordance with changes in relative supply and demand. In other words, I proposed to give to a properly selected and proportioned group of basic commodities the same monetary status as that then enjoyed by gold. This meant that new money would be issued to producers against, and backed by reserves of, basic commodities.

My meditation about the consumer's situation led me to similar conclusions. The chief cause of depressions in the modern world, I felt, was the public's lack of purchasing power to absorb the increased production resulting from preceding economic booms. I was much impressed by J. A. Hobson's classic work *The Economics of Unemployment*[2] which theorized about the impact of insufficient purchasing power somewhat as I had. (Hobson's book undoubtedly was an important precursor of the revolutionary thinking of J. M. Keynes.)

This idea came to me during the 1921 to 1922 depression, but I did nothing about it at the time except to discuss it with my Uncle Maurice Gerard, who thought it a good one. I was encouraged also, and surprised as well, to read in *The Sunday New York Times* an article describing a related idea of no less than Thomas Edison, the great inventor. He, too, proposed that new money be created against the deposit of raw materials in warehouses and that the farmers and other producers be compensated with it. But the details of his plan were different and more amateurish than mine: my plan would be simpler to effect and more practical in its consequences. Edison's plan fell into oblivion.

I put the plan aside during the ensuing boom years: I was too busy making money on Wall Street. (These years, by the way, were marked by unusual stability in the price index.)

It was not until ten years later that I published my plan. We were then in the midst of the greatest depression in our history. All the paradoxical malaises of 1921 to 1922 were now being repeated, but to a highly intensified degree. One of the results was an intellectual ferment, marked by the formation of numerous discussion groups, an outpouring of proposed remedies of the greatest variety, and the launching of various movements for bringing about radical changes in the economy. The chief of these was a really radical takeover idea, known as *technocracy*; another was Upton Sinclair's "bootstrap project" in California, known as *EPIC*; a third was the famous Townsend Plan, which advanced the then revolutionary proposal of giving people over sixty a pension of $60 per month.

A group interested in economics was formed and met regularly at the New School for Social Research in lower New York City, under the sponsorship of the school's distinguished president, Dr. Alvin Johnson. I immediately joined the group, which called itself "The Economic Forum." Our purpose was to exchange ideas about how to improve "the sorry scheme of things"—a phrase from *The Rubáiyát* that became our designation for the current economic mess. At one of the sessions in 1932 I presented my plan, in mimeographed form. Actually, I presented four separate plans I had dreamed up. One was the Commodity Reserve Currency Plan, pretty much in its final form but without the mass of statistics and calculations that were to be added. A second was an idea for large-scale slum clearance and its replacement by low-cost housing, with subsidies for the former slum tenants to the extent needed to meet the new rents. A third was a plan whereby people who had lost their jobs were entitled to personal credit based on their skills and experience, credit to be advanced to them by the federal government in the form of unsecured loans, bearing small or no interest and repayable on appropriate terms when they found jobs. While the latter two proposals appeared radical in the extreme to believers in the laissez-faire philosophy of the pre-Roosevelt days, they are not far different from schemes actually adopted in later years.

As a lighter note in my otherwise ponderous memorandum, I included a fourth proposal suggesting a way that France could repay the interest and principal on its war debt to us. I proposed that they do so by annually shipping 40 million bottles of wine, including champagne, and that every American citizen of voting age receive one such bottle gratis for Christmas. The allocation of wines was to be made by lot, seniority, or in some other equitable way. It was not a bad idea at all, introducing both reality and gaiety into the otherwise metaphysical financial relations of the two countries and at the same time would dispose of the war-debt question in a practical and pleasing fashion.

Two of the members of our group boldly decided to publish a magazine which would use our excellent name—*The Economic Forum*—and which would publish as many of the new proposals as the editors deemed worthy of attention. The senior editor was a young man named Joseph Mead, whose later career I know nothing about. The other editor and publisher was a still younger man, who—although already a member of that stronghold of conservatism, the New York Stock Exchange—had a keen interest in and an open mind for new economic ideas. His name was William McChesney Martin.

Little did we suspect that our Bill Martin was destined in a few years' time to be chosen the youngest president of the exchange in history, and thereafter was to become head of the U.S. Federal Reserve System, and thus one of the most powerful financial influences in the world. (I have just read in *Time*, July 2, 1965, that a speech made last month by Bill Martin which referred very briefly to some similarities between the stock markets of 1965 and 1929 led to a paper shrinkage of $34 billion in stock values on the Big Board.)

Editors Mead and Martin asked our forum to submit articles for their magazine. I wrote up my Commodity Reserve Currency Plan under the title "Stabilized Reflation" ("reflation" had then become a popular term to describe a return of conditions from deflation to normal without bringing on the counterevils of inflation). The article was published in the second issue of *The Economic Forum* in 1933. This was the first official presentation to the public of CRC.[3]

In the three decades since I invented it, my brainchild has brought me both gratification and disappointment. One of the psychological high points came at the very start. There was a brief moment of great excitement at the moment of the 1933 inauguration, when I learned that my friend David Podell, the lawyer, had interested his classmate, President-elect Franklin D. Roosevelt, in the idea, and that it was under serious study in Washington as part of the anti-Depression program. Something in the new president's inaugural address led me to think that he favored the commodity-reserve idea; naturally, I was in seventh heaven. I envisaged myself as the famous and honored savior of America's economy and perhaps of the world's. But nothing came of it. However, about two years later, I was visited by an important member of the Department of Agriculture, Louis Bean, a noted statistician and adviser to Secretary of Agriculture Henry Wallace. Roosevelt had formed the Commodity Credit Corporation to support the prices of agricultural products, and it had been buying up large amounts of various farm commodities. Bean saw in my plan a method of financing these commodities by issuing money directly against them, with stimulation to the general price structure by the increase in money in circulation. He gave me considerable personal encouragement about my idea and provided some useful data on prices for the book I ultimately wrote on the subject; but no official action was taken by the Department of Agriculture.

Evidently the CRC was regarded in Washington as too radical an innovation. Certainly it was opposed by Bean's teammate and rival Mordecai Ezekiel, who had other economic nostrums to peddle. So again, nothing happened—and this was to become a familiar sequel over the years. Bean never publicly endorsed the CRC plan, as far as I know; probably it would have been impolitic for him to do so. But he gave me various forms of moral encouragement from time to time and even sent me some historical data which he allowed me to include in my book.

On one occasion Bean had me come to Washington for a meeting with Secretary Henry Wallace. It's funny how certain minuscule details remain in one's memory through the years. As I mounted the main staircase of the imposing Department of Agriculture Building to reach the chief's office, my eye fell on a large mural depicting a varied scene of rural activity and happiness. Beneath it is engraved a Latin saying which begins "Felix si...": "O happy farmer, if you only knew your good fortune." And in the lower right-hand corner the printer had written the source of his verse thus: Virgile, *Géorgiques*. I asked myself in wonderment what these *French* names were doing under a Latin inscription in an American government building? Evidently, a French artist had been commissioned to do the mural, and he hadn't bothered to write "Virgil, *Georgics*," and no one in charge in Washington had even noticed the anomaly. It was as if the building itself had borne on its portals the inscription: *Département de l'Agriculture*.

(A parallel anecdote: the walls of the library of UCLA once bore the familiar words: "Haec studia adulescentiam alunt, senectutem oblectant" ("These studies nourish our youth and comfort our age"). The first time I saw them, I was horrified that Virgil was inscribed as author. To what depths has American culture fallen if a great university doesn't know the difference between Virgil and Cicero? Poor Cicero, who in the very oration in which these words appear, "Pro Archia Poeta," had insisted that all men seek posthumous fame and that even those who wrote tracts entitled "On Despising Glory" took care to add their names as author. Perhaps that vainest of orators rests a bit easier now that "Virgilius" has been erased from the library wall and replaced with his name.)

I don't remember anything of my short conference with Henry Wallace. It must have been quite fruitless; Bean, as a sort of consolation prize, no doubt, gave me the copy of Irving Fisher's *Stable Money* which Fisher had presented to Wallace. The book is still somewhere in my library. Bean later became one of the leading experts in predicting election results and then proceeded to write a book predicting the future movements of the stock market.

In 1936 and 1937 I worked up a book-length presentation of my idea for the CRC. It appeared under the title *Storage and Stability* in 1937. In selecting the title, I had in mind Henry George's alliterative title *Progress and Poverty*. I dreamed that one day *Storage and Stability* would occupy a place in economic literature beside George's masterpiece. I lavished much labor on the book. Facts and references to other writers are supported by a host of notes appearing in the appendix. The book also includes various calculations covering price variations in the proposed commodity unit; these were made by my young niece, who is now Dr. Judith Pool, an authority on hematology. I first asked Macmillan to publish the book, but they politely declined. Though McGraw-Hill had justifiable doubts about the commercial prospects of the book, they agreed to do it—out of deference, no doubt, to the success of *Security Analysis*—but on condition that I guarantee them against loss by taking over unsold copies of the First (2000-run) Edition. This was a far from dignified arrangement, but I acceded to it quickly enough in my eagerness for publication.

How many authors have felt compelled to do the same for works *they* thought would be milestones in the history of thought!

As the book was being completed, another possible entrée to President Roosevelt seemed to arise. Herman Baruch had talked to his brother Bernard about my plan, and it seemed to correspond to some of the great financier's own thoughts. Baruch invited me to his home to talk over my idea. This invitation came just when the galley proofs of *Storage and Stability* had been completed. Our talk went very well. Baruch said he was sure that this was the solution the economy had been waiting for. He would like to associate himself with it, and to present it to President Roosevelt as soon as possible. I agreed to provide him with a set of galley proofs the next afternoon.

I waited as patiently as I could for the result of the Roosevelt-Baruch discussion of the Graham Plan. In a sense I am still waiting, for I have never received any direct information about it. After a week or so my galley proofs were returned to me with a brief and noncommittal note. But Herman Baruch did tell me later, with some embarrassment, that a conversation had taken place, but, apparently, Roosevelt felt that he had introduced so many novelties into the economy that it would be politically unsound to try to pull another rabbit out of the hat. Baruch got the message: there were no practical results or prestige to be gained from my plan so he dropped the matter without a word. I can't help adding: "Just like him."

The hopes I attached to *Storage and Stability* are expressed in a sonnet I composed at the time and entitled "On the First Publication of an Ambitious Work." It begins:

> These are the wings that through the nights and years,
> Upon the unyielding anvil of my brain,
> I forged oblivious...

And it ends with the sestet:

Upon such pinions soared the unlucky one
Who fell lamented in the Icarian sea;
The youth who drove the coursers of the sun
Fell headlong from the upper air—but me
These wings must bear with better luck and higher,
To snatch for man a new Promethean fire.

These comparisons were indeed pretentious; they tempted Fate, and Fate revenged itself in the usual way. I often think of my sonnet when my eyes happen to fall on a copy of Brueghel's sardonic picture "The Fall of Icarus." There, you will recall, a large peasant in the foreground follows his plow, oblivious of anything else, while the son of Daedalus—quite tiny in the distance—is falling helplessly into the water.

A number of academic economists favored my plan, and I was persuaded to launch a publicity campaign to present it to the general public. We needed someone to act as executive director or man-of-all-work for the committee. I found him in an engaging fellow by the name of Norman Lombard. One would have sworn that this was a nom-de-plume, compounded perhaps from Montagu Norman and Lombard Street; but it seems that our man had actually been born with that fascinating moniker. I never knew exactly how he made his living, though I remembered that he was married to a schoolteacher, which no doubt helped a lot. He had been associated with Irving Fisher in the Stable Money Association and later had run some regular monthly economic discussions. We incorporated the Committee for Economic Stability, of which I was chairman. Its name sounds like an imitation of the well-known Committee for Economic Development; not so, because we adopted our name first, just as Pepsi-Cola came before Coca-Cola. We sent out literature and membership blanks, and managed to get fifty or more professors of economics—many with important names—to become members of the committee. But we achieved no results to speak of, despite efforts to make the committee an effective force. I quickly learned that a new economic proposal cannot get financial support from the public unless—like the Townsend Plan for old-age pensions—it promises direct and immediate financial benefits to a specific group, or unless the general emergency is great enough to induce people to approve any idea or slogan that makes vast promises of relief—as was the case with "Technology in the Great Depression." The Committee for Economic Stability has still a sort of legal existence, and even has about a thousand dollars in its bank account, but actually it has been dormant for some twenty years.

Each Sunday for a whole year I looked at the first page of *The New York Times Book Review,* to see if some important economist was hailing *Storage and Stability* as a major solution to the problem of economic depression. After all, the *Times* had done very nicely for me in their review of *Security Analysis,* and this new work was far more important. But apparently the *Times* considered my book just another excursion in the dismal science. They included its name among the new publications—as a matter of form—but did not bother to review it. My disappointment was keen, and only partly lightened by the fact that the book received notices of various lengths in several economic journals, though they were slow in coming.

I was made exceedingly happy when a review appeared in the most important of learned publications, *The American Economic Review*—in the same issue that contained my own article on the subject. It was written by another Graham, Frank D. Graham, professor of economics at Princeton University, and it was favorable, even enthusiastic. Frank Graham was to become an enthusiastic advocate of my idea. His book *Social Goals and Economic Institutions*[4] made a strong plea in favor of a commodity-reserve currency.

Needless to say, Frank Graham and I were not related. However, through contacts following his review, we got to be very close friends, and he became an investor in the Graham-Newman Fund. The similarity of our names produced great confusion in that part of the economic world that took an interest in CRC. Some writers thought we were the same person, others that we were related. Only last month, a professor from Cambridge, a strong advocate of CRC, told me he always thought that Frank Graham and I were brothers. In a footnote to my second book on the subject, I refer gratefully to Frank Graham's support, saying I am glad about a confusion that makes our names almost indistinguishable in this economic sphere. Since Frank Graham had originally been a professor of classics in Canada, I inserted a modified quotation from Horace, which read *Ambos una manet laus.* Horace had actually written, pessimistically, *omnes una manet nox*——"one night awaits (us) all." I changed it to the more hopeful "one praise awaits (us) both" (and added "I hope"). In a gracious note acknowledging my book and its reference to him, Frank Graham wrote modestly "But the 'laus' will go to you alone." His espousal of my scheme and the similarity of our names caused considerable confusion later about which Graham was responsible for the idea.

I recall going down to Princeton at Frank's invitation to take part in a faculty discussion of CRC. In a borrowed academic gown, I dined in hall at the faculty table that evening and listened to a Latin prayer before the meal. I couldn't help contrasting the Victorian atmosphere of the university with that in which modern economists strive to go beyond Adam Smith's economic axioms. That night I slept at Frank's home and made the acquaintance of his gracious wife.

Frank's modest investment in Graham-Newman Corporation was in his wife's name. After his death, his widow let the investment continue. Some years later, she wrote me a charming letter from Europe, telling me how indebted she was to us for her financial independence and her ability to spend the rest of her life as she pleased.

During the years that followed publication of *Storage and Stability,* quite a number of economists, of various degrees of eminence, showed interest in and support of my proposal.

Some of my good friends insisted that a movement should be launched to popularize the CRC idea, in order to bring about its adoption. From the beginning I was convinced that there were only two ways to realize my proposal. The first would be through the advent of another world depression, of the intensity of 1931 to 1932 or even 1921 to 1922, which would force world economic leaders to search openmindedly for a radically new solution to the paradox of want in the midst of potential plenty. The second might be a purely monetary crisis—based, say, on a shortage of international reserves. I could imagine certain financial advisers becoming convinced of the overall soundness of CRC as a means of creating "good money" when it was sorely needed. If ever expert world opinion should become ready for a new and improved formulation of sound money, my idea might be accepted as the best of its kind. On the other hand, I had little confidence in the ability of a propaganda campaign to sell a technical idea like mine to a preponderant segment of the public, nor did I think that mere popular demand—like that for the Townsend Plan—was likely to have much influence on the makers of economic-financial policy.

Epilogue

Benjamin Graham's Self-Portrait at Sixty-Three
May 1957

It is a clue to his character that B. has a host of loyal friends, very few if any enemies, but not a single chum or crony. Let's examine his inner life to see why. As a boy, he was bright, winsome, awkward, impractical, and morbidly sensitive. He was careful never to wound anyone, and he could not understand how others, including those who loved him dearly, would so often wound him, with nonchalance or even with malice. Very early in life he set to work, like a beaver, to build a breastwork around his heart. He embraced stoicism as a gospel sent to him from Heaven.

B's character was fully formed by his late teens. Superficially, it appeared wholly admirable. He had adopted all the self-advancing virtues with youthful ardor—industry, temperance, reliability, and a host of others. His natural kindliness was reinforced by what he fancied was a sense of *noblesse oblige*—for he always thought himself fortunate in his intellectual gifts—but it might just as well have been an overeager desire to make a good impression on the world about him. Con-

fident of his mental powers, he took for granted that he must
do everything honorable to attain success.

B's inordinate sensitivity to criticism worked on his character to produce two traits so marked as to be almost idiosyncracies. The first was his urge to escape any sort of censure by
showing exemplary and pleasant conduct. The other was a
basic reluctance to criticize others, and this was quickly transformed into an unwillingness to sit in judgment upon them. He
set before himself an ideal pattern of behavior towards those
around him. He must be invariably courteous, agreeable,
patient; he must avoid conflicts of all kinds, even those of
abstract opinion if any emotion might be involved.

As he grew older, B. achieved a degree of independence in
any area in which his judgment told him that his conduct ought
not to be dictated by mere convention or prejudice. He became
somewhat impatient with outer forms of etiquette when their
result was merely to prevent him from following his inclinations. But the change here was merely a superficial one; it did
not affect or reflect his essential relationship with the surrounding world.

The relations were not as brilliantly successful as, earlier,
he would have desired and expected. A large area of comparative failure was his dealings with women. Throughout his life
he had no difficulty in finding women who attracted him and
for whom he had sufficient appeal. Nor was his sex life inadequate or unvaried, after he had overcome the copybook puritanism of his first manhood. In *his* view his troubles with
women came about merely because they chose to take um-
brage at his good qualities—particularly his even temper and
his intellect. In return he developed some feeling of persecution and exploitation at their hands. Partly out of real experience, partly perhaps out of imagination, he felt that nearly all
women were unreasonable, dominating, unappreciative of his
kindness and patience, too insistent on penetrating into the
forbidden sanctum of his private self.

Only very late in life did B. meet a woman who possessed

the qualities of soul and mind, of character and temperament, which he had sought vainly in many others. To her, he felt, he could lower the barriers that had separated him from the rest of humanity. Under this new influence he inquired for the first time into the nature of these barriers. Why, since the end of his college years, had he admitted no one—man or woman—into a true intellectual and emotional intimacy? Why had he no pals, no chums?

B. examined his character afresh, and what he found was not too flattering. He saw smugness, selfishness, snobbery, a certain contrived artificiality in his generous gestures, a touch of calculated egoism in his unruffled serenity. His third wife said of him that he was humane, but not human—the phrase struck home. He lacked genuine sympathy, a true sharing of the joys and sorrows of others. His enthusiasms were either entirely impersonal—for ideas, for artistic creations—or else for those things that contributed to his own development, his inner glory. He "turned from praise" with unfeigned modesty, but that modesty was itself a manifestation of a pride so perfect as to be indistinguishable from vanity. His was Horace's *mens sibi conscia recti*—"a mind conscious of its own rectitude"—wrapped in the insulation of confident superiority. Like Landor, he strove with none, for none was worth his striving—at least in his own estimation. He recognized only one close companion, only one kindred spirit—himself.

His affability to others was unforced and unfailing, truly a second nature. But his first nature was remote and inaccessible to others. B. saw this all at last. He felt the need for less superiority and more humanity. A new personage from *outre mer* was entering his life and profoundly moving it. At age sixty and beyond he was to begin his emotional development all over again; he must accept Love not as an experience of life, but as *the* experience of life. He recalled a poem that he had written as a college sophomore, in the glow of his first romantic passion. Now the rather hackneyed sentiment took on a new dimension of meaning for him:

Inspiration

As a brook slumbers, hushed its tinkling song,
By March's icy cloak held prisoner,
My soul has music, too, that cannot stir,
Frozen to silence by a witless tongue.

But lo! the bar melts in the breath of Spring,
The water wakes into a melody;
So by the warmth this new love sheds on me
The bonds of speech are burst, and I may sing!

Benjamin Graham's
Eightieth Birthday Speech
April 11, 1974

Dearest Malou, brother Vic, children and grandchildren, and the other dear ones who are here with me, welcome to La Jolla and to my eightieth birthday celebration. First I want to thank my daughter Marjorie for arranging this gathering; also thanks to brother Victor for his artistic souvenir edition of some of my poems; and thanks to each of you for your valued contributions to my new scrapbook.

Mark Twain, whom, in my early youth, I saw resplendent in his white suit and curly white hair, once agreed to attend a banquet providing he not be asked to speak. But the crowd was so insistent that he finally got up. Very slowly and in the most mournful of tones, he pronounced the following: "Alexander the Great is dead, Julius Caesar is dead, Napoleon is dead—and I'm not feeling so well myself." Then he sat down.

I too can say "I'm not feeling so well myself," and I too am going to sit down. But first I have a bit to say.

In his eloquent if somewhat exaggerated tribute to his father-in-law, our eminent Irving [Janis, Marjorie's husband] mentioned a little sketch about Ulysses that I wrote only a few months ago. The story and the character of Ulysses made an indelible impression on me when I was a little boy—or "yittle" boy, as I used to pronounce it in those days. It is strange that the *Odyssey* has meant so much to me, since Ulysses' character is so different from my own. He was a great fighter and plunderer, while I have never fought with anyone or plundered anything in my life. He was crafty and devious, while I pride myself on being straightforward and direct. Yet he has attracted me all my life, as he has attracted countless readers for the last 2,500 years.

In my amateur literary critical view, based on a recent reading of the *Odyssey*, I find the story wonderful, but the poetry mostly second-rate. For one good quotable line in Homer, I find twenty or more in Virgil. And so, even if I'm the only man on earth to say so—*Athanasius contra mundum*[1]—I will insist that Virgil is the better poet of the two. (Perhaps Tennyson agreed with me, for he called the Roman poet "wielder of the mightiest measure ever molded by the mind of man.")

But while Ulysses has ever been my fantasy idol, there is another flesh-and-blood character after whom I have consciously modeled my life. By coincidence we have the same first name. The man is Benjamin Franklin. He had all the characteristics to which I aspire—high intelligence, application, inventiveness, humor, kindness, and tolerance of others' faults. Perhaps too—without trying—I shared some of his weaknesses, especially for the fair sex. If my life can be compared somewhat with his—for both inward and outward success—I should be well pleased.

Looking back over my eighty years, I am struck by a contrast between the outlook of my youth and that of my old age. As a youngster, I was often pessimistic about how my life was

going; it seemed full of mistakes, mishaps, and disappointments. But I was very optimistic about the future of the world;
I was sure that with the aid of science it was progressing
rapidly toward peace and a more comfortable existence for
everybody. Now from the vantage—or disadvantage—of four-
score years, the picture seems completely reversed. My own
life has been unusually successful and even happy; but the
world seems to me to be going to Hell in a hansom—as they
used to say when Sherlock Holmes rode around London in a
hansom cab. In the common groupthink and groupspeak of
today, my ten grandchildren at this table are expected in due
course to take on the responsibility for running the world.
That's a pretty big order for you kids to carry out in the fabulous year 2000. Let me wish you luck in that endeavor—but
with something of a headshake.

Now I have a last subject—and a more cheerful one—to
touch on before I close. I want to say that at least half of all the
pleasures that I have enjoyed in life have come from the world
of the mind, from things of beauty and culture, especially literature and art. These things are available to everybody, virtually free of charge: all one needs is the interest to start with
and a minimal effort to appreciate the riches spread out before
us. Grandchildren, take that initial interest, if possible; make
that continued effort. Once you have found it—the life of culture—never let it go.

In his defense of the poet Archias, Cicero pays a famous
tribute to the benefits conferred by humane studies. Let me
recite it now, a little in the Latin, and then in my English
translation:

Haec studia adulescentiam alunt, senectutem oblectant...

(These studies nourish our youth and comfort our age;
they adorn our prosperity and provide a refuge and a

solace in adversity; they delight us at home and are no hinderance abroad.)

Pernoctant nobiscum, peregrinantur, rusticantur.

(They pass the night with us, they travel with us, they go to the country with us.)

I have long thought that this eloquent tribute, in the very same words, could be paid as well to kind and lovely ladies in general, and especially to those I have known in my life—from my dear mother, who nourished my youth, to my priceless Malou, who comforts my old age. "Pernoctant nobiscum": more often than our studies do the ladies pass the night with us; they peregrinate with us, they rusticate with us.

Now for my final message. What better one can I choose than the closing lines of Tennyson's "Ulysses," those words well loved and oft repeated in the Graham family:

> Come, my friends, 'tis not too late to seek
> A newer world. Push off, and sitting well in order, smite
> The sounding furrows; for my purpose holds
> To sail beyond the sunset and the baths
> Of all the western stars, until I die.
> It may be that the gulfs will wash us down:
> It may be we shall touch the Happy Isles,
> And see the great Achilles, whom we knew.
> Though much is taken, much abides; and though
> We are not now that strength which in old days
> Moved earth and heaven; that which we are, we are;
> One equal temper of heroic hearts,
> Made weak by time and fate, but strong in will
> To strive, to seek, to find, and not to yield.[2]

Chronology

1894 Born May 9, London, England.

1895 Moves to New York City.

1900 Begins first grade at six and one-half.

1901 Visits England. Queen Victoria dies.

1903 Living at 244 116th Street, New York City. Begins grammar school P.S. 10. Sells *The Saturday Evening Post*. Goes to various summer resorts where Father sells imported chinaware at auctions. Father dies, aged thirty-five.

1906 Attends Townsend Harris Hall high school, a branch of CCNY. Studies French with Constance Fleischmann.

1907 Market panic: U.S. Steel fails; Mother loses her entire margin account. Enters Boys High School.

1910 Graduates Boys High, chosen Class Critic. Summer job on farm. "Loses" Pulitzer Scholarship to Columbia.

1911 Goes to CCNY, but leaves discouraged. Works at many different part-time jobs—classified-ad salesman, movie cashier, telephone assembler. Dean Keppel apologizes for administrative error, and he enters Columbia on an Alumni Scholarship.

1912 At Columbia, studies mathematics, philosophy, English, Greek, and music. Works at various part-time jobs. First girlfriend, Alda Miller.

1913 At Columbia, works at U.S. Express adapting Hollerith card-punch and card-sort machines leased by the Calculating-Tabulating-Recording Company (later IBM). Is promoted to manager. Takes a leave of absence from Columbia. Publishes article in *Vogue*. Tutors army officers' children at Governors Island.

1914 Graduates Columbia, Phi Beta Kappa, second in class.

On Dean Keppel's advice decides to follow a career in finance. Refuses three possible teaching jobs at Columbia. Tutors General Leonard Wood's son. Teaches English to foreign students at Bronx night school. Moves to luxurious Hunt's Point Palace apartments. Is invited by Carl Van Doren to be instructor at Brierly School but refuses. Hears Yvette Guilbert reciting a war poem. Because of anti-German sentiment, family changes name from Grossbaum to Graham. Joins brokerage firm of Newburger, Henderson, and Loeb. Writes evaluation of Missouri Pacific Railroad that prompts an offer from J.S. Bache and Company as security analyst, but Newburger refuses to let him go.

1915   Meets Hazel Mazur. Gives up night school job, but continues teaching officers' sons on Governors Island. Works as board-boy in customers' room at Newburger. Speculates in Missouri Pacific stock and is censured by Newburger. Completes successful arbitrage analysis of Guggenheim Exploration Company. Buys first auto jointly with Cousin Lou. Donates his sets of Hebbel and Lessing to Columbia University Library.

1916   Announces engagement to Hazel. Salary is raised to $50 per week. U.S. Express in bankruptcy. Negotiates purchase of house securities for Newburger Company; also acts as the company's bookmaker for bets on the presidential election.

1917   Marries Hazel. Brother Leon also marries. Opens unsuccessful phonograph shop venture with brothers, selling at a loss in 1919. Draft board grants deferment. Joins army reserve. Invests money for Professor Tassin, and loses it in mini-crash, then repays Tassin at $60 per month. Publishes article in *The American Mathematical Monthly.*

1918   Mother moves in; tension between her and Hazel. Makes brief effort as business consultant with Maurice Gerard, his mother's elder brother. First child, Isaac

Newton, born. Writes article for *The Magazine of Wall Street* explaining how to determine value of goodwill; will write dozens more for this magazine over the years.

1919   Finishes army reserve training. Does comparative analysis of railroad bonds. Rises in Wall Street. The bull market of 1919. Makes killing on Savold Tire, then loses money to syndicate organizer's trickery. After negative analysis of Chicago, Milwaukee, & St. Paul, meets Robert J. Marony, its vice-president, who becomes lifelong friend and later associate. Manages successful call operation with Pierce Oil bonds.

1920   Becomes junior partner in Newburger, Henderson, and Loeb. Conducts highly successful dealings in Japanese bonds with his friend Junkichi Miki. Starts a circular newsletter with assistance of Leo Stern. Analyzes tire industry. Accepts $20,000 investment from Uncle Maurice Gerard, who wishes to retire and live off the income. Becomes naturalized American citizen. Moves to Mt. Vernon. First daughter, Marjorie, born.

1921   Recommends trade of short-term U.S. Victory bonds for longer-term U.S. bonds and is proven correct. Idea for commodity reserve currency plan fermenting.

1922   Maurice Gerard and family move back to New York to be near Graham and Wall Street.

1923   Leaves Newburger and sets up private investment account, the Graham Corporation, with Harris family. Executes successful Du Pont–General Motors arbitrage. Buys stock in U.S. Express, now in liquidation.

1924   Takes a ski vacation in Mahopac with Hazel and two children, Newton and Marjorie.

1925   Graham Corporation dissolves as the Harrises drop out. Also dissolves Graham-Cohen account (with Benjamin V. Cohen). Second daughter, Elaine, is born. Spends summer in Deal, New Jersey.

1926   Sets up new structure, the "Benjamin Graham Joint

Account," in which he gets percentage of profit only. Investors put in $400,000. Jerome Newman joins firm, then becomes partner. Discovers undervaluation of Northern Pipeline. Summers again in Deal.

1927   At stockholders' meeting, requests that Northern Pipeline pay out surpluses to stockholders but loses because of lack of a second. Meets John D. Rockefeller. Son Newton dies of meningitis. Begins to teach at Columbia. Meets Bernard Baruch. Meets Winston Churchill. David Dodd becomes his student, then colleague. Hazel goes to Europe.

1928   Wins proxy fight with Northern Pipeline, becoming a director, as the company agrees to distribute excess holdings to stockholders. Becomes codirector of the ill-fated Unexcelled Fireworks Company. Newton II is born. Visits Europe. Moves to an expensive duplex in Beresford Apartments. Starts teaching enormously popular Advanced Security Analysis at Columbia (and continues till 1954).

1929   Joint account worth 2½ million; Bernard Baruch offers him partnership, which he refuses. Vacations on Baruch's brother's yacht. Agrees with Baruch that Crash is imminent, but unlike Baruch, leaves portion of portfolio in stock market. Account shows 20 percent loss for year.

1930   Joint account's worst financial year, down 50 percent. Receives no income from the joint account for five years. Lives by teaching, writing, and consulting. Marriage to Hazel is becoming shaky.

1931   Joint account down 16 percent.

1932   Joint account down 3 percent (70 percent of the original 2½ million has been lost). Chairs protective committee to secure proceeds of preferred stock in Aeolian record company. Moves to less luxurious apartment, the El Dorado. Dow Jones average is 42. Makes presentation to Economic Forum at the New School for Social

Research on Commodity Reserve Currency Plan. Publishes three-part series called "Is American Business Worth More Dead Than Alive?" in *Forbes*.

1933 Account is worth $375,000. Makes 50 percent profit. Publishes article in *Economic Forum*. Writes plays *China Wedding* and *The Day of Reckoning*, but they are not produced. Appears in court for first time as expert witness; will do forty more over the years.

1934 First Edition of *Security Analysis* published by McGraw-Hill (later editions appear in 1940, 1951, 1962, and 1988). Third daughter, Winifred, is born. Fund proposes to pay Graham and Newman straight 20 percent of profits. His play *Baby Pompadour* (earlier called *True to the Marines*) appears on Broadway on December 27 at the Vanderbilt Theatre and closes after four performances. The Fund adopts new financial accounting methods. Is consulted by government about the proposed Securities Exchange Act.

1935 All Depression losses have now been made good. Helps found New York Society of Security Analysts.

1936 Under IRS pressure, changes the joint account to "The Graham-Newman Corporation." Meets Carol Wade on cruise.

1937 Publishes *Storage and Stability* (McGraw-Hill) and *The Interpretation of Financial Statements* with Charles McGolrick (Harper and Row, Second Edition, 1955). Carol becomes his mistress. He proposes divorce to Hazel. When she refuses he goes to Reno over his lawyer's protest. Hazel finally agrees, and she obtains a divorce in Reno.

1938 Marries Carol at Sherry Netherlands Hotel in New York City.

1940 Divorces Carol. Revised Edition of *Security Analysis*. A lonely bachelor, he takes up roller-skating and attending Brooklyn Dodgers' baseball games. Starts a relationship with his secretary Estelle Messing, whom he later marries.

1941 Addresses American Statistical Association in Hart-
ford on "A Program for Stabilizing the Purchasing
Power of the Dollar."

1942 Proposes a board of qualifiers for the New York Society
of Security Analysts.

1943 Has final contact with Carol Wade. First grandchild,
Cathy Janis, is born to Marjorie (will have ten more
grandchildren).

1944 Mother is murdered in robbery on walk home from her
bridge game. Marries Estelle Messing. Publishes *World
Commodities and World Currency* (McGraw-Hill).

1945 Meets John D. Rockefeller for third time at New York
State Chamber of Commerce banquet. Defends Full Employment Act to this unreceptive audience. Benjamin Jr.
is born. Begins to write articles for *The Analysts Journal*
(later called *The Financial Analysts Journal*), first under
the pseudonym "Cogitator" and later under his own name.

1946 Addresses Summer Institute for Social Progress, Welles-
ley, Massachusetts on "Our Economic Future, Its Direction and Control." Engages in a public debate with Floyd
Odlum (chairman of the Atlas Corporation, friend of
Howard Hughes, and husband of Jacqueline Cochran)
about the wisdom of buying distressed companies.

1947 Meets Dwight D. Eisenhower. Speaks at the first
annual conference of the Financial Analysts Federation
(later the Institute of Chartered Financial Analysts),
urging formal certification examinations and standards
for the profession.

1948 Buys controlling interest in GEICO, then takes it public.

1949 Writes and publishes *The Intelligent Investor* (Second
Edition, 1954; Third, 1959; Fourth, 1973, the last with
help from Warren Buffett). Forms the Graham-Newman Partnership.

1950 Becomes member of board of P & R Company, owner of
coal and railroad properties.

1951   Serves as president of the Jewish Guild for the Blind (until 1953). Moves course to the Columbia Graduate School of Business.

1952   Addresses Institute of Chartered Financial Analysts on "Toward a Science of Security Analysis."

1953   Writes "Stock Dividends" for *Barron's*.

1954   Hires Warren Buffett. Graham-Newman now capitalized at $6 million. Travels to France to retrieve belongings of Newton II, a Korean War veteran, who has committed suicide. Begins a correspondence with Malou, with whom he falls in love. Over the years they spend more and more time together.

1955   Explains his success in testimony before a Senate committee chaired by James Fulbright. Elaine receives Ph.D. in Psychology at Yale University.

1956   Dissolves Graham-Newman Corporation and Graham-Newman Partnership and retires to Beverly Hills with Estelle and Benjamin Jr. Lives at 611 North Maple across the street from his cousin Rhoda Gerard Sarnat and her husband Dr. Bernard Sarnat. Becomes Regents Professor at the Graduate School of Business of UCLA, where he teaches without pay for fifteen years.

1957   Writes autobiographical vignettes.

1958   Testifies before House Ways and Means Committee on dividend policy, margin rules, and capital gains taxes (which he favors preserving).

1959   Gives up tennis.

1960   Visits London home.

1962   His effort to professionalize security analysts leads to the creation of the Financial Analysts Federation, later named the Association for Investment Management and Research, which gives certification by examination to financial analysts. Publishes Fourth Edition of *Security Analysis* with Sidney Cottle and Charles Tatham. (A Fifth Edition published in 1988 under auspices of Frank Block.)

1963   Sits for a portrait by the Dutch painter Jan Hoowig, paid for by Buffett and other ex-students and donated to the Financial Analysts Federation.

1964   Marjorie publishes *A Two-Year-Old Goes to Nursery School: A Case Study of Separation Reactions* (Tavistock Press). His friend's son Andrew Goodman, like Benjamin Jr., a volunteer in the Southern Voting Rights movement, is killed in Mississippi.

1965   Resigns from GEICO Board of Directors.

1966   Moves to La Jolla (7811 Eads Avenue) with Malou. They continue to live there for part of the year and divide the rest of their time between Malou's home in Aix-en-Provence and (for a time) Funchal, Madeira.

1967   Publishes his translation of a Uruguayan novel, Mario Benedetti's *The Truce*, with Harper and Row.

1968   Warren Buffett and other old students of Graham make a pilgrimage to seek his advice about the market. They meet at the Hotel Del Coronado. Corresponds with "Adam Smith," author of *The Money Game*.

1970   Takes trip to Australia.

1971   Jerry Newman resigns from GEICO Board of Directors.

1974   Eightieth birthday celebration: delivers speech and is presented by his brother Victor with a printed volume of his poems. Gives lecture on the "Renaissance of Value" to Institute of Chartered Financial Analysts, urging analysts to buy stocks at "fire-sale" prices (Dow is at 600) (excerpts printed in *Barron's*, September 23, 1974).

1975   Receives the Molodovsky Award, the highest given by the Financial Analysts Federation.

1976   With James Buchanan Rea cofounds the Rea-Graham Fund. Dies September 21, in Aix-en-Provence, France. Malou, Marjorie, and Elaine arrange for his cremation, and Marjorie carries his ashes back to the United States. The family holds a memorial and buries his ashes at Stephen Wise Free Synagogue Westchester Hills Cemetery at Hastings-on-Hudson, New York. A memorial service is held at Faculty House, Columbia University. Benjamin Jr. receives M.D. from University of California Medical School. GEICO on verge of bankruptcy, Buffett buys heavily into it, owning 48 percent by 1990 (and buying balance in 1995).

1977   First wife Hazel dies.

1979   Daughter Winifred Graham Downsbrough dies.

1981   Third wife Estelle Messing Graham dies.

1982   Rea-Graham becomes a public mutual fund.

1984   McGraw-Hill gives fiftieth anniversary celebration for *Security Analysis* at Columbia. Dodd is awarded honorary doctorate.

1986   Warren Buffett gives his famous speech, "The Superinvestors of Graham and Doddsville" (later published in *Hermes*, and in the last edition of *The Intelligent Investor*).

1987   David Dodd dies.

1988   Elected to the U.S. Business Hall of Fame in Atlanta. Other laureates include: Stephen Bechtel, Andrew Carnegie, Walter Chrysler, Walt Disney, Pierre Du Pont, George Eastman, Thomas Edison, Henry Ford, A. P. Giannini, Conrad Hilton, Henry Kaiser, Henry Luce, Andrew Mellon, J. Pierpont Morgan, Adolph Ochs, William Paley, J. C. Penney, John D. Rockefeller, David Sarnoff, Alfred Sloan, not to speak of Benjamin Franklin and George Washington. The award is accepted for the Graham family by Benjamin Jr. Robert Heilbrunn establishes a Professorship of Asset Management and Finance at Columbia Business School as the "cornerstone of a Graham and Dodd Research Institute."

Notes

Introduction

1. A fuller account of his later years appears in Janet Lowe, *Benjamin Graham on Value Investing* (Chicago: Dearborn Financial Publishing, 1994).

2. Gore Vidal, "How I Survived the Fifties," *The New Yorker*, October 2, 1995, p. 62.

3. New York: Schocken Books, 1989.

4. Chapter 3.

5. An article entitled "The Immortals," by Jennifer K. Brown, *California Business*, September–October 1991, contains a wonderful drawing of Graham, in the form of a Byzantine icon, holding a scepter in his right hand and a bejewelled book (presumably *Security Analysis*) in his left. A cherub with the face of David Dodd perches on his shoulder, playing a hymn to Value on the lute.

6. John Train, *The Money Masters* (New York: Penguin, 1980), p. 95.

7. "Portrait of an Analyst: Benjamin Graham," *Financial Analysts Journal*, January–February 1968.

8. See the "Self-Portrait," pp. 309–312. Here—and in the quotations from this crucial document that follow—Graham characteristically refers to himself in the third person, a stylistic marker of his desire to write a fair and objective account of himself.

9. See Chapter 16 infra.

10. The letter to Marjorie is dated February 10, 1971.

11. *The Wall Street Journal*, August 1995.

12. *World Commodities and World Currency* (New York: McGraw-Hill, 1944), pp. 1–2.

13. Ibid. p. 4.

14. *Fortune*, Fall 1987, p. 48. In fact, Graham reported that "many people had mistaken me for him" (see pp. 290–291), But Robinson himself found Graham more attractive: "I'll always remember Eddie's response to my remark, for it flattered my vanity so. 'Mr. Graham, if I looked like you, I'd play glamour parts.'"

15. Ibid.

16. A parody written on February 25, 1965, in his little notebook, or "pillow book": "The planes in Spain fly mainly in the rains."

17. *The Intelligent Investor* (New York: Harper and Brothers, 1949), p. 157.

18. Interestingly enough, relatives, friends, and students don't concur about his standoffishness. They remain deeply devoted to him. Perhaps he *felt* lonely and isolated, even though he was widely liked.

19. Epilogue, "Benjamin Graham's Self-Portrait at Sixty-Three" (May 1957), p. 310.

20. See Epilogue, pp. 310–311.

21. With something like boyish glee, he mentions George Gershwin, Edward G. Robinson, Sam Jaffee, Isaac Asimov ("who may one day rank with Jules Verne"), Caruso (singing "Una furtiva lagrima"), Frieda Hempel, Gatti-Cazzaza, Beniamino Gigli, and other singers like Schumann-Heink, Sembrich, Mary Garden, Geraldine Farrar, Jeritz, Chaliapin (singing "Boris Godunov"), Polacco, the original Alice of *Alice in Wonderland* (Alice Liddell Hargreaves), Nicholas Murray Butler, Buffalo Bill, Mark Twain, Churchill, Eisenhower, John Maynard Keynes, Babe Ruth, Pavlova (dancing "Le Cygne"), Nijinski in "Le Spectre de

la rose" and "L'Après-midi d'un faune," Yvette Guilbert, and so on. "I also once interviewed Albert Einstein, and received a letter from him in his own handwriting—in German, for some reason. I have it somewhere, pasted on cardboard among my papers; alas! the ink has faded to illegibility. It was about his sponsoring the annual appeal for funds by the Jewish Guild for the Blind, of which I was then president. I well remember seeing him come down the stairs of a friend's house in Westchester, wearing a disreputable sweater and with his hair every which way."

22. Mario Benedetti, *The Truce*, translated by Benjamin Graham (New York: Harper and Row, 1967), pp. 2–3.

23. But his daughter Elaine writes, in a letter of January 16, 1966: "It interests me that although Dad's self-insights were not at all psychoanalytic, they achieved (with Malou['s help]) as much change in his character as they did. It interests me too that three of his children were significantly immersed in psychoanalysis: I became [a psychoanalyst], Marj has grounded her professional and personal life within its tradition, and Buz went through a phase of intense interest in Freud during his late adolescence. I might add that in my own case, despite his 'deafness' to psychoanalysis...he paid without comment all the bills of my first five-year analysis."

24. Quoted from a letter of January 20, 1996, from his daughter Marjorie.

25. Marjorie writes: "He was a marvelous father. I was crazy about him as a child and young adolescent, and loved him deeply—if more critically—all my life. When I was a youngster, he was my 'walking encyclopedia.' He knew everything. Always he brought poetry into the life of the mind and the heart, into our everyday lives. It was a privilege to be with him. He was funny, charming, enthralling."

Chapter One

1. Unless otherwise indicated, the translations seem to be Graham's own.

Chapter Three

1. See pp. 215–216.
2. The whole passage was quoted by Graham in his eightieth birthday speech. See p. 315.

Chapter Four

1. Irving Howe gives an excellent portrait of Cohen in *World of Our Fathers* (New York: Schocker, 1989), pp. 283-286.
2. Howe characterizes Barondess as "the figure who best embodies [the] awkward turbulence—its pathos, its hysteria, its selflessness" of the Jewish labor movement at the turn of the century (pp. 112–115).

Chapter Six

1. See Chapter 9 for details.

Chapter Seven

1. Germany sent a gunboat to Agadir, Morocco, in 1911, ostensibly to protect its citizens' rights, but really as an act of aggression against France. War was only narrowly averted by a treaty.

Chapter Eight

1. "Graham is best known for establishing principles for the

fundamental valuation of assets, that is, estimating the *intrinsic* value of an asset (and hence its future value) as a function of observable characteristics, such as the asset's book value and earnings growth. Much of the progress in financial technology in the 1980s involved the basics of arbitrage-free valuation of assets whose value is contingent upon the values of other assets or variables. It is interesting that already in 1917, Graham seems to have recognized the basic ingredients of arbitrage-free valuation even as he was an early pioneer of 'risk arbitrage.'" (Note by Professor Terry Marsh, Haas Business School, University of California, Berkeley.)

2. Lucy Gates was a famous American opera singer of the 1920s. The only Lucy Marsh I was able to find was a socialite and amateur artist who published an illustration to a 1928 issue of the *The New York Times* and donated the proceeds to charity.

Chapter Ten

1. A good characterization of the Graham-Newman operations appeared in "Portrait of an Analyst: Benjamin Graham," *The Financial Analysts Journal*, January–February 1968:

Graham-Newman's operations were restricted to a few well-defined categories, each of which promised a satisfactory rate of profit—say, 20% per annum, or better—against relatively minor risks. The latter were further minimized by wide diversification. The categories were entitled: arbitrages; cash payouts (liquidations); related hedges; unrelated hedges; current-asset stocks ("bargain issues"), and controlled companies—the special province of J. A. Newman. A careful check was kept on the result of each operation and class of operations.

One consequence of this continuous evaluation of results may seem surprising. The "unrelated hedges"—in which a "cheap issue" is bought and an entirely disconnected "dear issue" is sold against it—were found to be more trouble than their overall profit was worth, and they were accordingly dropped. The Graham-Newman "value approach" did not work well enough in the short-selling of highly popular and hence apparently over-valued issues, *unless* there was adequate protection through holding of a senior, convertible issue of the same company.

The "bargain issues" were practically all restricted to the purchase of common stocks at less than two-thirds of their net-current-asset value. Remarkably few final losses were shown in this category, comprising [sic: "considering"?] the purchase of many hundred such issues over a period of more than thirty years. However, it is both paradoxical and typical of financial experience generally that the most profitable Graham-Newman operation of all did not meet this exacting requirement. This was the purchase of a 50% ownership of Government Employees Insurance Company at a price only slightly below its asset value.

Chapter Twelve

1. Andrew Goodman was one of the three voter-registration workers murdered in Neshoba County, Mississippi, in the summer of 1964; the others were Michael Scherner and James Chaney.

2. Ben wrote himself a note to quote the passage and to translate it. He was probably referring to Book VI, ll. 47-49 of the *Aeneid*.

3. Aldous Huxley, *Point Counterpoint* (New York: Doubleday, 1928), chapters 34–35, pp. 396–420.

Chapter Thirteen

1. *Inferno*, Canto V, ll. 121–123: "There is no greater sorrow/ Than thinking back upon a happy time/In misery—" (Allen Mandelbaum's translation, New York: Bantam Books, 1980, p. 46).

2. "I'm the boss; my wife is the one who commands."

3. A man named Montmirel: he also invented the "pudding à Chateaubriand" (later called "pudding diplomate"). See André Maurois, *Chateaubriand* (New York: Harper, 1938), p. 246, for details.

Chapter Fourteen

1. A wish, apparently, that was never fulfilled, since the manuscript does not contain such a chapter.

Chapter Fifteen

1. "The other person hears only the 'No,'" *Iphigenie auf Tauris*, Act 1, Scene 3.

2. The reader will note the enduring attractiveness of this kind of plot in efforts like *Born Yesterday* and *Bullets Over Broadway*.

3. *The Best Plays of 1934–35* lists the following information about *Baby Pompadour:*

BABY POMPADOUR

(4 performances)

A comedy in three acts by Benjamin Graham. Produced by Arthur Dreifuss and Willard G. Garnhardt at the Vanderbilt Theatre, New York, December 27, 1934.

Cast of characters—

George Armstrong	Scott Kolk
Margie	Virginia Deane
Ferdinand Dike	Robert Lowe
General Sancho Guiterrez	Joseph Monneret de Villard
Elmer Tweed	Maurice F. Manson
Rear Admiral Wilfred Butler	Charles Wellesley
Señor Miguel Arboleda	Daniel Ocko
Daniel P. Atkinson	John Murray
Dr. Calloway	A. M. Putnam
E. Silas Buchanan	Herbert Rawlinson
Dorothy Hamilton	Gladys Shelley
Cora Hunt Buchanan	Nana Bryant
Angela Dike	Gladys Feldman
Herbert Woolsey	Ralph Locke
Genevieve	Lillian Brown
Jeffries	Maurice F. Manson

Staged by Clarence Derwent; settings by Nicholas Yellenti

E. Silas Buchanan is an editorial columnist with two women in his life. One his wife, the other a blonde, Dorothy, from the chorus. It is Dorothy who has the greater influence with him and who keeps him up to snuff as a writer. Politicians and business tycoons seek her out in order to win her endorsement of their plans that she may pass the word on to E. Silas. Buchanan is indirectly responsible for sending the Marines to Nicaragua. Dorothy runs away with her boss's private secretary and ditches him for a sailor. Buchanan's work goes off and Mrs. Buchanan is forced to scheme to restore Dorothy to her husband's arms to get him in form again.

Chapter Sixteen

1. There was recently a United Nations Conference on Trade and Development held in Geneva. One of the papers submitted to that meeting was the joint effort of three illustrious professors of Economics: Hart of Columbia, Kaldor of Cambridge (England), and Tinbergen of Rotterdam (Holland). After considering various current economic problems of the world and rejecting certain possible solutions, they began their main argument with the words: "This brings us to Benjamin Graham's old plan for a commodity-reserve currency..." I own to a strange feeling as I read the phrase "Benjamin Graham's old plan." Could an idea which only yesterday (as memory has it) seemed completely novel and revolutionary now be viewed by economists as "old"? Yet it was not yesterday but more than thirty years ago that the idea was published; thirty years in the modern world bring more changes than many "cycles of Cathay." [Graham's note]

2. London: G. Allen & Unwin, 1922.

3. Almost the identical idea of directly stabilizing the price level of a group of basic commodities had occurred to an honest-to-goodness economist in Holland. He was Jan Goudriaan, professor of economics at the University of Rotterdam, later director of the Dutch railroad system, and still later, a professor at the University of Pretoria in South Africa. His proposal was published in London in 1932 in a little pamphlet entitled "How to Stop Deflation." As far as I know, that pamphlet was never circulated or reviewed in the United States, and I did not learn about its existence or that of Goudriaan until many years later, when he became my friend. Goudriaan is entitled to credit for prior publication of the idea. However, my own presentation in book

form was the first to attract the general attention of economists, and insofar as there were differences in details, my version has generally been preferred. The plan is usually referred to under my name alone, but I would prefer that it be called the Goudriaan-Graham (or Graham-Goudriaan) Plan. [Graham's note]

4. Frank D. Graham, *Social Goals and Economic Institutions* (Princeton: Princeton University Press, 1949, originally published 1942).

Epilogue

1. St. Athanasius (c. 295–373) was bishop of Alexandria. His tenure was always problematic, and he spent more than seventeen years of his episcopate in exile.

2. The last four words appear on Benjamin Graham's tombstone.

Bibliography

Writings by Graham

"Are We Too Confident About the Invulnerability of Stocks?" *The Commercial and Financial Chronicle,* February 1, 1962.

"The Art of Hedging," *The Magazine of Wall Street,* vol. 25, February 7, 1920, pp. 252–253.

"Bargains in Bonds," *The Magazine of Wall Street,* 1919.

"The Coal Situation and Coal Stocks," *The Magazine of Wall Street,* vol. 24, July 5, 1919, pp. 509–511.

"The 'Collapse' of American International," *The Magazine of Wall Street,* vol. 26, December 11, 1920, pp. 175–176, 217.

"A Conversation with Benjamin Graham," *The Financial Analysts Journal,* September 1976.

Current Problems in Security Analysis [Transcripts of Lectures, 1946–7] (New York: New York Institute of Finance, 1947).

The Flexible Work-Year: An Answer to Unemployment (Santa Barbara: Center for the Study of Democratic Institutions, 1964).

"The Future of Financial Analysis," *The Financial Analysts Journal,* May 1963.

"The Goodyear Reorganization," *The Magazine of Wall Street,* vol. 27, March 19, 1921, pp. 683–685.

"The Growth of Corporate Working Capital, 1939–1945," *The Financial Analysts Journal,* First Quarter 1947.

"The Hippocratic Method in Security Analysis," *The Financial Analysts Journal,* Second Quarter 1946.

"Inflated Treasuries and Deflated Stockholders," *Forbes,* vol. 29, no. 11, June 1, 1932, pp.10–12.

The Intelligent Investor: A Book of Practical Counsel, First Edition, New York: Harper Brothers, 1949; Fourth Revised Edition, with preface and appendix by Warren Buffett, 1985.

With Spencer B. Meredith, *The Interpretation of Financial Statements*, First Edition: New York: Harper Brothers, 1937; Third Revised Edition, with Charles McGolrick, Harper and Row, 1975; First Perennial Library Edition, Harper and Row, 1987).

"Is American Business Worth More Dead Than Alive?" *Forbes*, June 1, 1932; June 13, 1932; July 1, 1932.

"The New Speculation in Common Stocks," *The Financial Analysts Journal*, June 1958.

"Northern Pacific Outstrips Great Northern," *The Magazine of Wall Street*, vol. 24, June 7, 1919, pp. 314–317.

"A Note on Corporate Working Capital 1939–1945," *The Financial Analysts Journal*, Fourth Quarter 1946.

"Our Balance of Payments—The Conspiracy of Silence," *The Financial Analysts Journal*, November 1962.

"On Being Right in Security Analysis," *The Financial Analysts Journal*, First Quarter 1946.

"A Profitable Switch—From Saint Paul at 41 Into Big Four at 43," *The Magazine of Wall Street*, vol. 24, May 24, 1919, pp. 222–225.

"A Questionnaire on Stockholder-Management Relationship," *The Financial Analysts Journal*, Fourth Quarter 1947.

The Renaissance of Value: The Proceedings of a Seminar on the Economy, Interest Rates, Portfolio Management, and Bonds (Charlottesville, Virginia: Financial Analysts Research Foundations, 1974).

"The Riddle of U.S. Steel's Book Value," *The Magazine of Wall Street*, vol. 38, July 17, 1926, pp. 524–525, 614–617.

With David Dodd, *Security Analysis*, First Edition, New York: McGraw-Hill, 1934; Fifth Edition is retitled *Graham and Dodd's Security Analysis,* revised by Sidney Cottle, Roger F. Murray, Frank E. Block, with the collaboration of Martin L. Leibowitz, New York: McGraw-Hill, 1988.

"The S.E.C. Method of Security Analysis," *The Financial Analysts Journal,* Third Quarter 1946.

"Severe Unsettlement in Stock Prices," *The Magazine of Wall Street,* 1927.

"Mr. Shareholder—Do You Know When Periodic Dividends Help and When They Hurt You?" *The Magazine of Wall Street,* vol. 38, no. 11, September 25, 1926, pp. 1032–1034, 1076.

"Should Rich but Losing Corporations Be Liquidated?" *Forbes,* vol. 30, no. 1, July 1, 1932, pp. 13–14.

"Should Rich Corporations Return Stockholders' Cash?" *Forbes,* vol. 29, no. 12, June, 15, 1932, pp. 20–22.

"Should Security Analysts Have a Professional Rating? The Affirmative Case," *The Financial Analysts Journal,* January 1945.

"Some Observations," *The Financial Analysts Journal,* November 1967.

"Some Structural Relationships Bearing Upon Full Employment," *The Financial Analysts Journal,* May 1955.

"Special Situations," *The Financial Analysts Journal,* Fourth Quarter 1946.

"Stock Dividends," *Barron's,* August 3 and 10, 1953.

Storage and Stability: A Modern Ever-Normal Granary (New York: McGraw-Hill, 1937).

"Strategic Switch in Railroad Issues," *The Magazine of Wall Street,* vol. 24, August, 16, 1919, pp. 759–762.

Translated from Spanish, *The Truce,* a novel by Mario Benedetti (New York: Harper and Row, 1967).

"Three Switches in New York Tractions," *The Magazine of Wall Street,* vol. 24, July 5, 1919, pp. 509–511.

"Toward a Science of Security Analysis," *The Financial Analysts Journal*, August 1952.

"The Two 'American Ships,'" *The Magazine of Wall Street*, vol. 25, January 10, 1920, pp. 291–292, 322.

"Two Illustrative Approaches to Formula Valuations of Common Stocks," *The Financial Analysts Journal*, November 1957.

"Two Ways to Making (and Losing) Money in Securities," *The Financial Analysts Journal*, Second Quarter 1948 supplement.

"The War Economy and Stock Values," *The Financial Analysts Journal*, First Quarter 1951.

"Which Way to Relief from the Double Tax on Corporate Profits?" *The Financial Analysts Journal*, February 1954.

"Will the Market Grow to the Sky?—Some Problems Ahead," *The Commercial and Financial Chronicle*, April 6, 1961.

"Which Is the Best Sugar Stock?" *The Magazine of Wall Street*, vol. 25, April 30, 1920, pp. 799–801.

World Commodities and World Currency (New York: McGraw-Hill, 1944).

Writings about Graham

Anon., "Portrait of an Analyst: Benjamin Graham," *The Financial Analysts Journal*, January–February 1968.

Arbel, Avner, "A Message from Ben Graham," *Forbes*, November 30, 1987.

Auxier, Albert L., "Happy Birthday, Ben," *Barron's*, vol. 74, no. 19, May 19, 1994, pp. 50–52.

"Ben We Hardly Knew Ye," *Worth*, June–July, 1992.

"Benjamin Graham, Securities Expert [obituary]," *The New York Times*, September 23, 1976.

Blustein, Paul, "Benjamin Graham's Last Will and Testament," *Forbes*, August 1, 1977.

Buffett, Warren, "Benjamin Graham," *The Financial Analysts Journal*, November–December 1976.

Buffett, Warren, "The Superinvestors of Graham and Doddsville," *Hermes*, 1984.

Butler, Hartman, "A Conversation with Benjamin Graham," *The Financial Analysts Journal*, November–December 1986.

Cook, Anthony, "The Stock Market Is Like a Pendulum," [Interview with Graham], *Forbes*, vol. 115, June 15, 1975, pp. 35, 37.

Davidson, Catherine, "Graham and Dodd's *Security Analysis*: The Fifth Edition," *Hermes*, Fall 1987.

Dorfman, John, "Updating a Classic Guide to Market Investment," *The Wall Street Journal*, March 10, 1988.

Guzzardi, Walter, Jr., "The U.S. Business Hall of Fame," *Fortune*, vol. 117, 1988, pp. 142, 147.

Hagstrom, Robert, *The Warren Buffett Way* (New York: John Wiley, 1994).

Harmon, Elmer Meredith, *Commodity Reserve Currency: The Graham-Goudriaan Proposal for Stabilizing Income of Primary Producing Countries* (New York: Columbia University Press, 1959).

Kahn, Irving, and Robert D. Milne, *Benjamin Graham, the Father of Financial Analysis* (Charlottesville, Va.: Financial Analysts Research Foundations, 1977).

Kilpatrick, Andrew, *Warren Buffett: The Good Guy of Wall Street* (New York: Donald Fine, 1992).

Lowe, Janet, *Benjamin Graham on Value Investing: Lessons from the Dean of Wall Street* (Dearborn Financial Publishing Company, 1994); reviews by Joseph Barth, *Library Journal*, October 1, 1994, and Daniel McGinn, "Benjamin Graham on Value Investing," *Newsweek*, November 21, 1994.

Lowenstein, Roger, *Buffett: The Making of an American Capitalist* (New York: Random House, 1995).

Loomis, Carol J., "The Inside Story of Warren Buffett," *Fortune*, April 11, 1988.

Moskowitz, Milton, "The Intelligent Investor at 80," *The New York Times*, May 5, 1974.

Oppenheimer, Henry, "Ben Graham's Net Current Asset Values: A Performance Update," *The Financial Analysts Journal*, November–December 1986.

Oppenheimer, Henry, "Remembering Uncle Ben," *Forbes*, October 15, 1975.

Oppenheimer, Henry, *Common Stock Selection: An Analysis of Benjamin Graham's "Intelligent Investor" Approach* (Ann Arbor, Mich.: UMI Research Press, 1981).

Oppenheimer, Henry, "A Test of Ben Graham's Stock Selection Criteria," *The Financial Analysts Journal*, September–October 1984.

Regan, Nancy, *The Institute of Chartered Financial Analysts: A Twenty-five Year History* (Charlottesville, Va.: The Institute of Chartered Financial Analysts, 1987).

Smith, Adam, *Supermoney* (New York: Random House, 1972).

Train, John, *The Money Masters* (New York: Harper and Row, 1985).

U.S. Senate, 84th Congress, *Hearings Before the Committee on Banking and Currency* (Washington, D.C.: U.S. Government Printing Office, March 11, 1955).

Vu, Joseph, "An Empirical Analysis of Ben Graham's Net Current Asset Value Rule," *Financial Review*, May 1988.

Index

Aeolian Vocalion records, 151–152
Agadir incident, 133
Ajax Tire Company, 170
Aldrich, Winthrop, 213
Alexander the Great, 312
Alger, Horatio, 49
Alghieri, Dante, 247–248
L'Alliance des Professeurs Français en Amérique, 94, 95
Alte Pinacothek, Munich, 243
American Coal Products Company, 178
American Economic Review, The, 305
American Light and Traction Company, 150–151, 153
American Scholar, The, 209
American Telephone and Telegraph Company, 191
Anabasis, 74, 83
Angell, Sir Norman, *The Great Illusion,* 124
Angry Flood (play by Graham), 179
Apollo, 83
Armour's Ham, 32
Arnold, Matthew, "Dover Beach," 244
Atchison, Topeka, and Santa Fe Railroad, 133, 170
Athanasius, 313
Augeas, 80

Bache and Company, 138–139
Bacon, Francis, *Magna Instauratio, or the Advancement of Learning,* 73–75, 77, 230
Bank of the United States, 249

Barman, Jacob, and family, 74, 78–85, 242
Baron, Nellie (Mrs. Leon Graham), 147
Barondess, Joseph, 65–66
Baruch, Bernard, 214, 216, 250–253, 303
Baruch, Dr. Herman, 173, 213–215, 303
Baudelaire Charles:
  "Le Balcon," 95
  "Le Voyage," 83
Bayne, Stephen F., 53
Bean, Louis, 300–302
Beckett, Samuel, *Waiting for Godot,* 291
Beethoven, Ludwig van, 68, 247
Belasco, David, *Madame Butterfly,* 281
Benjamin Graham Joint Account, 173, 191–192, 249, 252, 254–255, 267
Berall, Lou, 164
Beresford Apartment House, 255–257, 263
Bergen-Belsen, 83
Bergson, Henri, 57
Bernstein, Lou, 104–106, 115
Bernstorff, Count Johann-Heinrich von, German Ambassador, 137–138
Bible, 2, 20
Bingle, E. V., 215–216
Boer War, 9
Bonaparte, Napoleon, 34, 247, 291, 312
Bonbright, James, *The Valuation of Property,* 270–271

Bonright and Company, 164
Boswell, James, *Diary*, 233
Boutroux, Raymond, 57
Boys High School, Brooklyn, 67–70, 74, 192
Brahms, Johannes, 68
Breton, Guy, 275
Brierly School, 99, 318
Brisbane, Arthur, 283, 288
Brontë, Emily, *Wuthering Heights*, 99
Brooks, Norman, 134
Brown, Chester, 48
Brueghel, Pieter, "The Fall of Icarus," 304
Bushnell, D. S., 201–211

Caesar, Julius, 42, 247, 312
Carbona Cleaning Fluid, 124
Carl Pforzheimer & Company, 200–201
Carter, Nick, 49
Catullus, 97
Cavalieri, Lina, 214
Cavallaria Rusticana, 152
Chamberlain, Lawrence, *The Principles of Bond Investment*, 138
Chamberlain, Neville, 276
Chase Bank, 213
Chateaubriand, François-René de, 256
   Souvenirs d'Outre Tombe, 232
Chemical National Bank, 274
Chicago, Milwaukee, & St. Paul Railroad, 170–172
China Wedding, 280–282
Christ, Jesus, 61–62
Churchill, Winston, 252
Cicero, 68
   Pro Archia Poeta, 302, 314
Clarence Derwent Prize, 286
Cleland, John, *Fanny Hill*, 233–234
Coffee, Rudolph I., 61
Cohen & Graham, 191
Cohen, Benjamin V., 191

Cohen, Morris R., 56–57
College of the City of New York, 55, 87–88
College Board Entrance Exams, 75
Columbia Alumni Scholarship, 92, 93
Columbia University, 57, 75, 87, 90, 93, 101, 192, 252
   Extension Division, 238, 249, 264
   Law School, 118
   School of Business, 268
   Teachers' College, 224
Committee for Economic Development, 304
Committee for Economic Stability, 304–305
Commodity Credit Corporation, 300
Commodity Reserve Currency Plan (CRC), 293–307
Computing-Tabulating-Recording Corporation (later International Business Machines Corporation), 103
Conrad, Joseph, *Heart of Darkness*, 117
Consolidated Stock Exchange, 27
Consolidated Textile Company, 179
Cook, Alfred A., 208–211, 260
Cook, Nathan, & Lehman, 207–208
Corcoran, Tommy, 191
Corneille, Pierre, *Le Cid*, 155
Credit Anstalt failure, 258
Currie, Bill, 215
Cutler, Bertram, 209

Daedalus, 231, 304
Daumier, Honoré, 271
Day of Reckoning, 282
De Bergerac, Cyrano, 68
Delf, Harry, *The Family Upstairs*, 282–289
De Lisser, Horace, 170
Derwent, Clarence, 286–287
Descartes, René, 98, 99

Dickens, Charles, 49
  Nicholas Nickleby, 118
Diller-Quaile School of Music, 224
Disraeli, Benjamin, 274
Dix, John, 257–258
Dodd, David L., 239, 264–265, 276
Don Quixote, 204
Dow Jones Industrial Average, 251,
  253, 255, 258, 267
Duke of Windsor, 2
Du Pont Corporation, 188
Dürer, Albrecht, 240

Economic Forum, The, 299–300
Economic Forum, The, 298
Edison, Thomas, 21, 298
Edward VII, King of England, 9
Egbert, James, 238
Eisenhower, Dwight, 252
El Dorado Apartment House, 261
Ellis Island, 4
Emerson School of Dramatic Art,
  117
Erskine, John, *The Private Life of
  Helen of Troy*, 99, 101, 123
Ertel Oil Company, 180
Euclid, 98
Euripides, *Iphigenia at Tauris*, 96,
  242
Ezekiel, Mordecai, 301

Fichte, Johann Gottlieb, 97
Fielding, Henry, *Tom Jones*, 113
Financial Analysts' Journal, 274
Fisher, Irving, 304
  Stable Money, 302
Fisher, M. A., 103–104, 106
Fleischmann, Constance, 58–59, 113
Flexible Flyer sled, 43
Fontaine, Camille, 95–96
Forbes Magazine, 264, 269
Fortune Magazine, 193
Franco-Wyoming Oil Company, 206

Franklin, Benjamin,
  Autobiography, 50, 313
Fujimoto Bill Broker Bank, 165
Full Employment Act of 1946, 212

Garbat, Fifi, 220
Gassner, Claude, 66
Gassner, Violet, 113
Gates, Lucy, 152
General Motors, 177, 188
Genesis, 2
George III, King of England, 5
George, Henry, *Progress and
  Poverty*, 302
Gerard, Elsie (cousin), 38
Gerard (Gesundheit), Eva (aunt),
  33–34, 38, 41
Gerard, Helen (cousin), 38
Gerard (Gesundheit), Maurice
  (uncle), 26, 29, 33–34, 38, 41, 57,
  65, 66, 67, 177–178, 297
Gerard, Ralph (cousin), 38
Gershwin, George, *Porgy and Bess*,
  290
Gesundheit, Grandfather, 9
Gibbon, Sir Edward, *The Decline
  and Fall of the Roman
  Empire*, 53, 86
Giordano, Umberto, *Madame Sans-
  Gêne*, 291
Goethe, Johann Wolfgang von, 236,
  281
  Iphigenia at Tauris, 96, 242, 281
Gohl, Louisa, 219, 222
Golden, John, 281
Golden, Sylvia, 281
Goncourt, Edmond and Jules, *Jour-
  nals*, 197
Goodbody & Company, 214
Goodman, Andrew, 228, 261
Goodman, Charles, 227, 261
Goodman, Robert, 227–228, 229, 261
Goodman, Sylvia, 158, 196
Gottshalk, Morrie, 55–56

Gouin method of language instruction, 117

Gourmont, Rémy de, *A Night in Luxembourg*, 61

Government Employees Insurance Company (GEICO), 161, 173

Graham, Benjamin Jr., "Buz" (son), 49, 228

Graham (nee Gesundheit), Dorothy (mother), 1, 2, 12–14, 16, 21, 24, 26–35, 38, 40, 41, 43, 54, 57–58, 65, 71, 74, 84–85, 87, 90, 92, 101–102, 113, 146, 154–155, 161, 231, 239, 241, 243, 263

Graham, Elaine (daughter), 217, 222–225

Graham, Estelle ("Estey," nee Messing, third wife), 157, 161

Graham, Frank D., *Social Goals and Economic Institutions*, 305–307

Graham, Hazel (nee Mazur, first wife), 113–115, 117, 119–121, 146–147, 154, 161, 163, 220, 222, 228–232, 234, 236, 239, 255, 257, 279–281, 287

Graham, Isaac Newton (first son), 25, 161, 163, 217–219, 222, 231

Graham, Leon (brother), 1, 8, 11, 14, 16, 26, 44, 47, 67, 108, 113–114, 147, 151–152, 160–161

Graham, Marjorie (daughter), 185, 217–221, 224, 257, 312

Graham, Newton (second son), 237–238, 239

Graham, Victor (brother), 1, 3, 8, 11, 16, 22, 24, 26, 38, 42, 44, 58, 85, 115, 152–153, 158–159, 160–161, 196, 230, 312

Graham Corporation, 187–191

Graham-Newman Corporation, 173, 192, 268, 307

Grape-Nuts cereal, 7

Graves, Robert, 50
    The White Goddess, 233

Gray, Thomas, "Elegy in a Country Churchyard," 88

Great Northern Railroad, 171

Greenman, E. F., 257

Greenman, Frederick F., 55, 86, 134, 186, 191, 207–208, 209, 244, 259, 260, 268

Grillparzer, Franz, 96

Grossbaum, Emanuel (uncle), 24, 26

Grossbaum, Ethel (cousin), 24

Grossbaum, Grandfather, 9, 19–20

Grossbaum, Isaac (father), 4, 6–9, 12, 20–21, 23–28, 37

Grossbaum, Louis (cousin), 41, 47, 91, 100, 115, 125, 159–160

Grossbaum, Sol (uncle), 19

Grossbaum, Wilfred (cousin), 125

Grossbaum, Will (uncle), 20

Guggenheim Exploration Company, 145, 150

Guilbert, Yvette, 95

H. Hentz & Company, 213, 214, 248–249, 250, 253

Hadassah, 226

Harding, Warren, 111

Harmsworth, Alfred, 86

Harris, Frank, 232

Harris, Lou, 186–187, 191

Harris Raincoat Company, 186

Hauptmann, Bruno, 272

Hawkes, Herbert E., 97–98, 123, 126

Hebbel, Friedrich, 96

Henty, G. A., 49

Herbert, Victor, 148

Hercules, 80

Hervey, William Addison, 96

Heuser, Frederick, 96

Heywood and Wakefield Company, 251

Hitler, Adolf, 97, 276, 290

Hobson, J. A., *The Economics of Unemployment*, 297

Holinshed, Raphael, *Chronicles*,
234
Hollerith method, 103
Holmes, Sherlock, 314
Homer, 68
Iliad, 50
Odyssey, 50, 313
Horace, 97, 306
Horvitz, Aaron, 186, 191
Housman, A. E., 59
Hughes, Richard, 26
Hugo, Victor, 50
"La Tombe et la Rose," 59
Huneker, James, *Painted Veils*,
95
Hunt's Point Palace Apartments,
118, 147, 196
Huxley, Aldous, *Point Counter-
point*, 231
Hyman, Maxwell, 182, 191

Ibsen, Hendrik, *Ghosts*, 242
Icarus, 231, 304
Intelligent Investor, The, 273
Internal Revenue Service, 268
Interstate Commerce Commission,
103, 142, 200–201
Irving, Washington, *The Legend of
Sleepy Hollow*, 49–50

J. K. Rice & Company, 215
Jaffee, Sam, 290–291
James, William, 56–57
A Pluralistic Universe, 61
Janis, Irving, 313
Jardine, Tom, 215–216
Jedermann, 242
Johns Hopkins University, 281
Johnson, Alvin, 290, 298
Jolson, Al, 115
Joseph, 1, 15, 295
Judaism, 60–64
Juilliard School of Music, 99

Kafka, Franz, *Letters to Milena*, 233
Kahn, Irving, 291
Kant, Immanuel, 98, 115
Karolik, Maxim, 221–222
Kaufmann Department Stores, 249
Kazantzakis, Nicos, 51
Kelly, Hugh, 264
Keppel, Frederick F., 91–92, 97, 105,
107, 119, 123, 127, 146
Keynes, John Maynard, Lord, 294,
297
Kipling, Rudyard, 157
Kleist, Heinrich van, 96
Kobe University, 168
Kosloff, Alexis, 225
Kresel, Isidore, 248–249
Khrushchev, Nikita, 2

Laemmle, Carl, 260
Laemmle, Max, 260
La Rochefoucauld, François, 32
Lehigh Valley Railroad, 70, 109
Lessing, Gotthold Ephraim, 96
Levy, Guy, 267
Levy, Saul, 289
Lewine, Jerome, 213, 248–249, 250
Lewis, Oscar, 248–249
Lincoln, Abraham, 87, 221
Lincoln School, 100, 219, 223, 224,
257
Lindbergh, Charles, 272
Lipton, Sir Thomas, 5
Loeb, Daniel, 132, 164, 179–180
Loeb, Jake, 132
Loeffler, L. J., 89–90
Lombard, Norman, 304
Louy, Pierre, *Aphrodite*, 233
Lucretius, 10, 97

MacLaughlin, Maury, 135
Macmillan and Company, 302
Magazine of Wall Street, The,
156–159, 175, 180, 185, 214

Malou, 312, 315
Major, Cedric, 70
Marlowe, Julia, 100
Marony, Robert J., 172–173, 191, 259
Marsyas, 83
Martin, William McChesney, 299–300
Matthews, Brander, 99
May, A. Wilfred, 274
Mazur, Sylvia, 114
McDonnell & Company, 230
McGraw-Hill Publishing Company, 264, 302
McNamee, Graham, 260
Mead, Joseph, 299
Mellon, Andrew, Jr., 209
Menuhin, Yehudi and Yalta, 220
Merrimée, Prosper, *Colomba*, 59
Merriwell, Frank, 49, 93
Metropolitan Museum of Art, 52
Mexican Petroleum Company, 178
Miki, Junkichi, 164–169
Miller, Alda, 100, 109, 115–117
Miller, Henry, *The Tropic of Cancer*, 233–234
Miller, Shirley, 285
Milton, John:
"L'Allegro," 49–50
"Comus," 114
Missouri, Kansas & Texas Railroad, 143–145, 153
Missouri Pacific Railroad, 138
Mitchell, John Purroy, 138, 148
Mitty, Walter, 50
Moissi, Alexander, 242
Molière, 247
Montefiore, Sir Moses, 66
Morrissey, Michael J., 95–97

National City Bank, 128
National Transit Company, 213–215
Neighborhood Playhouse School of Dancing, 225

Neiman-Marcus Department Store, 261
Neumark, Arthur, 214
New Jersey Tax Equalization Board, 270
New Milford, New York, 74
New School for Social Research, 290, 298
New Testament, The, 62
New York Central Railroad, 270
New York City Athletic Club, 225
New York Curb Market (later American Stock Exchange), 131–132, 180, 181, 183
New York Evening Journal, 288–289
New York Guild for the Jewish Blind, 195
New York Highlanders (later New York Yankees), 48
New York Hippodrome, 218
New York State Chamber of Commerce, 212
New York Stock Exchange, 27, 117, 126, 131, 135, 163, 171, 175, 213
New York Times, The, 298
New York Times Book Review, 305
Newburger, Alfred, 126–127, 129, 143–144, 155, 158, 163
Newburger, Henderson, and Loeb Brokerage (N.H.&L.), 126, 138, 143, 144, 150, 163, 166, 169, 173, 185, 186, 213, 214, 226, 290
Newburger, Lester, 133, 169
Newburger, Samuel, 126, 133–134, 138–139
Newman, Douglas, 178, 192
Newman, Estelle (nee Reiss), 192, 194–195
Newman, Jerome, 131, 192–195, 250, 259, 267
Newman & Graham Co., 192
Nizer, Louis, *My Life in Court*, 269
Northern Pacific Railroad, 171

Northern Pipeline Company, 201–212

Omar Khayyam, *The Rubáiyát*, 13, 88, 298
"On the First Publication of an Ambitious Work," 303
Optic, Oliver, 49
Osaka Stock Exchange, 168

Palmer Method for Perfect Penmanship, The, 75
Pan American Petroleum Company, 178
Parker, Bert, 230
Pascal, Blaise, 63
Pepperell Manufacturing Company, 250–251
Petronius, *The Golden Ass*, 233
Phi Beta Kappa, 125, 133
Phi Beta Kappa Foundation, 209
Pierce Oil Company, 176
Platt, Seleno, 106, 109
Plymouth Cordage Company, 250–251
Podell, David, 300
Pool, Dr. Judith, 302
Pope, Alexander, 23
Powers, Barnard, 156, 175, 180–182
Prince of the House of David, A, 61
Proust, Marcel, 51
  A la Recherche du Temps Perdu, 274
Public Bank, 274
Public School No. 10, 22, 37, 46, 54
Pulitzer Scholarships, 47, 75, 85–87, 91–92

Rabelais, François, *Gargantua*, 95
Raleigh, Sir Walter, "O eloquent, just, and mighty Death," 220
Raging Flood, The, 289–290
Reade, Charles, 49

Recess Club, 209
Reiss, Elias, 192, 259
Renan, Ernest, "Prayer on the Acropolis," 96
Ricci, Ruggiero, 220
Rilke, Rainer-Maria, *The War Letters*, 233
Robinson, Edward G., 290–291
Robinson, James Harvey, 101
Rockefeller, John D., 209–213
Rockefeller Foundation, 201, 208, 210–211, 213
Rogow, Sydney, 40, 53, 176–177
Ronsard, Pierre de, 17
Roosevelt, Franklin D., 191, 265, 267, 300, 303
Rosenthal, Alexander, 25, 151–152
Rostand, Edmond, 95
Rouse, Harold, 132, 145, 164
Rousseau, Jean-Jacques:
  Confessions, 232
  Emile, 69
Royce, Josiah, 56
Rubens, Peter Paul, 243
Russo-Japanese War, 164

St. Louis & Southwestern Railroad ("SS"), 170–172
St. Pierre, Bernardin de, *Etudes sur la Nature*, 66–67
Sanders, Henry, 274
San Giovanni, Eduardo, 56
Sardou, Victorien, *Madame Sans-Gêne*, 34
Sarnoff, David and Lisette, 256
Saturday Evening Post, The, 39
Savold Tire Company, 180–184
Schiller, Friedrich von, 96
Schnader, Henry, 210
Securities and Exchange Commission, 276
Securities Exchange Act, 191
Security Analysis, 239, 264, 272–273, 276, 284, 302, 305

Septimius Severus, 52–53
Shakespeare, William, 69, 247
    Julius Caesar, 179
    King Lear, 290
Shapiro, Karl, 234
Shattuck Corporation (Schrafft's
    restaurants), 188
Sigma Xi, 126
Simenon, Georges, 229, 233
Sinclair, Upton, EPIC, 298
Slade, Helen, 273–275
Smith, Adam, 306
Stable Money Association, 304
Standard Oil Company, 199, 201,
    204
Standard Oil Pipeline Companies,
    199
Steinman, Irving, 284–287
Stern, Leo, 169
Stern, Morton, 138
Steuer, Max, 249, 260
Stevenson, Robert Louis, 49
Storage and Stability, 302–307
Strauss, Nathan, Jr., 256–257
Strauss, Oscar, 256
Svevo, Italo, *The Confessions of
    Zeno*, 52
Sweyd, Freddy, 124–125

Tacitus, 97
Tammany Hall, 41, 138
Tanzola, J. J., 125
Tassin, Algernon Duvivier, 100,
    150–151, 153–154, 159, 176, 289
Tchaikovsky, Peter I., 220
Technocracy, 298
Tennyson, Alfred Lord, 51, 313
    "Idylls of the King," 217
    "Ulysses," 315
Theatre Magazine, 281
Theatre Program Company, 287
Thimig, Helen, 242
Time Magazine, 300
Tony Pastor's Theatre, 42

Toulouse-Lautrec, Henri, 95
Townsend Harris Hall, 55–56, 65,
    67, 94
Townsend Plan, 298, 305, 307
True to the Marines (renamed *Baby
    Pompadour*), 283–289
Twain, Mark, 312

UCLA, 239, 301
Ulysses, 50, 313
Unexcelled Manufacturing Com-
    pany, 199, 215–216
United States Express Company,
    103–107, 109–110, 127, 293
United States Federal Reserve
    System, 300
United States Steel, 27, 172, 176
United States Treasury Depart-
    ment, 268, 295
Universal Pictures Company,
    260–261

Vanderbilt, Cornelius, 148
Vanderbilt Theatre, 286
Van Doren, Carl, 99–100
Venner, Clarence, 204
Victoria, Queen of England, 9
Virgil, 53, 68, 75, 247, 248, 302, 313
    Aeneid, 89, 276
    Georgics, 301
Vogue magazine, 155

Wade, Carol (second wife), 273,
    275–276, 277
Wagner, Cosima, 240
Wagner, Richard, 239
    Götterdämmerung, 241
    Meistersinger von Nürnberg,
    239
    Ring of the Niebelungen, 239
    Siegfried's Idyll, 240
    Tristan und Isolde, 239

Wagner, Siegfried, 240
Wagner, Winifred, 240
Wagner, Wolfgang and Wieland, 240
Wahnfried, 240
Walker, Jimmy, 103
Wallace, Henry, 300–302
Washington, George, 5
Wertheim & Company, 213
Whitman, Walt, "Oh Captain, My
    Captain," 8
Whitney Manufacturing Company,
    268
Wilding, Anthony, 135
Williams, Norris, 134
Willstatter, Richard, 137, 138, 139
Wilson, Dr. May, 237

Wilson, Woodrow, 150
Wood, General Leonard, 49, 111,
    146
Woodbridge, Frederick A., 98–99,
    101, 123
Wyckoff, Carrie, 156–159
Wyckoff, Richard D., 156–159

Yokohama Specie Bank, 167
Yourcenar, Margaret, *Memoirs of
    Hadrian*, 53

Zeta Beta Tau fraternity, 101
Zion, Irving, 151–152